THE BUYOUT OF AMERICA

THE BUYOUT OF AMERICA

*How Private Equity Will Cause
the Next Great Credit Crisis*

JOSH KOSMAN

PORTFOLIO

PORTFOLIO
Published by the Penguin Group
Penguin Group (USA) Inc., 375 Hudson Street,
New York, New York 10014, U.S.A.
Penguin Group (Canada), 90 Eglinton Avenue East, Suite 700, Toronto,
Ontario, Canada M4P 2Y3 (a division of Pearson Penguin Canada Inc.)
Penguin Books Ltd, 80 Strand, London WC2R 0RL, England
Penguin Ireland, 25 St. Stephen's Green, Dublin 2, Ireland
(a division of Penguin Books Ltd)
Penguin Books Australia Ltd, 250 Camberwell Road, Camberwell,
Victoria 3124, Australia (a division of Pearson Australia Group Pty Ltd)
Penguin Books India Pvt Ltd, 11 Community Centre,
Panchsheel Park, New Delhi–110 017, India
Penguin Group (NZ), 67 Apollo Drive, Rosedale, North Shore 0632,
New Zealand (a division of Pearson New Zealand Ltd)
Penguin Books (South Africa) (Pty) Ltd, 24 Sturdee Avenue,
Rosebank, Johannesburg 2196, South Africa

Penguin Books Ltd, Registered Offices: 80 Strand, London WC2R 0RL, England

First published in 2009 by Portfolio, a member of Penguin Group (USA) Inc.

3 5 7 9 10 8 6 4 2

Copyright © Joshua Kosman, 2009
All rights reserved

LIBRARY OF CONGRESS CATALOGING IN PUBLICATION DATA
Kosman, Josh.
The buyout of America : how private equity will cause the next
great credit crisis / Josh Kosman.
p. cm.
Includes bibliographical references and index.
ISBN 978-1-59184-285-9
1. Private equity—United States. 2. Leveraged buyouts—United States.
3. Credit—United States. 4. Financial crises—United States. I. Title.
HG4751.K673 2009

338.5'420973—dc22   2009019877

Printed in the United States of America · Set in New Caledonia

This book is dedicated to the millions of Americans working for private-equity–owned companies.

Contents

Prologue

You've heard the term, but do you know what it means?

Private equity.

I didn't in 1995 when I applied to work for a private-equity-owned company. I didn't even *know* it was a private-equity-owned business, but something seemed odd.

At the time, I was twenty-eight years old and beginning a career in journalism. The *Middletown Press* daily newspaper in central Connecticut listed several openings on the Columbia University Journalism School hotline. It was rare that a paper would suddenly have several positions open. I applied and started to do some research.

Newspaper conglomerate Journal Register Co. had just bought the 111-year-old paper and was cleaning house. They were planning to run some stories from their other area papers in the *Middletown Press* to reduce editorial expenses. I read in the Hartford alternative weekly that the Journal Register fired experienced reporters, replacing them with those who worked for less. This was troubling. But I got the job and felt maybe there was logic to the cost cutting.

After I arrived, I started viewing things differently. I met a fired longtime political reporter. He seemed like a solid veteran who delivered real news to the community. Where would he go?

I didn't know that PE firms had the companies they acquired borrow most of the money to finance their own sales, forcing them to reduce staff so they could repay their loans.

Within six months I, too, was fired.

Back in New York, I saw a blind-box classified advertisement in the *New York Times* for a reporter who could deliver scoops. It turned out to be the *Buyouts Newsletter*, a trade publication covering private-equity firms like Warburg Pincus, which owned Journal Register.

I soon realized the rapacious leveraged-buyout (LBO) kings of the 1980s were still around. They had just adopted a new name, now calling themselves private-equity investors. And I was one of the few reporters following their activities. In the late 1980s, the press closely covered the buyout kings, and Hollywood vilified them in movies like *Pretty Woman* and *Wall Street*. But when I joined the *Buyouts Newsletter* in 1996, they were operating under the radar. They didn't have the money to buy large public companies like RJR Nabisco, so they were quietly acquiring hundreds of smaller businesses, ranging from the Sealy mattress company to J. Crew. I could see that the former LBO kings were staging a comeback. Part of me wanted in.

After about one year of reporting for the *Buyouts Newsletter*, I wrote to several private-equity executives who had been helpful to me, asking them how one might make the switch from PE journalist to PE professional. Béla Szigethy, who co-ran the private-equity firm The Riverside Co., said he would be glad to offer his thoughts. We met at the ground-floor Rockefeller Center café and gazed at the ice rink that was just on the other side of our glass partition.

He asked, "Why are you interested in joining my firm?"

"I think you guys are sharp, and what you do is interesting."

"That's not the right answer," he said. "The only reason you should want to join us is because you love making money."

This exchange forced me to look at why I wanted to join the industry, and I soon dropped the idea.

By this time, I had started to question the PE firms' practices. They ran something of a legal shell game. They bought companies with other people's money by structuring acquisitions like mortgages: The critical difference was that while we pay our mortgages, PE firms had the businesses they bought take the loans, making *them* responsible for repayment. Typically PE firms put down cash equal to between 30 percent and 40 percent of the purchase price, and their acquired companies borrowed the rest. They then tried to resell the businesses within five years.

The idea that PE firms put cash into companies was a widely held misconception. PE firms almost always saddled them with the bill and subsequently larger debt. This led to layoffs, like those at the *Middletown Press*.

PE firms acted differently from hedge funds, which often bought currencies, shares, and debt securities—not companies. Private-equity firms weren't venture capitalists, either. Venture capitalists invest in growing companies, and they maintain an active oversight role as these companies grow and change. Private-equity firms buy businesses through leveraged buyouts, which means the majority of the money for the buyout comes by loading the company down with debt.

I started seeing, too, the connections between PE barons and important Washington power players, and I began to wonder if that was why they were escaping government regulation. Former president George H. W. Bush and Colin Powell, as well as Clinton cabinet members Erskine Bowles, George Stephanopoulos, and Federico Peña, were working on behalf of private-equity firms. One of the things I found really interesting about the industry was how it reached the highest corridors of power.

Now I switched tactics. I decided to learn as much as I could about private equity to write a book about the industry aimed at a general readership. I felt the public needed to know that many companies were being mortgaged and that they would be the ones paying the price.

In 1998 I broached the idea with fellow *Buyouts Newsletter* reporter Robert Dunn. We considered titles like *The Secret Empire*. The plan was to profile three PE barons: Leon Black, Tom Hicks, and Mitt Romney. The son of former Michigan governor George Romney, Mitt Romney even then had barely disguised political ambitions, but this was years before he was ready to run for president.

We began investigating the industry, looking beyond stories that fit only the *Buyouts Newsletter*, exploring, for example, how PE firm DLJ Merchant Banking Partners had built a company called Decision-One by acquiring many small companies that serviced computers for corporations and combining them. DLJ had a reputation for firing the heads of most of these businesses, and repricing customer contracts, angering clients. As a result, clients left, and the company eventually went bankrupt.

Soon Robert and I parted ways, taking different career paths. I kept at it—learning more about private equity. After two and a half years at the *Buyouts Newsletter*, I left for the more widely read *Daily*

Deal newspaper, continuing to report on the sector. The *Deal* closely covered mergers for a business audience.

In some ways, I felt like a spy. Cozying up to industry sources and trading information on what PE firms were buying and selling, while gathering notes on how PE barons were affecting people and companies.

In 2003, mergermarket, an online news service for Wall Street bankers and lawyers, recruited me to head its North American operations because of my track record of breaking PE stories. I took the job but still thought about the book. Meanwhile, I was one of the few journalists who got to closely witness the PE industry's explosive growth.

By 2007 private equity was the hottest Wall Street craze since the tech boom. It was symptomatic of an era when the faith of both the government and public investors in the stock markets had been shaken by the scandals at Enron and other publicly traded companies and by the tech bust. Corporate managements were reigned in, and stock prices for many businesses went sideways. PE firms armed with cheap debt, though, could pay ever higher multiples of earnings for businesses. They soon found many public businesses within their reach, and from 2001 to 2007 acquired nearly a thousand listed companies.

Media interest in private equity grew. The PE firms claimed they were operational managers who had a longer-term vision for the businesses they bought than publicly traded companies that were focused on meeting quarterly earnings targets. PE firms also said they empowered the executives who ran their businesses by making them owners.

My desire to write the book increased as I listened to these misrepresentations. I knew from my personal reporting that these faceless PE firms, with names like Blackstone Group and Carlyle Group, were not helping the companies they acquired. Just the opposite—the PE firms put the companies they acquired under more intense pressure than they would ever feel in the public markets. Their actions hurt the companies they owned, their customers, and employees. Furthermore, private-equity firms from 2000 through the first half of 2007 bought companies that employed close to 10 percent of the American private sector (roughly ten million people).

Once I had a book contract and began to work full time on the project, I set out to test my previous observations. Would I find my impression was correct that PE firms mostly made money by hobbling businesses and hurting people? Or, on closer examination, would I find they weren't really so pernicious after all?

One of the first meetings I arranged was with Scott Sperling, co-president of PE firm Thomas H. Lee Partners, to discuss his 2004 buyout of Warner Music, an American icon and the world's fourth biggest music company.

Consumers were buying fewer CDs, while downloading more songs. The traditional music-company model was not working anymore, and Sperling had focused Warner more on content distribution, like ring tones, instead of producing albums. He reduced the workforce in three and a half years by 28 percent to 3,800 from 5,300. This allowed Warner Music to borrow more money on top of the original loan that financed the buyout. Warner used the new loans to help pay its PE owners $1.2 billion in dividends, about the same amount they had put down to buy the business. These job cuts also helped Warner come up with the money to pay the PE owners a $73 million management fee.

Sperling's Boston office was in a tall glass tower at 100 Federal Street, near Amtrak's South Station. His secretary greeted me at the firm's thirty-fifth-floor entrance. She led me into his office and said I should wait there for Sperling, who would be back in a few minutes. I looked around.

Through the floor-to-ceiling windows, I could peer down at the planes flying into or out of Logan Airport. There were pictures of Sperling's teenage children everywhere throughout the office: on his desk, on the walls, on a shelving unit that covered the bottom third of the glass window, and on an end table. Wherever I turned, I was looking at his kids. Almost hidden from view, just right of the entrance, was the framed front and back cover of what looked to be a 1970s-era record album. The front picture showed men wearing leather jackets and standing on a dirt road. The group had been renamed Hurdle Rate, the record was now called *Cash on Cash*. Sperling's face and those of some of his partners had been superimposed on the bodies of some legendary band.

Song titles on the fake album cover's back included "Leaving on a Private Jet Plane," "Take These Bonds and Shove 'Em," and "Edgar, Don't Miss Those Numbers," a reference to Warner Music CEO Edgar Bronfman Jr.

Sperling arrived and proceeded to spend the next hour saying things like "Cost restructuring was not just to save costs. It was to make Warner a much more efficient and effective competitor."

But his explanation was hard to believe. I kept thinking about how the PE firms had taken more money out of the business than the company was saving through cost cuts. The faux album's last track was "Money for Nothing." It could be, I thought, the anthem for the whole industry.

Introduction

It is late 2011, months before President Barack Obama will run for reelection. The U.S. economy is gradually recovering from four years of hovering on the brink of disaster. Banks are lending money again, at least to strong companies, and employment is stabilizing.

President Obama has finally begun to breathe a bit more easily, when the secretary of the Treasury walks into his office one day.

"You better sit down," the secretary says. "I've got bad news. First Data, the largest merchant credit card processor, has defaulted on $22 billion in loans. Clear Channel Communications, which owns more than twelve hundred radio stations, is on the brink. The other credit tsunami that we knew was out there has begun."

The Treasury secretary is talking about private equity. It's not the private-equity firms themselves but the companies they own that are defaulting. During the boom years of 2001–7, private investors bought thousands of U.S. companies. They did it by having the acquired companies take on enormous loans using the same cheap credit that fueled the housing boom. That debt is now starting to come due.

"Considering what we have already been through, how bad can it be?" Obama asks.

"Well," says the Treasury secretary, "PE firms own companies that employ about 7.5 million Americans. Half of those companies, with 3.75 million workers, will collapse between 2012 and 2015. Assuming that those businesses file for bankruptcy and fire only 50 percent of their workers, that leaves 1.875 million out of jobs.

"To put that in perspective, Mr. President, NAFTA caused the displacement of fewer than 1 million workers, and only a slightly higher 2.6 million people lost jobs in 2008 when the recession took hold.

"A spike in unemployment will mean more people will lose their homes in foreclosure, and the resulting nosedive in consumer spending will threaten other businesses. The bankruptcies will also hit the banks that have financed LBOs and the hedge funds, pensions, and insurers who have bought many of those loans from them."

"Is this bigger than the subprime crisis?"

"It is similar in size to the subprime meltdown. In 2007, there were $1.3 trillion of outstanding subprime mortgages. As a result of leveraged buyouts, U.S. companies owe about $1 trillion.

"Sir, we are on the verge of the Next Great Credit Crisis."

Obama is no longer smiling.

The picture painted by the Treasury secretary in this imaginary scene, as dire as it is, is not total fantasy, nor is it a worse-case scenario. There are people in the financial world, including the head of restructuring at one of the biggest banks, who predict this outcome. Some knowledgeable observers say the carnage will start sooner. In December 2008, the Boston Consulting Group, which advises PE firms, predicted that almost 50 percent of PE-owned companies would probably default on their debt by the end of 2011. It also believed there would be significant restructuring at these companies leading to massive cost cuts and difficult layoffs.

A rain of defaults is already starting. From January 1 through November 17, 2008, eighty-six companies defaulted globally on their debt. That is four times the number in 2007, and 62 percent of those companies were recently involved in transactions with private-equity firms.

The tsunami of credit defaults described by the imaginary Treasury secretary is not inevitable. If the U.S. economy manages to recover from the credit crisis that began in the mortgage markets in 2007 before the big PE debts come due, more of the PE-owned companies will be able to refinance their debt. In that case, we won't see a full 50 percent of them go under. Although if history is any guide, many of them will collapse anyhow, regardless of any easing in the credit markets, thanks to the greed and grossly shortsighted management policies of their private-equity owners.

First a little primer on how private-equity firms operate. Private-equity firms buy businesses the way that homebuyers acquire houses. They make a down payment and finance the rest. The financings are structured like balloon mortgages, with big payments due at some point in the future. The critical difference, however, is that while homeowners pay the mortgages on their houses, PE firms have the businesses they buy take out the loans, making *them* responsible for repayment. They typically try to resell the company or take it public before the loans come due.

Played out within reasonable limits regarding the amount of the debt, the strength of the acquired company, and the continuation of some threshold level of investment to maintain that strength, it's a strategy that can offer big payoffs. But private-equity players are quintessential Wall Streeters whose grasp of the concept of reasonable limits is quite limited. For them, the whole purpose of doing business is to make money, so if a strategy works, each success is just an encouragement to raise the ante and be a bit more daring next time.

So here's why buyouts done from 2003 to 2008 could soon sink our economy. In the early years of the latest private-equity boom (there have been others before), the PE strategy worked well. The PE firms were gambling they could buy low and sell high, and for a while, they were right. If a firm bought a business in a 2002 LBO and the business's earnings grew just at the rate of the overall U.S. gross domestic product, the PE firm could sell the business in early 2007 and get its money back 3.4 times over.

Attracted by these rich returns, PE firms began to do more and more deals. KKR (Kohlberg Kravis Roberts & Co.) cofounder Henry Kravis announced in May 2007 that private equity was on the threshold of a golden age. PE firms, which in 2003 led buyouts of U.S. businesses that totaled $57 billion, just three years later, in 2006, quadrupled that figure to rack up $219 billion in LBOs. Buyouts in 2007 jumped to a staggering $486 billion. There was a feeding frenzy as PE firms gobbled up companies ranging from telephone firm Alltel to hotel chain Hilton.

One Trillion Sold

Private-Equity LBOs of U.S. Companies 2000–8

	Number of Deals	Value of Deals (in millions)
2000	203	$29,019
2001	113	$17,050
2002	143	$27,811
2003	209	$57,093
2004	326	$86,491
2005	615	$122,715
2006	804	$219,052
2007	581	$486,090
2008	194	$136,127
Total	3,188	$1,181,448

Sources: Government Accountability Office Analysis of Dealogic Data;
Thomson Reuters

Banks like Citigroup, which underwrote loans to finance the buyouts, loved the business. They collected fees on the overall balance of the loans they made and then resold more than 80 percent of the loans to the same hedge funds and insurance companies that were buying up subprime mortgages. As banks were reselling more of their loans, they were also relaxing lending standards.

By 2007, PE firms were paying earnings multiples that on average had risen 45 percent since 2000. And the amount of cash PE firms were putting down to buy businesses was actually falling from 38 percent in 2000 to only 33 percent in 2007. It had become possible for PE firms to arrange loans for publicly traded companies at higher earnings multiples than those businesses were trading at in the public markets.

Kohlberg Kravis Roberts and TPG Capital (formerly the Texas Pacific Group) announced plans in February 2007 to lead the biggest buyout ever—a $44 billion acquisition of Texas utility TXU Energy. KKR and TPG wanted the deal despite the fact that there was little chance TXU could ever repay the loans it was taking on to fund the buyout.

When Texas Republican state senator Troy Fraser said he believed KKR was overpaying by a considerable amount, the buyers had former U.S. secretary of state and Houston resident James Baker press their case for approval.

Baker told the Fort Worth and Greater Dallas Chambers of Commerce he was lobbying for the deal because the PE firms were not going to build the dirty-coal plants TXU was planning to construct and because they were buying TXU in a way that was economically responsible in that they had agreed to cut electric prices for TXU customers and freeze them until at least September 2008. There was little talk about what TXU might have to do after that or how it would repay its loans.

In fall 2007, TXU shareholders met to consider the sale. Protesters from ACORN (Association of Community Organizations for Reform Now), which advocates for low- and moderate-income families, gathered outside the Adam's Mark Hotel (now the Sheraton Dallas). Many wore red T-shirts with flyers taped to their backs reading "KKR and TPG are throwing $24 billion in debt on my back. Vote no on the buyout."

Still, shareholders owning 74 percent of the stock voted for the deal because the $69.25 share price offered a 28 percent premium over where the stock was trading a month before the buyout was announced. Soon after the shareholder vote, the U.S. Nuclear Regulatory Commission gave its approval. It was a perfect emperor's-new-clothes deal; its fundamental economics were pure fantasy, but that was an issue no one addressed.

A mutual-fund manager said he bought some TXU—now renamed Energy Future Holdings (EFH)—debt, believing that regulators concerned about global warming would stop the building of new coal plants. This would cause electricity prices to rise and improve profits to the point where it could refinance. Instead, electricity prices unexpectedly fell. For the year ending December 31, 2008, when subtracting a one-time accounting expense, EFH lost $900 million from continuing operations. If it had not have had to make $4.9 billion in interest payments it would have been profitable. Moody's Investors Service in February 2009 said it was concerned EFH might not be able to pay its $43 billion in debt, about $20 billion of which was coming due in 2014.

Leveraged buyouts increased in both size and number during this decade, and the KKRs of the world have become more powerful than the biggest American corporations. KKR itself in 2008 owned or co-owned companies that employed 855,000 people, which made it effectively America's second biggest employer, behind Walmart. In fact, five PE firms were among the ten biggest U.S. employers.

KKR Versus World's Biggest Employers

Employer	Employees
Walmart Stores	2,055,000
State Grid Corporation of China	1,486,000
China National Petroleum	1,117,345
Kohlberg Kravis Roberts	855,000
U.S. Postal Service	785,929

Source: *Time* magazine, which compared KKR to *Fortune* magazine's list of the world's biggest 2007 employers.

As long as the PE firms could refinance, or turn around and sell off their holdings before the biggest loan payments came due, spectacular flameout bankruptcies could be avoided. But even without the financial meltdown in mid-2007 that made financing almost impossible, there was another time bomb ticking: PE owners' short-term management practices cripple businesses, so eventually a significant number of them become noncompetitive and die.

Because the strategy of PE firms is to sell their businesses within several years, they focus on quick, short-term gains and give little consideration to long-term performance.

The LBO playbook is full of tactics for raising short-term cash. One is to cut costs by lowering customer service. Clayton, Dubilier & Rice did this from 1996 through 2004, when its company Kinko's got such a bad reputation for ignoring customers that comedian Dave Chappelle did a nationally televised skit spoofing the chain. Another is to raise prices, as when KKR-owned Masonite charged Home Depot so much for its doors during the housing boom that it eventually lost much of the Home Depot account and went bankrupt.

PE firms also starve companies of operating and human capital. They reduce 3.6 percent more jobs than peers during their first two years of ownership. Then there are companies like Energy Future Holdings that cut back on capital spending and research and development. When EFH finishes building the three plants it is required to construct by 2010, it will not have the money to add more capacity. EFH may move from losing money to being slightly profitable, but even this improvement would mean that there will still be no extra money for building new environmentally friendly plants or paying its principal.

PE firms would like to have us all think the reason they try so hard to raise earnings in their businesses is so that companies can use those profits to pay down the money they borrowed to finance their own acquisitions. But the records show that during the 2003–7 buyout rush, that wasn't generally the case.

Instead, they used the profits as a basis to borrow more money. The new loans, which were piled on top of the original debt taken on to finance the LBO, were used to issue dividends. The money from the loans went straight into the PE owners' pockets. The fourteen largest American PE firms declared dividends in more than 40 percent of the U.S. companies they acquired from 2002 through September 2006. Many of these eighty-three businesses are now in particularly precarious positions because they slashed budgets and then borrowed more money during the credit bubble.

If history is any indicator, there are rough times ahead. Junk bond king Michael Milken fueled a smaller buyout boom in the 1980s that ended with the savings-and-loan crisis and a mild 1990–91 recession. Of the twenty-five companies that from 1985 to 1989 borrowed $1 billion or more in junk bonds to finance their own LBOs, 52 percent, including wallboard maker National Gypsum, eventually collapsed. The biggest deal of that era was KKR's $30 billion buyout of RJR Nabisco, chronicled in *Barbarians at the Gate,* the bestselling book about greed gone berserk. KKR eventually traded half its shares in RJR for Borden Inc., and much of what Borden became went bankrupt.

A real possibility exists that KKR may soon hold the dubious distinction of driving both the biggest buyout of the 1980s, RJR/Borden, and the biggest one in this generation, TXU, into bankruptcy.

The coming buyout crash, like the mortgage meltdown, will have global dimensions. American and British private-equity firms since the 1980s have backed companies in England that employed about 20 percent of the private sector there. Multiples paid for those businesses this decade are even higher than for American companies. Jon Moulton, who heads British PE firm Alchemy Partners, concedes that many of the companies will struggle, but he diminishes the importance of the failures, predicting that the number of lost British jobs will be only in the hundreds of thousands, not the millions. "Now two hundred thousand to three hundred thousand jobs lost in the U.K. is a big deal, but it is not catastrophic," he said.

Of course, PE firms will be just fine if all these companies collapse. That's because most of them earn enough from the management fees they charge their investors and the companies to more than cover any losses. And that's not counting the huge dividends they haul in. Despite the credit crisis in 2009, PE firms were sitting on roughly $450 billion in unspent capital and itching for more deals.

PE firms—many of which are the ones about to cause the Next Great Credit Crisis—are trying to profit from the current one by buying distressed assets in the United States and Europe, like banks, mortgages, and corporate loans at deep discounts. During the recession, they cannot borrow much money to finance buyouts and therefore are seeking dislocations in the debt and equity markets where they believe a flood of sellers is causing assets to trade too cheaply. Mostly, this means they can appear to be saviors to governments, banks, and financial services institutions that are anxious to reduce liabilities. The U.S. government sees PE firms as part of the bank-rescue solution. It wants PE firms to partner alongside its $700 billion Troubled Asset Relief Program (TARP) bailout fund in buying troubled banks at relatively low prices.

All of this activity continues despite the likely collapse of half of the 3,188 American companies that PE firms bought from 2000 to 2008. If the credit markets remain restricted, the fall will be more dramatic. Many overburdened PE-owned companies will go under when their balloon debt payments come due, which in most cases will not happen until 2012 unless they break loan covenants first. Millions of jobs could be lost. If that happens, however, it will be because we have been living through at least five years of recession, so maybe, if there is a bright side, it will be that by then we will have learned how to live with financial disaster. But even if the credit markets reliquify and an era of relatively easy money returns, there is still a wave of bankruptcies coming. They will just occur over a longer time. It won't be a tsunami, only a hurricane.

These failures are going to occur because PE firms put their companies into crippling debt and, unlike entrepreneurs, who manage their businesses to succeed in the marketplace and grow, they manage their companies largely for short-term gains. They care about the futures of their PE firms but not about the viability of the companies they buy. So they make deep cuts in spending on current operations and on research to develop new products. They fire not only redundant workers but also many who are essential to producing competitive goods and providing customer service. They raise prices on noncompetitive goods to unsustainable levels. And they use the brief windows when they have nice-looking financial statements from the cost cutting to take on huge new loans to pay enormous dividends.

I believe the record shows that PE firms hurt their businesses competitively, limit their growth, cut jobs without reinvesting the savings, do not even generate good returns for their investors, and are about to cause the Next Great Credit Crisis. Leadership is needed to rally opposition to close the tax loopholes that make this very damaging activity possible.

PART ONE

THE BUYOUT
OF AMERICA

CHAPTER ONE

How Private Equity Started

In the late 1960s, a new kind of empire builder emerged in the United States. He wasn't a twenty-something geek whose "new new thing" turned the heads of venture capitalists. Nor was he a visionary businessman determined to revolutionize his industry. He didn't even see himself as in the business of running businesses. He was a Wall Streeter through and through, an established player in the high-stakes world of corporate mergers and acquisitions.

The most successful of these new empire builders was Jerome Kohlberg Jr. At the time, he co-ran the corporate finance division of Bear Stearns. For more than ten years, Kohlberg had been advising companies on mergers and acquisitions, and raising capital on behalf of these clients. In 1964, he suggested that instead of restricting itself to helping other businesses prosper, Bear should start buying companies itself. Kohlberg's plan relied upon a creative interpretation of the tax code that just might make the firm millions.

He had in mind the purchase of several manufacturing companies in partnership with their management teams. These companies were generating stable and steady revenue by filling dependable but generally unglamorous marketplace niches. Kohlberg focused on these types of companies because he intended, as part of the purchase process, to saddle them with huge new debt obligations. His plan was to make the companies pay for their acquisitions by having them take out loans equal to approximately 90 percent of their own purchase price, with Bear putting down only 10 percent. The target companies were generally willing to accept this unusual arrangement because Bear often came in with a competitive price.

Good business sense suggests that buying companies by weighing them down with huge debt is not a winning strategy. But according to First Chicago banker John Canning Jr., whose firm helped fund some of those early deals, here was the genius of the plan: Kohlberg saw a way to make debt far less onerous for a company being acquired. He would have the company treat its debt the way other businesses handle capital expenditures—as an operating expense deducted from profits through the depreciation tax schedules, thereby greatly reducing taxes. With far less to pay the government, his companies could use the money that formerly went to Uncle Sam to retire these huge loans at an unusually fast rate. Bear's equity would rise with every dollar the companies paid back in debt, even if the value of the businesses only remained the same. The final step in the plan was to sell these companies as soon as possible, usually within four to six years.

But the key unanswered question was: Would lenders buy into this arrangement? Would they agree to provide this debt? After all, if a company weighed down with loans hits a downturn in demand for its product or finds itself up against new competition, there could be a high risk of default. Still, it was worth trying, because the potential existed for huge returns. According to banker Canning, Kohlberg and his partners were "shocked" when they applied to Prudential Insurance Co. for one of their first buyout loans and, Prudential returned their call.

Most businesses Kohlberg bought this way were manufacturers like Vapor Corporation, formerly a division of Singer Sewing Machine. Vapor produced the door-opening systems for mass-transit networks, an unglamorous but steady source of predictable revenue. Once the company was acquired, Kohlberg did what any good manager would do for a business saddled with huge debt. He sought additional ways to save money by belt tightening—including cutting staff. We thought the companies could be run a little leaner, focus on generating more cash and paying down their debt faster, Canning said.

Kohlberg's plan worked. That 1972 investment in Vapor Corp., in which Bear put down $4.4 million, would produce a twelve-times return in six years. A 1975 buyout of Rockwell division Incom, which made gears and filters, would result in a twenty-two-times return. Of course, not all the deals turned out this profitable. But many were. In 1976, when Kohlberg made the decision to strike out on his own, taking along with him younger bankers Henry Kravis and George Roberts to form Kohlberg Kravis Roberts, First Chicago, which had been partnering on some of these deals, gave them money to set up an office and then helped finance every KKR deal right through the middle of the 1980s.

At first, a handful of "buyout groups," as these firms came to be known through the media, including KKR, Forstmann Little, and what would become Clayton, Dubilier & Rice, acquired companies worth no more than $350 million, because only four to five lenders, such as Bank of America and Security Pacific, were willing to finance these "leveraged buyouts" (LBOs), and the amount they would make available for such deals was limited.

This changed when the Wall Street bank Drexel Burnham Lambert, under the leadership of Michael Milken, popularized junk bonds (bonds that offered a relatively high return because they were unusually risky), and Leon Black, the head of Drexel's mergers and acquisitions practice, in 1982 started selling them to companies financing leveraged buyouts. (Leon was the son of Eli Black, who had run United Brands, which owned the Chiquita banana company. In 1975, when it was about to be revealed that Eli Black had bribed Honduran officials to lower the tax on banana exports and was himself facing financial ruin, he returned to his office on the forty-fourth floor of New York's landmark Pan Am Building, and took his own life by smashing a window and then jumping out.)

Under Milken and Black, each buyout process began the same way. Drexel agreed to lend the acquired company much of the difference between the amount the buyout king put down and the purchase price. Once the deal was closed, the savvy team at Drexel went out and resold its loan in the form of junk bonds. Citing the past successes of firms such as KKR and others, Drexel was highly successful in selling these bonds by suggesting that despite their name, the risk in these bonds was fairly low. Primary customers turned out to be savings and loan associations and insurance companies.

It wasn't Drexel's pitch about the low risk that caused the S&Ls to sit up and pay attention, but the fact these bonds were offering an 11 percent return. At this time, S&Ls were very worried about their future. Most of their money was being invested in residential mortgages, paying approximately 6 percent, while the S&Ls offered their customers 3 percent. The spread was not great, but the real problem began when the commercial banks started issuing CDs that paid customers 6 percent. Drexel's junk bonds, offering an opportunity to invest at 11 percent, seemed like a lifeline to the S&Ls, so they did not bother with much due diligence.

"The S&Ls were, I think, naive, and so they bought a lot of this stuff," cynically observed Joseph Rice, a cofounder of LBO firm Clayton, Dubilier & Rice, in a 2007 interview. "I mean, it's not dissimilar from what we've just gone through [with the banks financing risky mortgages and reselling them] in CLOs."

Armed with this new infusion of money, in 1986, KKR and Leon Black at Drexel engineered the $8.7 billion buyout of Beatrice Companies, the largest LBO up to that date. This marked the first time KKR bought a business despite its management's reluctance to sell. Hostile buyouts such as this were soon to become more frequent and more hostile. In the case of Beatrice, KKR reached above CEO James Dutt and went straight to the Beatrice board of directors, persuading them to negotiate. After Dutt quit, KKR continued its discussions with Beatrice. When the deal was closed, KKR put down $402 million of its own money against a purchase price of $8.7 billion.

Once again, targeting Beatrice had more to do with KKR's ability to scan the tax codes for loopholes than normal business acquisition strategies. KKR now believed it could buy a conglomerate like Beatrice, immediately sell off divisions, and according to the tax codes not pay a penny in taxes on the profits made by divesting those pieces.

Within a few years of purchasing Beatrice, KKR dismantled it, selling most—but not all—of the pieces for about the same price it had paid for the entire company. The pieces sold off included Tropicana to Seagram's; the Beatrice Dairy Products division to Borden; Avis car rental company to LBO firm Wesray; and Coca-Cola bottling operations that spanned nine states to Coca-Cola. Nine other divisions, including Samsonite luggage, were folded into one separate publicly traded company. Then, in 1990, KKR sold off what was left of Beatrice—the Swift, Wesson, and Peter Pan brands—to ConAgra for $1.3 billion. In doing so, KKR made about three times its money, proving that Beatrice's parts were more valuable than the sum of the whole.

Initially, the success of this deal was the talk of the town. The company was dismantled; KKR made a nice profit. But as more of these hostile takeovers hit the press, and the layoffs that came with them rose, the media began referring to the LBO kings as a new breed of robber baron. In the iconic 1987 movie *Wall Street,* a Henry Kravis–inspired Gordon Gekko proclaims: "Greed is good." The movie's hero, a stockbroker and son of a union man, eventually realizes leveraged-buyout kings unfairly victimize workers who have loyally helped build a company. Using the duplicity learned when he was playing with the big boys, he helps Gekko's rival buy his father's company. If only life imitated art. Alas, nothing of the sort happened.

But there was growing concern about the long-term consequences of leveraged buyouts. By the late 1980s, United Food and Commercial Workers Union members were picketing outside KKR-owned Safeway supermarkets, and others were crying out for Congress to act against what was widely perceived as an unfair exploitation of the tax code.

The government in 1987 ended the ability of new owners to sell off business divisions without paying taxes on the gains, making it unprofitable to buy a business like Beatrice and smash it to pieces (by this time it had also stopped companies from claiming the money borrowed to finance takeovers as depreciation, the original loophole that Kohlberg identified). But even these actions did not quell the growing fear in executive offices that someone at KKR had identified their company as the next takeover target.

The timing of the LBO spree could not have been worse for corporate America. After decades during which America's manufacturing products were accepted as the standard of excellence, its businesses suddenly had competition. In certain fields, such as electronics and automobiles, consumers in the United States were turning more and more to foreign goods. United States corporations were ceding market share not to other American corporations but to British and Japanese companies. And now they had to worry about these hostile takeovers.

LBO pioneer Rice would later argue that LBO firms like his helped American businesses by buying some of their noncore divisions. That, in turn, made them better able to compete against foreigners.

That argument was not totally convincing. It was true that many of the targeted businesses were conglomerates that did have extra layers of corporate fat, and some had too many divisions, which didn't get the managerial attention they needed. But piling huge amounts of debt on companies or divisions that were already having problems didn't seem to many people to be a helpful strategy.

There was, however, one thing that clearly was true: The buyout kings were making piles of money. The 1989 Forbes list of the four hundred richest Americans included the three KKR founders, Jerome Kohlberg, Henry Kravis, and George Roberts, who combined were worth $1.1 billion.

By 1989 there was even some evidence the LBO firms were helping to soften up American companies for foreigners. In 1979, KKR bought publicly traded industrial conglomerate Houdaille Industries. Soon the Japanese pounced, aggressively competing against the debt-laden business's division that made machine tools. Houdaille found it hard to protect itself against this new market threat while still meeting its loan obligations. Houdaille, after splitting off seven divisions, though, borrowed yet more money to buy KKR's stake for more than four times what it had paid. In 1986, British conglomerate Tube Investments Group acquired Houdaille, then nearly bankrupt.

It was now twenty years since the first Kohlberg buyout, and it was becoming clear that many of the companies loaded down with debt needed to make damaging cuts to meet their payments. As the layoffs of workers increased, so too did public outrage. Where was Congress to protect ordinary Americans against these Wall Street parasites?

In October 1987, House Ways and Means Committee chairman Dan Rostenkowski (D-IL) proposed closing the last big LBO loophole—changing the tax code to disallow deducting bank interest of more than $5 million from a company's tax obligations if money was borrowed to buy a majority of a company's stock. He wanted to keep the deduction for real business expenses, such as borrowing money to build a factory, not for subsidizing LBOs.

A few days after Rostenkowski proposed limiting interest deductions, the Dow Jones Industrial Average fell 23 percent, the largest one-day percentage decline in stock market history. Rostenkowski, who some believe caused "Black Monday" by his proposal, dropped it from the tax finance bill.

Emboldened, the buyout kings now began targeting businesses like Federated Department Stores, whose profits were unpredictable. LBO activity increased from $3 billion in 1981 to $74 billion in 1989. KKR was the buyout champ, acquiring RJR Nabisco in a $30 billion LBO, the era's biggest.

Buyout firms were so successful in acquiring companies because they were prepared to pay very high price-earnings multiples. Thus, for instance, in 1989 when LBO firm Gibbons, Green, van Amerongen paid $980 million for Ohio Mattress, which owned the Sealy brand, the purchase price was fourteen times earnings before taxes and interest. What made the offer even more appealing to the board was, as Ohio Mattress board member Ken Langone said, "A stretch price was paid for a company in an industry that had zero growth."

Observers looked at the sale and scratched their heads, wondering how the numbers could possibly work out. Because the LBO firm had put down roughly 16 percent of the purchase price, Ohio Mattress now had to meet debt payments equal to twenty-eight-times annual earnings when factoring in interest payments and do so over ten years without any real plan for growth. But in the booming 1989 buyout market, the purchaser could hope that Ohio Mattress's value would rise or at least stay the same, and if push came to shove, it could always refinance the debt and get a longer payoff period.

Rostenkowski's withdrawal in 1987 of his proposal to deny companies the right to deduct loan interest from taxes did not end public scrutiny or concern about the LBO industry. Two years later, in 1989, nine congressional hearings were planned on the impact of leveraged buyouts. Once again, politicians seriously considered ending the interest deductibility. Treasury Secretary Nicholas Brady, who served under President Reagan and stayed on with new President George H. W. Bush, thought changes were necessary. "When you put together a leveraged buyout," he argued, "what you essentially do is eliminate the 34 percent that used to go to the Federal Government in the form of taxes . . . maybe we ought to go to some sort of a balanced system of limiting the interest deductions [and reducing the tax on dividends]."

The Treasury secretary, who also was the former chairman of the
Wall Street investment bank Dillon, Read & Co., understood the LBO
business well. He knew that the tax breaks weren't the only incentive. There were also the enormous fees that buyers and arrangers
received up front and the fact that LBO firms had little at risk. The
firms formed buyout funds and committed capital equal to only about
2 percent of those pools, raising the rest from investors like state pensions. They also got a 20 percent commission on fund profits, so they
had the incentive to buy bigger and bigger businesses.

Banks encouraged buyouts because they received fees for brokering
deals and for making loans. Lenders like Drexel resold most of the loans
they made and were guaranteed profits as long as there were enough
S&Ls and insurance companies willing to buy the loans from them.

As Brady saw it, there were few incentives for self-regulatory cau-
tion. "A contributing factor in the proliferation of LBO activity is the
ability...to earn substantial up-front fees...[that] can total nearly six
percent of the corporation's purchase price," Brady observed. "These
fees are earned up front, largely divorced from the long-term risks of
the transaction. The LBO sponsor, investment banks, bond underwrit-
ers, syndicating banks, and others earn substantial income if an LBO
is completed and thus have strong incentives to identify LBO candidates, arrange financing, and conclude transactions. Sadly, these same
parties may have relatively little, if any, investment in the long-term
success of the new enterprise.

"While shareholders may..." walk away with "large premiums from
an LBO, the corporation's employees, bondholders, and community in
which the corporation is located may be adversely affected. Employees may lose their jobs if a corporation is forced to retrench or if divisions are sold in order to retire debt. Such job losses have significant
collateral effects in the communities in which the employees work.

"[If LBOs] went to an extreme and we did this to the whole United
States, I think it would be a bad thing," Brady concluded.

But attempts to rein in the LBO kings would not get very far. Newly
elected President George H. W. Bush was certainly not going to invest
any time in restricting their activities. The Bush and Kravis families
(Henry Kravis co-ran KKR) were very close. Ray Kravis, Henry's

father, had offered Bush his first postcollege job. Henry became a big fund-raiser for his presidential campaign, cochairing a Manhattan dinner at which guests contributed $550,000. KKR founders Kravis and George Roberts each gave $100,000 to GOP Team 100, a Republican National Committee fund dedicated to making the party competitive in every major election, and KKR's RJR Nabisco even donated $100,000. To thank them for their help, Bush named Kravis cochair of his 1989 inaugural dinner.

During congressional hearings, the LBO kings put forth the argument that if government took away tax interest deductibility, it would hurt America's global competitive position, explaining that Japanese businesses borrowed large amounts of money from local banks and deducted the interest from their taxes. What they left out of their argument was the fact that Japanese business owners were not flipping out of their companies. Another witness was Federal Reserve chairman Alan Greenspan, who was a great believer in the self-correcting nature of free markets. When asked by Oregon Republican senator Bob Packwood what he recommended in the way of action, Greenspan suggested that we "are probably looking at the peak of this activity.... This could lead me to try to do very little with respect to legislation but a lot with respect to supervision."

LBO activity did soon fall off, but not because of a change in attitude among the leveraged-buyout firms. Instead, the funding environment changed sharply. Then–U.S. Attorney Rudolph Giuliani hit Drexel's Michael Milken with racketeering charges that included insider trading. Milken eventually pleaded guilty to six felonies. Judge Kimba Wood sentenced him to ten years in prison, and he served twenty-two months. Drexel also pleaded guilty to mail, wire, and securities fraud, agreeing to pay $650 million in fines.

At the same time that Milken's and Drexel's legal problems were restricting the market, the savings and loans that had been some of the primary purchasers of junk bonds ran into trouble. Squeezed by bad real-estate loans, they no longer had the funds to invest in the junk-bond market. Then, to make matters worse, the government forced them to sell the bonds they still owned at any price they could get, which flooded the market. By 1990, the junk-bond market was moribund, and Drexel, unable to pay its fines, filed for bankruptcy protection.

More than half of the companies acquired in the twenty-five biggest buyouts eventually collapsed into bankruptcy and were taken over by creditors. In addition to the devastation within the companies that were reorganized or liquidated in bankruptcy, the carnage from the 1980s LBOs was also widespread elsewhere.

Major Buyouts Done in the 1980s That Failed

Of the twenty-five companies that issued $1 billion in junk bonds related to buyouts between 1985 and 1989, 52 percent filed for bankruptcy.

1.	Allied Stores
2.	Burlington Industries
3.	Charter Medical
4.	E-II Holdings
5.	Federated Department Stores
6.	Gillett Holdings
7.	R. H. Macy
8.	National Gypsum
9.	Owens-Corning
10.	SCI Holdings
11.	Southland
12.	USG
13.	Wickes

Sources: reprinted from *New York Times* chart that credits KDP Investment Advisors, Securities Data Corporation, New Generation Research.

The buyout fund investors, such as state pensions, who put cash down in buyouts lost much of their money. S&Ls and other junk-bond buyers, who funded 33 percent of the transaction price, also came away with very little. Eventually, as part of its bailout of the savings and loans, the government covered roughly $5 billion (or $15 billion counting interest) in junk-bond losses. So taxpayers lost. Commercial banks like First Boston and Chemical Bank financed the rest of these deals, and they were the last to lose their money, but even they sometimes got burned. Still, the LBO kings, who had long ago been paid their fees, consistently made money on these deals, and lots of it.

As the money for new buyouts dried up at the end of the 1980s, many observers came to believe that Alan Greenspan had been right. Even though LBOs had done a lot of damage, there was little need to worry because they were about to vanish. This expectation seriously underestimated the industry. As long as huge up-front fees could be made and investors could be lured with the argument that companies could still deduct the interest on the huge loans they took to finance their own takeovers, the industry was not about to go away.

In the early 1990s, the LBO kings disappeared from public view. They continued to operate, but on a diminished scale and in a less flamboyant fashion, turning their attention to rebuilding and giving themselves and their activities a professional makeover. First, the industry adopted a new name in an effort to erase its ties to the soiled history of LBOs. "It went from leveraged buyout to management buyout to private equity," said Canning, the banker who had funded the first Kohlberg deals and in 1992 formed his own private-equity firm, Madison Dearborn Partners. "It was really a marketing concept."

Fortunately too, interest rates came way down from where they were in the 1980s, so PE firms could refinance some of their struggling businesses, lowering debt payments and allowing companies to survive awhile longer.

At about the same time that LBO groups became private-equity firms, junk bonds were renamed high-yield bonds, and investment banks like Donaldson, Lufkin & Jenrette, full of former Drexelites, began to sell them increasingly to mutual funds, money managers, and insurers. The funding spigot was on again.

To an even larger degree, the PE firms began to raise money for their down payments from the state pensions that needed higher returns to pay all of the soon-to-be retiring Baby Boomers, and from high-net-worth individuals, as well as corporate pensions and endowments. The Blackstone Group, which had raised most of its money in the late 1980s from insurers, in 1993 raised about half of the money for a new $1.1 billion buyout fund from pensions. Groups like them said they were not like KKR, pointing to the fact that most of the companies they had bought had not gone bankrupt.

State pensions at the time had most of their investments in securities, like bonds, and their consultants were advising them to redirect some of that money to real estate and private-equity funds that could deliver better returns.

During much of the 1990s, funding for buyouts was still somewhat constricted. As a result, in this next iteration, private-equity firms (often referred to now as PE firms) turned to targeting more privately held businesses that produced steady earnings, spent little on capital expenditures, and could be bought for the right price.

The math was relatively straightforward. A company that generated $100 million in EBITDA (earnings before interest, taxes, depreciation, and amortization) and spent $15 million annually on capital expenditures could be bought for a six-times-EBITDA multiple, $600 million. If you then put down $180 million, 30 percent of the purchase price, and had the target company borrow the rest, it could pretty quickly reduce debt. The company would generate perhaps around $53 million annually in free cash flow (EBITDA minus capital expenditures, interest on the debt at a roughly 7 percent interest rate, and minimal taxes) and could give it all to lenders. In three years, the company would then pay $159 million in debt ($53 \times 3$). If the PE firm resold that business for the same $600 million price, it walked away with a $159 million profit on its $180 million cash investment, almost double its money, over three years. Imagine how much more the PE firms and their investors would collect if the company's profits grew and they were able to sell it at an even higher multiple!

In the late 1990s, the credit markets loosened a bit, and more investors with fatter wallets began turning once again to buyouts. In part, this was because the industry had succeeded in remaking its image. No longer were the big market players the greedy LBO kings whose excesses had cost investors so much and driven some S&Ls to the brink of collapse in the late 1980s. Now they were private-equity firms whose prudent investments in cash-rich companies in the early 1990s had yielded handsome returns.

Sellers were people like Ronald Berg, the scion of Philadelphia T-shirt distributor Alpha Shirt. In 1998, he had been running the company, which his grandfather had founded, for twenty-five years. A former student of existentialism, Berg had a knack for marketing, and his business was growing—perhaps too fast. Alpha bought T-shirts in bulk from the biggest makers, like Anvil Knitwear, and then sold them to hundreds of mom-and-pop screen printers. It was opening new warehouses in California, Indiana, and Texas. Berg was growing his business, but he was no financial whiz. He said, "I'm up to $350 million a year in sales and we are the biggest, and I knew nothing about words like budget and EBITDA. Even if you spelled out the words they didn't mean anything to me." Lenders, though, told Berg that Alpha was running out of money and needed to bring in additional capital. Merrill Lynch introduced him to private-equity firm Linsalata Capital Partners. Soon it became clear what Alpha was worth. "The number of what I would attract in a sale blew my mind," Berg said.

Though he had twins, they were only teenagers and not ready to take over the business. Berg—knowing very little about private equity—moved forward. "I had no second thoughts."

The company put itself up for sale, and several PE firms took interest. "They all told us how much they respect family businesses and team spirit. All the buzzwords they thought I wanted to hear." He sold to Linsalata, and though company growth under them was not remarkable by Alpha standards, the PE firm made Alpha much more profitable.

But as more and more ex–Wall Street bankers decided to get into the LBO game by forming their own private-equity firms, finding cash-rich companies like Alpha or divisions of businesses that mainly needed better cost controls became increasingly difficult. By the decade's 1999 peak, seventy-five PE firms globally managed individual funds bigger than $1 billion (compared to five in 1989).

With so much money chasing too few opportunities, the definition of a "good deal" started to change. Ideally, PE firms continued to target companies with a steady cash flow. But when these were not available, they started going after businesses that could be "squeezed" into this profile. For the companies bought in the 1990s, the ones that did have healthy cash flow, stripping away all of their surplus cash to pay down debt required them to restrict spending, but they could maintain operations. When the buyouts turned to the companies that needed to be "squeezed" just to create a profile that would support the debt payments, the picture changed.

"Squeezing" came to mean looking for ways to boost revenue as well as cutting costs. At the Iasis hospital chain, according to hospital insiders, the squeezing took a frightening form. PE firm JLL Partners bought the fifteen-hospital and one behavioral medical center chain in 1999 and allegedly put financial considerations ahead of everything else, including life and death.

I investigated conditions at its 350-bed St. Luke's hospital in Phoenix, Arizona. In 2003, St. Luke's reached an agreement with a cardiac practice that allowed it to operate without being under hospital peer review. (Since 1986, when Congress passed the Health Care Quality Improvement Act, all physicians with hospital memberships have been required to face peer review.) St. Luke's leased the practice space so it could operate without hospital oversight.

"I have never seen that happen in my years in the profession," said a person who was a St. Luke's administrator at that time.

Dr. David Hoelzinger, who was then head of cardiology, told us, "This arrangement was just not typical, not usual, and the rest of us cardiologists felt very uncomfortable with that and made that known at committees, but the practice somehow seemed to sidestep all of that with this arrangement."

According to a member of the St. Luke's executive committee, when the committee fought the administration and voted to put the practice's doctors under hospital peer review, Iasis froze spending for the hospital. Only after the staff a few weeks later approved new by-laws transferring peer review from physicians to hospital administrators (who allowed the cardiac practice to police itself) did Iasis start funding the hospital again, he said. An Iasis spokeswoman, Tomi Galin, said the allegation that Iasis hospitals amended by-laws so certain physicians could operate outside peer review is "untrue."

In any event, a senior physician who was then on the executive committee, said the practice soon started seeing patients and installing intra-aortic balloon pumps, which relieve heart pressure and are normally only given to the very ill, at about ten times the average rate.

Jerre Frazier, the former Iasis vice president of ethics and business practices and chief compliance officer, alleged in a 2005 complaint against Iasis under the False Claims Act that doctors at four of Iasis's sixteen hospitals performed unnecessary cardiac procedures, including the cardiac practice at St. Luke's of putting a number of patients on balloon pumps so it could bill an additional $1,000 per patient per day for maintenance of the balloon pumps. These allegedly unnecessary procedures resulted in millions in reimbursement for St. Luke's, which Frazier claimed charged for leasing the space and got paid a set amount for surgeries performed at its hospital.

The U.S. District Court for Arizona in 2008 dismissed the suit partly because Frazier did not state why the procedures were medically unnecessary or identify any cases of patients with unnecessary procedures.

JLL managing director Jeffrey Lightcap told me he didn't know about the allegation of unnecessary surgeries until Frazier brought it to Iasis's attention in 2004, months after he was fired. Lightcap said Iasis investigated and found there was nothing serious enough to report.

Still, Dr. Cordell Esplin, who currently heads the St. Luke's radiation safety committee, said Iasis, when reaching the deal with the cardiac practice, put money over patient care.

After boosting Iasis's revenue by 25 percent and EBITDA by more than 50 percent, JLL sold control of Iasis in 2004 to fellow PE firm TPG Capital Partners and better than doubled its money.

In the late 1990s, as the prices of deals rose and the availability of companies with extra cash diminished, purely dollar-based decisions such as these became increasingly the norm. These decisions, which diminish the quality of the companies' goods and services, eventually damage their reputations and ultimately their economics. But especially in health care where patients are reluctant to change providers, it can take quite a while before the economic damage hits the bottom line. The full impact might not be felt for five to ten years, and that will be long after the PE firm expects to be out.

About half of the big companies acquired in the LBO frenzy of the late 1980s eventually collapsed, but the deals of the 1990s were, in a sense, more destructive. Not as many of the companies acquired in the 1990s ended up in bankruptcy, but whereas many of the LBOs of the 1980s destroyed companies that were bloated, PE firms in the 1990s took companies that were decent performers and made them sick by squeezing them to produce higher earnings and burdening them with crippling debt.

My investigation of the ten biggest 1990s LBOs reveals that six of the companies clearly were worse off than they likely would have been had they never been acquired; three were largely unaffected; and only one came out ahead. What most of the buyouts have in common is they made millions, if not hundreds of millions, for the private-equity firms that put them together (see appendix).

These LBOs were in industries ranging from technology to packaging. Many companies were bled of capital to boost earnings and retire debt more quickly. And because they were in industries that required investment, they fell behind their competitors. In 1999, when Thomas H. Lee Partners and Evercore Partners acquired what they renamed Vertis Communications, it was the fifth largest North American printer. By 2006, when many peers had expanded to offer other services, such as marketing, it was ninth. Vertis filed for bankruptcy in 2008.

Meanwhile, the U.S. government, by failing to end the tax deductibility of interest on debt, lost about $22.5 billion on companies bought during the decade. Many workers, some who had loyally worked for these companies their entire adult lives, lost their jobs. And investors rarely did much better.

Despite the promises of riches, investors in buyout funds did not collect huge returns. Steven Kaplan, a University of Chicago professor of entrepreneurship and finance, co-wrote a study that showed PE funds from 1980 to 2001 produced returns—after fees—lower than the S&P 500 stock-market index. The PE firms delivered better than stock-market numbers, but not after subtracting their 25 percent commissions.

Still, while the PE industry staged an impressive comeback during the 1990s, it was during the mid-2000s that it really took off. People who never imagined themselves targets, like rent-stabilized tenants in Manhattan apartments, ended up in the crosshairs of the hunters.

CHAPTER TWO

The Next Credit Crisis

One thing we learned from the mortgage crisis that began in 2007 is that lenders bore at least as much responsibility for the bad loans that swamped the credit markets as the borrowers. True, the borrowers often lied about their assets and incomes on loan applications. But many of them were doing so with the full encouragement of lenders.

Because lenders were packaging and reselling their loans, they didn't really care if the borrowers could repay. The banks and mortgage brokers were making their money on fees, so what mattered to them was volume. Bankers were actually pushing loans on people they *knew* probably couldn't pay, because their institutions weren't going to be holding the loans by the time the borrowers defaulted, and the more loans they generated, the more the banks earned in fees. The situation was made worse by the fact that the writing of mortgages was driven not by demand from potential homeowners but by demand from investors buying loans from banks.

In the private-equity arena, the same dynamic was at work. Here the demand was magnified by an influx of pension money flowing into the buyout funds that provided the down payments in LBOs. All through the 1990s, private equity had courted pension-fund managers and had had some success. Most fund managers, though, invested at least equally in venture capitalist firms, which offered high returns along with a reputation for driving new technology. But in the early 2000s, venture-capital firms began returning money to their investors unspent, reporting that they could not find enough new companies worth funding. And when they did raise new investment funds, the pools were generally much smaller than before. By 2002, the technology bubble had burst, and the venture capitalists had taken to the sidelines. Now private equity became one of the only games in town for pensions seeking high returns, especially since faith in the stock markets had been shaken by the corporate scandals at Enron and other high-flying companies.

Most pension-fund managers had allocated no more than 5 percent of their funds to venture capital and other "alternatives" to traditional stocks and bonds. But that 5 percent played a critical role in their investment strategies. The higher-than-average returns they expected from venture-capital investments made up for the fact many of these pensions were becoming underfunded. So the fund managers reluctantly turned to private equity to look for the higher returns they needed. What sealed the deal for those who wavered was the Federal Reserve's determination to spur consumer spending by lowering interest rates. Between January and November 2001, the Fed cut interest rates ten times, from 6.5 percent to 2 percent. This allowed the PE firms to promise that the companies they bought through LBOs would generate higher than typical returns because they could borrow at historically low interest rates. Pension managers were convinced.

Armed with new pension money and having easy access to increasing amounts of credit, private equity went on a buying spree. A study by the World Economic Forum covering the period from 1970 to 2007 reported that the estimated value of LBOs globally totaled $3.6 trillion. A careful examination of this data, however, shows that 75 percent of those dollars, or $2.7 trillion, was the result of deals that happened between 2001 and 2007.

Big banks financed the post-2000 PE activity. At first, the banks were careful. Especially during the "difficult 2001 and 2002 period [when bankruptcy rates were high]," said Robert Barnwell, vice president of Royal Bank of Scotland, the banks attempted to restrict the activity of PEs to creditworthy firms. Even in 2003 and 2004, he observed, "there was a lot of attention paid to credit quality."

Then the banks, taking a leaf from the private-equity playbook, started letting their guard down. By 2006, a loan from a bank like RBS came with an up-front fee of 1.5 percent to 2 percent of the total loan. RBS figured it could earn enough from the fees to offset any risks associated with the money it actually had on the line. And the amount it risked was limited because it was reselling 85 percent to 90 percent of the loans almost as soon as it made them. Besides reducing the bank's exposure and freeing money for the bank to lend again, the resales reduced the amount of reserves banks were required by law to hold against outstanding loans. This gave the banks extra money to make loans for more PE buyouts, for which they could charge more fees.

Meanwhile, many of the people buying the loans from the banks weren't holding on to them either. They were repackaging and reselling them to people who would often repackage and resell them yet again. The loans were passed around like hot potatoes, each holder trying to get rid of them before they got burned.

Much of the most senior debt, which would be paid back first if the borrower went bankrupt, was sold to CLOs, or collateralized loan obligation funds. CLOs were similar to the CDOs, or collateralized debt obligations, which were instrumental in the meltdown of the mortgage market in 2007–9 and paid similar rates. In creating CDOs, fund managers bundled together unrelated mortgages and then sold off pieces of the bundle. The idea was that, while a few of the debtors might default, the vast majority of the loans in the bundles would be good, and this would make the CDOs safe assets to hold.

The problem in the mortgage market was that once the CDOs made it possible to sell off loans so easily, the banks originating them became almost indifferent as to whether the borrowers could pay them back—that is, until a wave of foreclosures hit in 2007. Then the investors who had bought into CDOs, thinking they were getting safe investments, stopped buying new loans. That meant the banks became more careful about making loans, which in turn caused the housing market to collapse.

As stated before, CLOs are basically the same thing as CDOs, only with corporate loans instead of mortgages. Every CLO consists of a little bit of debt from perhaps 150 to 200 different loans, the idea being that if one of these "pieces" of debt fails, the others can more than make up the difference. As with subprime mortgages, no one ever discussed the possibility of more than a small percentage of the loans in any one CLO package defaulting at the same time.

CLO managers had cover when reselling CLOs to investors. They paid the two biggest credit-rating agencies, Standard & Poor's and

Moody's, to rate their CLOs, and the agencies gave the part of CLOs that represented about 75 percent of the money raised AAA ratings, which meant very little risk of default. The agencies, however, did not examine the creditworthiness of the loans in the portfolios. Rather, they based these ratings on whether the CLO manager had systems in place to monitor the loan portfolio and their computer models that considered historical default rates and seemed to overlook the historical default rates on loans for highly leveraged buyouts made during boom times. More than half of the companies that borrowed more than $1 billion in junk bonds to finance buyouts in the 1980s went bankrupt.

Rating agencies worked with little formal regulation or oversight. The Securities and Exchange Commission (SEC) was prompted by the mortgage crisis in September 2007 to start regulating the rating agencies, but that was after the damage had already been done.

The SEC in July 2008 concluded a formal investigation into the agencies. It found some of them were overwhelmed by the increased volume of work that came from the flood of CDOs, and they cut corners when rating securities. It also found that the agencies may have considered their own profits when issuing ratings. Both Moody's and McGraw-Hill, the parent of Standard & Poor's, saw their stocks soar on the strength of the rating fees.

Most of the loans in the CLOs haven't come due yet, but it is very likely that a substantial number of them will fail. And because there are several layers of even more derivative securities built behind the CLOs, these loans are just as widely distributed as the toxic mortgages. CLO investors range from Sub-Saharan African countries to state municipalities. If and when they go down, the result is likely to be another global tsunami.

The main point here is the CLOs and the other derivative securities created a huge new market for loans and unleashed a torrent of funding for leveraged buyouts in the middle of the first decade of the new century. In 2003, CLO fund managers raised $12 billion. Two years later, in 2005, they raised $53 billion; one year after that, $97 billion. By 2008, U.S.-based CLOs held $270 billion in loans, mostly for private-equity–owned companies.

Who Bought Bank Loans?

The following is a list of investors that bought the fifteen biggest slices of a 2007 bank loan from the banks that financed one of the largest buyouts. The composition of buyers is typical for buyouts completed from 2005 through the first half of 2007.

1.	Hedge Fund 5.1 percent
2.	Mutual Fund Manager/Insurance Company 4.4 percent
3.	CLO 4.1 percent
4.	Mutual Fund Manager/Insurance Company 3.7 percent
5.	Mutual Fund Manager/Insurance Company 2.6 percent
6.	Mutual Fund Manager/Insurance Company 2.4 percent
7.	Hedge Fund 2.2 percent
8.	CLO 2.2 percent
9.	CLO 1.8 percent
10.	CLO 1.7 percent
11.	Mutual Fund Manager/Insurance Company 1.6 percent
12.	Hedge Fund 1.5 percent
13.	Mutual Fund Manager/Insurance Company 1.4 percent
14.	CLO 1.4 percent
15.	CLO 1.2 percent

TOTAL: These fifteen buyers bought 37.3 percent of the bank loan.

As the demand for CLOs surged, the managers who packaged them looked to the banks to produce more loans. The banks, as a result, became willing to lend money at higher and higher earnings multiples. The bankers figured that if CLOs were willing to buy a loan funding the buyout of Toys "R" Us equal to 9 times its earnings before interest, taxes, and depreciation (EBITDA), the banks would lend at that multiple and resell the loan. This was even though a year earlier they were only willing to lend Toys "R" Us money equal to 7.7 times those earnings. The fact that Toys "R" Us might have trouble repaying the loan was not a major concern.

The average EBITDA multiple paid by a PE firm for a company in an LBO increased 40 percent, from 6.0 in 2001 to 8.4 in 2005.

A lending head at a major global bank described it, saying, "It was just fantastic markets. When a company like ServiceMaster [which cleans houses through its Merry Maids branches and whose Terminix agents kill bugs] raised 7.75 times debt to EBITDA or whatever the leverage was [in July 2007] to finance a $5 billion buyout, you might think those guys were nuts for buying at 7.75 times, but that's where the market was and that's where your competitor was, so that's where you went."

At the same time that the banks were lending more, the PE firms were also raising more money from their investors, collecting more fees, and buying even more businesses. The more they raised and spent, the more they made, even if the investments failed. Sometimes they bought from each other. In 2005, 16 percent of the U.S. companies acquired by PE firms, excluding the ones they bought to combine with their existing businesses, were purchased from their peers.

Investors who put money into deals in the early 2000s did well. Capital invested in 2001 and 2002 generated good returns, so pension-fund managers responded positively when PE firms came with new offerings. The percentage of U.S. pension plans with $5 billion or more in assets that invested in private equity rose from 71 percent to 80 percent from 2001 through 2007.

As the pension-fund money poured in, demand for new companies began to exceed supply. PE firms were competing with each other for deals. Sellers, sensing desperation, took control of the situation, significantly shortening the sales process by giving buyers less opportunity to study their books and operations.

Before the sellers seized the market, an auction for a business typically unfolded for several months. The seller, working through a financial adviser, sent a teaser letter, which contained only the most basic financial information about the company, to potential suitors. Suitors who wanted to see more signed a confidentiality agreement and in exchange received a sales book with more detailed information.

Then the seller set a date for preliminary bids, which were not binding but indicated how much suitors might be willing to offer for the company. After receiving those offers, the seller let a handful of bidders, usually no more than six, into a second auction round. During this phase, the suitors got to visit the company, meet management, and pore over its financial statements. A PE bidder would notify a lender to see if it could finance a deal, and would give it two to three months to decide whether to fund the buyout.

Under the new rules imposed by sellers, PE firms had to bid for companies based on financials provided by the seller, not their own homework. This became more important as sellers started telling buyers to bid based on earnings derived not from historical numbers but on what their companies *would* earn after making certain improvements. Barnwell, whose bank sometimes represented sellers, said they often fed suitors earnings figures that were inflated by 20 percent to 30 percent over what they actually were. Private companies, he noted, were less constricted than public companies in coming up with more optimistic projections, because they did not have to make sure the stories they told suitors were compatible with the ones they told shareholders. Although sellers hired outside accountants to verify the financial strength of their businesses, these reports were often just as suspect.

Jon Moulton, the founder of London PE firm Alchemy Partners, believes only one third of the numbers were based on reality. The rest were optimistic projections. For example, these projections might include savings on overhead that might not be achieved for five years.

"My favorite was a PricewaterhouseCoopers report I got in May 2007 for a company which started off... 'We have had no access to the books and accounts of the company,'" Moulton said. "PWC was paid a fortune for taking no risk. It's pretty hard to sue off a report that says this is what the company told us."

The banks lending the money to fund the buyouts were similarly pressed, especially after 2005, when they were asked to make commitments in as little as a few weeks, as opposed to a few months, Barnwell said. By then, when a PE firm called a bank to see if it could finance a deal, the banks understood they needed three internal teams—a leveraged-loan group, a syndication group (the people who resell the loan), and a credit team—to start working on the project. "Any institution that is going to respond within ten days needs to have all these teams working in tandem," Royal Bank's Barnwell explained, adding that they had to start their analysis with the copy of the financials the seller provided the buyers.

"Now what you would like to have happen is that someone goes on the Internet downloading comps from similar companies so you can see how their peers have performed through a bad business cycle. You would like to download research reports; you would like to purchase $5000 industry studies from various consultancies.

"The reality is you are trying to populate memos. What you are doing is telling a story to get approval to satisfy your regulators that you have done your diligence. A good part of your time is spent creating a document, rather than formulating and analyzing information."

Still, it was clear that some loans were very risky, even if you planned to resell them. For example, Moody's Investors Service reported that the seven- or eight-year loans taken out in 2006 by a group of specialty retailers, which included Michaels stores, to finance buyouts could not be paid back for a thousand years at the firms' current rate of earnings. By comparison, specialty retailers bought in 2004 were assessed as being able to pay back their similar loans in a mere fifteen years.

Moody's raised the possibility that the retailers bought in 2006 would never be able to repay their debts without sizable increases in cash flow. It gave Burlington, Michaels, and PETCO right after their respective buyouts a B2 rating, which means that assurance of loan compliance over any long period of time might be small.

Why would PE firms arrange such risky loans for their companies? Because they believed the companies' value would rise, and then they would be able to resell the businesses or refinance the loans within several years. From 2002 through the first half of 2007, they were right, as the debt markets kept rising, Moulton said. "You got rewarded for taking ever more ludicrous risks, and for swallowing ever less attractive companies with less legitimate numbers."

Speaking at a 2006 industry conference, former Drexelite Leon Black was one of the first to publicly express reservations about the actions of private-equity firms. "Most of us in this business are deal junkies...so I worry about us as an industry keeping our investment discipline." Still, his firm, Apollo Management, in 2006 led a $1.3 billion buyout of one of those specialty retailers, Linens 'n Things, which went bankrupt in 2008. After collapsing, the company was unable to find a buyer willing to acquire it out of bankruptcy, so it liquidated its inventory and closed operations. The buyers lost the $648 million they put down to buy the business. Linens 'n Things five months before filing for bankruptcy had 589 stores and 17,500 employees.

Apollo and its bidding group, though, likely did fine. Apollo put up about 2.2 percent of the money in the buyout fund that made the down payment, so if its coinvestors put up similar amounts in their funds they lost a combined $14.3 million when the business collapsed (the bidders put $648 million down to buy Linens and $648 \times 2.2 = 14.3$). But the firms (not the fund investors) collected a $15 million transaction fee from Linens 'n Things, plus out-of-pocket expenses when closing the deal, and an annual $2 million management fee for overseeing the business, which it probably received for two years. It likely shared that $19 million in fees equally with fund investors, netting the firms $9.5 million. Apollo charged its fund investors an annual 1.5 percent management fee. If the rest of the bidding group did the same even after they reduced the management fee by an amount equal to half the money they collected for themselves in fees (common practice in the PE world), it still totaled another $14.7 million over two years. *Ka-ching!* In total, the PE firms made a better than 50 percent return on Linens 'n Things, even though they quickly drove the business into bankruptcy and their fund investors were essentially wiped out.

Purchase multiples that had risen 40 percent from 2001 to 2005 took another 15 percent leap between 2005 and 2007. Meanwhile, the amount of cash that PE firms were putting down to buy businesses was actually falling (from 38 percent cash down in 2000 to only 33 percent in 2007).

An investor in PE firm Bain Capital's funds said Bain conceded it was overpaying for companies in 2006 and 2007 but claimed it was buying such good businesses that it would figure out how to make money on the investments.

Sometimes Barnwell says credit teams like the one he helped lead at RBS raised concerns. "We were careful the way we issued warnings, as credit committee meetings were recorded and reviewed by regulators. You can look at a deal and say from a risk return point of view it is not something I want to do. On the other hand I think it will distribute." Translation: If we had to hold on to the loan, it would make no sense. Given that we will resell it, we may be able to get away without losing our shirts and possibly even make money.

Barnwell said he did not agree with the credit decisions but understood the rationale. "When you stand in front of the revenue train, you are going to be run down. In a financial institution, the CEO is compensated on stock price appreciation."

By 2007, five to ten banks, including JPMorgan and Goldman Sachs, were generating roughly 20 percent of their revenue from private-equity–related business, such as financing buyouts. Banks feared that if they did not agree to finance a particular buyout, the PE firm making the request would never call on them again, because there were always several other banks ready to make the same loan at the terms they wanted.

In earlier eras, there were kingmakers like Michael Milken of Drexel Burnham Lambert or James Lee at Chase who controlled much of the buyout-financing markets. While aggressively approving loans, they also kept their PE clients in check. If a PE firm wanted a buyout loan, it would likely have to go through them. But in 2007, just about all the major global banks were financing buyouts, and none had a dominant market share (from 2005 through 2007, JPMorgan Chase held a leading 15 percent share of the U.S. LBO loan market). For example, RBS was providing the largest amount of money backing buyouts of European companies, and was making a strong push to be one of the biggest in America. RBS bankers felt an immense amount of pressure to lend at higher levels than its peers. This competition between the banks put them in a weak bargaining position when negotiating with PE firms.

Lenders Providing Biggest Bank Loans Financing
U.S. Buyouts 2005–7

	Deal Value (in billions)	Market Share
JPMorgan Chase	95.3	15%
Goldman Sachs	58.3	9.2%
Citigroup	56.2	8.9%
Credit Suisse	54.9	8.7%
Bank of America	49.6	7.8%
Deutsche Bank	47.4	7.5%

	Deal Value (in billions)	Market Share
Lehman Brothers	40.2	6.4%
Merrill Lynch	33.5	5.3%
Morgan Stanley	28.9	4.6%
Wachovia	24.4	3.9%
Total	$488.7	77.3%

Source: Government Accountability Office Analysis of Dealogic Data.

Even when they were already getting what they wanted, PE firms pitted banks against each other to drive better terms. "There virtually was always push back for a variety of reasons," Barnwell said. "One is the banks were competing, so you want to set the banks against themselves before you accept the first offer. The other thing is the market for CLOs [which were buying the loans from the banks] was so strong at the time. CLOs were having a real problem getting enough loans to fill demand. And there was an understanding that very few deals didn't get done. So therefore you continually pushed the market to see what the market would and would not accept."

As a result, private-equity–owned companies were able to get loans that carried few performance requirements. James Coulter, the cofounder of PE firm TPG Capital, said at a 2006 conference while addressing his peers that when retailer PETCO borrowed money in 2000 to finance a $600 million TPG and Leonard Green & Partners buyout, it was required by its lenders to maintain its earnings. If the retailer's EBITDA fell by 8 percent, the company might break an earnings covenant and default. The PE firms eventually listed PETCO on the stock market and made a huge gain—4.5 times their money. PETCO's share price from the time of the early 2002 IPO through the summer of 2006 stayed the same. In 2006 TPG led a $1.8 billion repurchase of the business. The terms of the bank loan this time were much different. PETCO's EBITDA could fall by 100 percent in two years, and the company would not be in trouble.

Banks basically agreed to stop monitoring PE-owned companies. They would allow them to fall well below any point at which the loans could conceivably be repaid before taking action. Some businesses bought in 2007 even got provisions in their loan agreements called

PIK toggles, allowing them, if they did not want to make interest payments, to instead exchange them for bonds with a higher interest rate that were not due for several years.

Brimming with confidence, PE firms bought companies they could not have dreamed of acquiring in years past. They had much more money to put down in buyouts than ever before. They quadrupled the amount they raised for their funds from $66 billion globally in 2003 to $258 billion in 2006. Because they only put 33 percent down in buyouts, in 2007 they essentially had $780 billion in buying power. They borrowed from banks that sometimes offered to finance buyouts of companies at higher earnings multiples than they were trading at in the public markets. With that fuel, PE firms in 2006 and 2007 did nine of the ten biggest buyouts of all time. These ranged from the $28 billion acquisition of casino operator Harrah's Entertainment to the $38 billion LBO of real-estate developer Equity Office Properties.

Biggest Buyouts of All Time

Date Deal Closed	Buyer	Company	Industry	Amount (billions)
10/07	TPG, Goldman Sachs, KKR	TXU	Utility	$44
2/07	Blackstone	Equity Office Properties	Real estate	$38
11/06	Bain, KKR, Merrill Lynch	Hospital Corp. of America	Hospitals	$32
4/89	KKR	RJR Nabisco	Tobacco and consumer foods	$30
1/08	Apollo, TPG	Harrah's Entertainment	Casinos	$28
5/07	Carlyle, Goldman Sachs, Riverstone Holdings, AIG	Kinder Morgan	Pipelines	$28

Date Deal Closed	Buyer	Company	Industry	Amount (billions)
9/07	KKR	First Data	Credit card processing	$27
11/07	Goldman Sachs, TPG	Alltel	Telecom	$27
10/07	Blackstone	Hilton Hotels	Lodging	$27
7/08	Bain, Thomas H. Lee Partners	Clear Channel Communications	Radio stations and billboards	$26

Source: Thomson Reuters.

PE firms in 2007 led buyouts globally worth $659 billion. They were executing about one quarter of all mergers in the United States and an even larger proportion in Britain. Overall, PE firms from 2000 through mid-2007 bought companies that employed close to one of every ten Americans working in the private sector, 10 million people, according to University of Chicago professor Steven Davis.

In 2004 the *Economist* hailed PE firms in a cover article, "The New Kings of Capitalism." TPG's Coulter, speaking to his peers at the 2006 conference, riffed off the classic tale of buyout greed gone berserk, *Barbarians at the Gate*. "Unlike in the 1980s when the Barbarians were at the gate," Coulter said, "they are now in our homes and dating our daughters."

Ironically, this rush of activity came to a crashing halt not because PE-owned companies went bankrupt but because CLO investors started losing money in subprime mortgages bought through the very similar CDOs. In July 2007, Bear Stearns announced that the hedge funds it managed had lost $1.4 billion as a result of its position in subprime collateralized mortgage bonds, and that outside investors in those funds would be essentially wiped out. Predictably, there was a spectacular overlap between those who bought collateralized subprime-mortgage debt and those who bought collateralized private-equity debt. The only difference was that the vast majority of collateralized private-equity debt would not come due for several years.

As a result of the mortgage crisis, a number of banks that had agreed to finance leveraged buyouts to the tune of $350 billion were left holding the bag in 2007. Investors weren't buying CLOs, so the banks couldn't unload the loans on them. Some of the banks were saved because the PE firms decided not to go ahead with their deals, realizing that their companies could not afford to pay the higher interest rates that would be charged during the credit crisis. Buyouts of companies ranging from student loan provider SLM (Sallie Mae) to car audio equipment–maker Harman International were scrapped. But occasionally banks had to stand by their commitments because the PE firms wouldn't let them out.

Most PE-owned companies do not need to worry about bankruptcy until their principal is due, which is seven or eight years into their loans. Until then, they have few performance requirements to meet and generally must pay only 1 percent principal annually. Even if they cannot make interest payments, those with PIK toggles can exchange interest payments for bonds, and others can tap revolving lines of credit they arranged when the credit markets were more forgiving. Principal will come due for most of these businesses anywhere between 2012 and 2014.

In spring-2008, Maria Boyazny, a managing director with private-equity firm Siguler Guff, said, "Over the next year, $500 billion in sub-prime mortgages are maturing…but even scarier is the $1 trillion in [U.S. corporate] leveraged loans that are maturing" later.

Chris Taggert of research firm CreditSights said, "By and large, unless the loans are paid down, which I don't think they will be in most cases, you can do two things: sell assets and pay back the loan, or refinance. It took a bubble to issue all this debt; it may not take a bubble to refinance it. But it will take a strong credit market."

In 2008, Taggert said he believed that if the credit markets returned to normal levels, where they were right before the mortgage and buyout booms took hold, then banks will refinance loans to the many companies that can pay higher interest rates and push out their principal payments, while they will force those that need cheap financing to survive into bankruptcy. Perhaps as many as 85 percent of the companies bought in LBOs during the buyout boom would then remain solvent past 2015.

If the credit markets stay frozen as they were in 2008, however, many PE-owned companies, even those that can make higher interest payments, will go bankrupt, because there will be no one willing to refinance their existing loans when they come due in three to five years. Then, Taggert predicts, half of the companies bought through buyouts could go bankrupt.

A complicating factor is that most of the loans PE companies took out to finance their buyouts were based on a floating London Interbank Offered Rate (LIBOR) of interest plus, say, 2 percent. If the LIBOR rises, the companies pay more. The LIBOR likely *will* rise soon because the U.S. government is borrowing money for bank bailouts and stimulus projects, and it will need to offer higher rates to attract investors.

There are some ominous signs. Of the fifty-six companies acquired in some of the biggest buyouts that have options to switch on PIK toggles, 35 percent as of December 2008, including Hispanic language broadcaster Univision, invoked them and issued bonds due in several years instead of paying interest. PE-owned companies in industries especially hurt by the recession are also already collapsing. For example, in newspaper publishing, Tribune Co., which owns the *Chicago Tribune* and *Los Angeles Times;* the *Star Tribune* of Minneapolis; and my former employer, *Journal Register,* have all filed for bankruptcy.

Despite the drop in advertising, *Star Tribune* executives said after the company declared bankruptcy in 2009 that the paper would have still been turning a narrow profit had it not been for interest payments on the money it borrowed to finance its own buyout.

The companies that did not have to meet performance requirements may be in the worst shape when reckoning day comes. If their loans had required it, they might have been forced to declare bankruptcy sooner. Once operating in bankruptcy, they would have had less debt and been able to invest more in areas that drive growth, such as research and development. But PE firms now will starve these businesses longer and as a result may kill them off before they have a chance to restructure.

Even if PE firms wanted to shore up these companies with cash infusions, many will not take money from new funds to bail out investments from older funds and risk angering new fund investors.

Some PE firms have brought in operating executives to help run the companies that they don't have time to manage adequately. Goldman Sachs, manager of one of the biggest PE firms, hired Jon Weber, who had been in charge of operational oversight for Carl Icahn's companies, to create value in the businesses it owned. But it isn't clear whether these operating executives' primary job is to improve the businesses over the long term or to pressure the management teams who run the companies to boost earnings faster.

James Whitney, managing director at Conway MacKenzie & Dunleavy, a corporate consulting firm that helps turn around businesses heading for bankruptcy, said PE firms often underestimate the work it takes to rescue companies. Predicting what will happen in the next few years, he draws a parallel with the housing market.

Many homeowners who bought in the middle of the real-estate boom now are stuck paying mortgages totaling more than the value of their homes. So they are filing for bankruptcy to avoid making payments. Similarly, PE firms that find their companies way over their heads in debt may just bail out of them and focus on maximizing returns from their better deals. Hugh MacArthur, a senior partner in consulting firm Bain & Co.'s private-equity practice, even suggested to PE firms at a 2008 industry conference that they not waste too much time on turning around struggling businesses. The head of restructuring at a major bank predicts 10 percent to 15 percent of PE-owned companies will default annually from 2012 through 2014.

The losses won't make the PE barons close up shop. They have made enough in fees to cover the money they personally put into their businesses. On top of that, they have roughly $450 billion they have already raised to invest, and they are ready to start buying companies through LBOs again when the economy recovers. But others will suffer.

The underfunded pensions that are counting on PE firms to help save them will be in bigger trouble than they already are. Big investors include the California Public Employees' Retirement System, the California State Teachers' Retirement System, and the New York, Michigan, and Washington state pensions.

Even though they have resold most of their loans, the banks that financed buyouts are also likely to be hurt. Their losses will be gradual, as they have to mark down the value of their loans every quarter. But if there is a rash of buyout bankruptcies, the banks could be sued for not doing proper due diligence. In an October 2007 speech (after the credit crisis started), Comptroller of the Currency John Dugan, who regulates and supervises all national banks, expressed disappointment in the way banks had acted, saying that going forward they should underwrite loans in a manner more consistent with the standards they would use if they held the loans themselves. Former Federal Reserve chairman Alan Greenspan testified before Congress in October 2008 that he was in "shocked disbelief" that the self-interest of banks had not kept them from making so many bad subprime loans.

Hedge funds that invested heavily in LBO financings and often raised CLO funds will also take a hit. CLO investors are vulnerable and are already selling their stakes to buyers of distressed debt, like Cerberus Capital Management, at deep discounts.

Even the CLO investors who took out credit insurance on their positions are likely to be out of luck, because many of the insurers (called monolines) themselves are going broke. Purchasers of the even more derivative investment vehicles built out of the CLOs will also be along for the downward ride.

The people who will suffer most, however, are likely to be the millions of people who will lose their jobs. If only half of the PE-owned firms file for bankruptcy and only half of their workers are fired—which is not a worse case scenario—that will still put 1.875 million Americans out of work.

And the really bad news is, even if the economy recovers so that more companies can refinance and there is not a cataclysmic meltdown, many of the PE-owned companies are still destined to fail. It will just take them a bit longer. That's because PE firms manage their businesses to satisfy short-term greed, not for long-term survival.

PART TWO

THE LBO
PLAYBOOK

CHAPTER THREE

Doctoring Customer Service

There was a time when patients looked forward to spending the night in one of Louis A. Weiss Memorial Hospital's rooms that faced Lake Michigan. It wasn't just the view. The food was excellent. The Chicago hospital, jokingly, became known as the Weiss Hilton. More important, patients received good care. Weiss was affiliated with the University of Chicago Hospitals, which gave it access to extensive medical resources.

Financially, though, it was suffering. So the university began to look for a buyer. In June 2002, private-equity–owned Vanguard Health Systems, which owned a handful of hospitals, bought the not-for-profit hospital and converted it into a for-profit facility.

Almost immediately, the new Weiss owner began to lay off staff. It started with a handful of people in 2002. Then it began to eliminate unfilled positions, and there was a second round of layoffs the following year.

Weiss's financial problems were not unusual. Thanks to the complexities and inadequacies of health-care financing in the United States, many hospitals struggle to survive. Rigorous management of revenue and costs is a key to success, and many nonprofit hospitals lack strong financial controls. The doctors who sit on their boards are generally more interested in caring for patients than in managing billing systems, negotiating with insurance companies, and controlling costs.

The managerial shortcomings of hospitals are, in fact, one of their attractions for private-equity firms. By simply sharpening management controls, the purchasers know they can improve cash flow. There are almost always uncollected or poorly negotiated bills, as well as redundant costs that offer real, valid opportunities for financial improvement.

If the new owners of a hospital are so inclined, they can use the increased cash that they generate from the tighter management to bolster the finances of the hospital and to improve patient care. When this happens, it is good for the staff, for the patients who rely on them, and in the long run, for the owners of the hospitals, as more doctors and patients are attracted by the quality of the service.

When the new owners are PE firms, however, the newly generated cash is rarely used for these purposes. As PE firms have made clear over and over again, they are not really interested in the long term. They have business models that call for them to own companies only briefly. Most available cash is used to pay down loans and pay out dividends, and if there isn't enough cash available, then they squeeze operations to produce more.

At Weiss, there certainly were opportunities for improvement, and the new management's initial cuts probably did make the hospital more efficient. But after the $59 million buyout, Vanguard needed all the money it could get out of Weiss to pay the debt and produce profits for Vanguard. So it made more staffing cuts. And as the cuts continued, the quality of Weiss's services began to decline. A Vanguard executive, who helped oversee Louis Weiss operations, later acknowledged, "They just cut, and care suffered."

In oncology, for example, where chemotherapy treatments were given, the hours of registered nurses were reduced, and nurses were replaced with nursing assistants. This led to a situation that Chief Nursing Officer Susan Nick described as "worrisome."

PE firms don't specifically set out to damage the companies they buy. But because they are more interested in the short term than the long term, they often cripple them for the future by squeezing them too hard to deliver in the present. Often the result of the squeezing is that the quality of goods and services that once attracted customers, like care for cancer patients, begins to decline. Reducing quality doesn't always hurt a company. If a reduction in quality is accompanied by a lowering of prices, it can result in a strategic repositioning into a new sector of the marketplace. But reducing quality without lowering prices cuts into competitiveness. It may take awhile for customers to notice the decline in quality, but eventually they do, and when they do, they start looking around for alternatives.

In the hospital industry, however, sick customers generally aren't in a position to shop around much. They tend to go where their doctors send them. And doctors don't change their affiliations all that frequently. So hospitals can often get away with declining quality longer than some other businesses. This may be one reason that PE firms have chosen to become significant players in the hospital industry. They now own seven of the fifteen biggest for-profit chains, and for-profit institutions represent about 20 percent of America's five thousand hospitals.

PE-Owned For-Profit Hospital Chains

Owner	Hospital Name	Number of Hospitals	Year Acquired
Kohlberg Kravis Roberts; Bain Capital; Merrill Lynch	HCA	170	2006
Cinven	Spire Healthcare (UK chain)	25	2007
Blackstone Group	Vanguard Health Systems	15	2004
Texas Pacific Group	Iasis Healthcare	14	2004
GTCR Golder Rauner	Capella Healthcare	14	2005
Cinven	USP Hospitales (Spain chain)	13	2007
Welsh, Carson, Anderson & Stowe	Ardent Health Services	12	2001
Vestar Capital Partners	Essent Healthcare	5	2003

Kohlberg Kravis Roberts, Bain Capital, and Merrill Lynch Global Private Equity in 2006 bought HCA, America's largest hospital group, with more health facilities than the Veterans Administration. The California Nurses Association formed the HCA Nurses Network because the buyout put HCA under enormous pressure to cut costs and there were growing concerns that HCA business practices were devaluing nurses, driving them from the bedside, and reducing the quality of care.

Meanwhile, former U.S. Senate majority leader Bill Frist, whose family founded HCA and who sat on the finance committee that oversees health care, joined Chicago PE firm Cressey & Company as a partner to buy more medical companies.

With so many pressures on the U.S. health-care system, including nursing shortages, high costs for malpractice insurance, and the need to provide care for millions of indigent and uninsured patients, the financial problems of hospitals cannot be blamed primarily on private-equity owners. Many of the hospitals that private-equity firms acquired have been available for acquisition precisely because they were having financial difficulties. But there are few indications that the management actions of private-equity firms have improved care or reduced costs to patients, and there is much evidence that private equity is making an already precarious health-care system even more dangerous.

On September 14, 2004, two years after Weiss was acquired by Vanguard, the U.S. Department of Health and Human Services arrived for a spot inspection. At 2 P.M., with a manager's help, inspectors put an activated infant sensor bracelet on a doll. They wrapped the doll in a blanket and started carrying it out of the labor area, tripping the alarm. No one stopped them. They proceeded to exit down a stairwell. One staff member tried to silence the triggered alarm, and that was the only reaction.

The HHS Centers for Medicare and Medicaid Services was so alarmed by this and other violations that it placed the hospital on conditional accreditation, which is essentially probation. Losing accreditation would have forced Weiss to shut down. In 2007, Weiss closed its maternity ward.

In the same year as the spot inspection, Diane Richards, a recovering cancer patient, lost her voice and went to Weiss for treatment. In 2002, Richards had gone to Weiss with chronic obstructive pulmonary disease, which made breathing very difficult. Richards spent two weeks in the intensive-care unit and survived.

In 2004, when she arrived, a Weiss physician drew blood and

scheduled a bronchoscopy, an examination of the airway, for several days later. The hospital called Richards the next day, asking her to return immediately. She was told that she had anemia (a low red blood cell count) and needed a blood transfusion. Richards's companion, Ted Erikson, recalls thinking at the time, "Uh, oh, something is really wrong here."

Richards, a retired nurse, kept a detailed diary of her experiences. In it, she noted, for example, that while the hospital believed she needed to come in immediately, the staff let her wait almost twelve hours after admission before transfusing the blood.

Later she returned to Weiss for the bronchoscopy and was sent home. The tests showed no cancer. Richards, though, soon was feeling weak and coughed up lung tissue, which never grows back. She went to Weiss and was admitted as an inpatient. The doctors, suspecting tuberculosis, gave her medications to fight the disease. They also put Richards on a ventilator.

As she lay in an intensive-care bed, she wrote in her journal: "Carbon dioxide level allowed to get too high." High carbon dioxide levels make taking in oxygen hard, and Richards, a nurse, was fully aware of this. "I can't breathe normally," she wrote. She wanted a nebulizer transfusion machine that delivers medicine as liquid mist so it can be breathed directly into the lungs. She called, but no nurse ever came; she tried again one hour later. Eventually, someone arrived. "Nurse responses are not the best," she wrote in her journal. When it came time to draw blood, nurses took at least six attempts, leaving bruise marks on Richards's arm.

Diane Richards died while still in the intensive-care unit. The autopsy revealed that she did not have tuberculosis, but chronic obstructive pulmonary disease, as she had had two years earlier. Erikson said he is convinced that with better care Richards would not have died.

Vanguard counsel Ronald Soltman declined to comment on the case, saying the company is prohibited under the Health Insurance Portability & Accountability Act (HIPAA) from sharing personal medical information without written patient authorization.

Susan Nick, the former chief nursing officer at Weiss, who stayed on a few years after the sale, said it was clear to her that Vanguard believed the most important person at each of its hospitals was the chief financial officer. "It's all about the money," she said, adding that she did think that Vanguard CEO Charles Martin was an advocate for good patient care.

Good patient care may have been Martin's intention, but Vanguard's operating systems weren't organized to promote it. Another former Vanguard executive who helped oversee Weiss said Vanguard had no formalized focus on measuring service. Rather, Vanguard would leave that up to hospital CEOs, who meanwhile were offered bonuses for hitting certain earnings thresholds.

Harvard professor Dr. David Himmelstein, a critic who believes for-profit hospitals should be banned, does not think Vanguard is an exceptional story. He said there is a 2 percent higher mortality rate at for-profit hospitals, resulting in roughly 2,250 more annual deaths than would occur if they were as safe as other facilities.

The cause, he says, is owners, often PE firms, that are too focused on earnings. His position is that hospitals, like fire departments, exist to provide community service and therefore should not be expected to produce profits.

Vanguard's biggest revenue generator is the Baptist System, based in San Antonio, Texas. It consists of five hospitals scattered throughout the city, serving about 30 percent of the population. Dr. Fernando Guerra, San Antonio's director of health, said care for expectant mothers after the 2003 buyout of the Baptist System fell from about a six to a three on a scale in which ten is the top quality.

Infection rates provide another sign that customer service fell in San Antonio after the Vanguard acquisition. Between 2002, the year before Vanguard acquired the San Antonio hospitals, and 2005, pneumonia cases rose 14.3 percent. Pneumonia is a lung infection caused by germs that can be contracted during hospitalizations for other illnesses. Poor disease prevention often leads to higher pneumonia rates.

During those same years, the number of Vanguard's San Antonio beds did not change significantly, and there was actually a 1 percent decline in pneumonia cases at other San Antonio hospitals, according to the Texas Department of Health Services.

Vanguard general counsel Soltman responded that this increase does not reflect poor infection control, and that nothing could be further from the truth: "In the San Antonio metropolitan area, Baptist Hospitals treat a disproportionate percentage of elderly, low-income, and chronically ill patients—precisely the populations that are most at risk for developing illnesses like pneumonia.... Deriving opinions about quality of care based on the conditions with which patients present themselves to the hospital simply defies logic." Texas only reports a total pneumonia number and doesn't indicate how many are hospital-contracted cases.

However, the Joint Commission, an independent nonprofit organization that accredits health-care facilities, found in 2008 that eight of the eleven Vanguard hospitals it inspected, including the San Antonio Baptist network, provided pneumonia care that was below other hospitals in the states in which it operated. None were above.

Also in a May 2006 internal paper to chief nursing officers regarding ways to improve care, Vanguard implicitly stated that cost cutting might have hurt quality. According to the paper, "managing staffing and supply costs tightly and maximizing reimbursement was the ticket to success" in the past when the "public accepted quality of hospitals at lower levels than almost any other industry."

Dr. Guerra said in 2007 that after initial problems, Vanguard has conferred with him and over the last several years has significantly improved service at the San Antonio Baptist hospitals.

Poor care has been a problem throughout the Vanguard chain, including at Phoenix Baptist, which it bought in 2000. "It was a well-respected community hospital," said Dr. James Kennedy, who practiced at Phoenix Baptist for twenty years and was medical director after the takeover. "Doctors liked it; the patients liked it. It was small enough and big enough at the same time."

About three months after buying the hospital, Vanguard started firing support staff and reducing nurses' hours. "They didn't do it all at once," Kennedy said. "You know you couldn't have done that. So then it took another year to get it down to fairly lean standards."

In meetings at Vanguard's Nashville headquarters, Kennedy said top Vanguard executives would explain that you could make cuts and maintain quality. At first, Kennedy said he thought they might be right. But the cuts went deep.

On a medical surgical floor, for example, staffing was reduced to one nurse for ten patients from one nurse for five patients. Kennedy said the proper level is no greater than six to one. He recalls nurses after the cutbacks spending much of their time filling out documents rather than attending to patients.

Complaints about Phoenix Baptist started mounting at the state's health agency. On average, Arizona's seventy-seven hospitals each had three complaints a year, and Baptist had fourteen. Arizona officials investigated. Virginia Blair, who oversaw state licensing, said most of the complaints were substantiated and were serious enough to inform Medicare. Kennedy left around this time.

In 2000, Vanguard also acquired MacNeal Health Network in the Chicago suburb of Berwyn, Illinois, where Kennedy said it applied management principles similar to those it used in Phoenix.

During summer 2007, I took a walk around MacNeal Hospital to see how local residents felt about its quality of care. I saw two middle-aged women sitting at a table outside an ice cream parlor and asked them what they thought about the hospital. They stared back, and then one of the women almost laughed: She said her daughter died at MacNeal due to poor care and was legally bound not to discuss the case.

Walking behind the hospital, I decided to see if I could catch some workers leaving their shifts. I approached Medical Assistant Marina Carrillo, a short young woman wearing glasses, and asked her if she had a minute to speak about what was going on at MacNeal. She stopped near her car in the outdoor parking lot.

"The ER is awful," she said.

"I was in the ER in June after hurting my foot, and waited four hours. The doctor sees me for five minutes, and without taking an X-ray, said it was a sprain, and sends me home with a Tylenol Three prescription.

"I tell my boss in Cardio, and he makes me an immediate appointment with the surgeon."

Out of courtesy, I asked Carrillo if she wanted her name attached to the story. She said she had already complained to MacNeal and didn't care.

I raised these concerns with Vanguard vice chairman Keith Pitts in New York at the public-relations firm that represented the chain. We sat on opposite sides of a round table that filled a small conference room. Pitts said there was no correlation between cost cutting and quality of care. He said a lot of its hospitals had improved service considerably since Vanguard acquired them.

Pitts would have a hard time proving this, as the Joint Commission changed its grading systems after Vanguard acquired most of its hospitals, making it difficult to compare before and after scores.

Nonetheless, many inspected Vanguard hospitals were still subpar in key areas, making the claim of improvement almost immaterial. The Joint Commission focuses on raising the level of care at hospitals, not including surgeries. It looks at things such as how long it takes certain types of heart-attack patients after admission to have their clogged arteries opened. In heart-attack care seven of eleven Vanguard hospitals it inspected in 2008 performed at levels below most accredited organizations in their states. Three were average, and one was better than most facilities (its three Massachusetts hospitals provided better than average heart-attack care when inspected in 2006 and have not had on-site inspections since).

The Vanguard lawyer pointed out that the independent agency HealthGrades, which tracks surgeries, in 2007 awarded MacNeal Hospital a five-star rating for coronary bypass surgery, higher than any other Chicago-area hospital. But when digging deeper into the HealthGrades report, one sees that it gives MacNeal only an "as expected" three-star coronary-bypass rating in hospitalization plus six months, a measure of patients who died during their stay plus those dying within six months of discharge. This indicates that MacNeal had good heart surgeons and poor after-surgery treatment. Further, Vanguard cited as an example of quality that the Society of Chest Pain Centers accredited San Antonio's Baptist System. However, in 2008, when evaluating chest-pain–related operations, HealthGrades gave Baptist a one-star "poor" pulmonary-embolism (blood clot) rating for hospitalization plus six months. Baptist was the only hospital in its nine-hospital peer group to be given a poor rating.

Despite its clinical record, Vanguard shines on the financial front. Two Vanguard facilities made the national 2006 top 100 list of the Thomson Solucient Ranking, which ranks hospitals by factoring in profitability as well as care.

Vanguard did two big things while it was owned by Morgan Stanley Capital Partners from 1997 to 2004: It beefed up its financial departments by hiring documentation specialists, who help physicians bill correctly, and it cut the nursing and maintenance staffs, the people who actually deal with patients. The moves paid off for the PE firm when it sold the chain in 2004 to fellow PE firm Blackstone, turning its roughly $325 million investment into $900 million over seven years, including the 30 percent stake it kept in the business. After exercising stock options, CEO Charles Martin in 2005 became America's most highly paid hospital executive, earning $24.3 million. He reinvested some of it to help fund the Blackstone buyout and kept running Vanguard.

Morgan Stanley got its profits before the cuts did much damage to Vanguard's market positions, but when Blackstone took over, the seven years of PE ownership started taking its toll. Doctors began leaving Vanguard hospitals. Jim Kennedy, former chief medical officer of Phoenix Baptist, said the complaints he heard from doctors grew: "'I don't have the same scrub nurse that I usually do... you put people in my rooms who don't know what I need, what I want, and it slows me down. I go up to the floor and see a different nurse taking care of my patients every day.... I don't trust this person to be taking care of my patients.... I don't even know who to look for when I come up here for rounds.'"

Unhappy doctors can present serious financial problems for hospitals. Even though they don't like to change hospitals, most doctors are not hospital employees, so they can relocate anytime they choose, taking patients with them. For the year ending June 30, 2005, the average number of Vanguard discharges per bed, a general measure of inpatient volumes, decreased by 6 percent.

Meanwhile, interest payments doubled because of the money borrowed to fund the second buyout. For the year ending June 30, 2008, Vanguard spent $122 million on debt payments, contributing to a $4 million loss from continuing operations. If something doesn't change, Vanguard may not be able to pay its interest and certainly won't be able to pay its principal, which is due in September 2011. Standard & Poor's in June 2008 rated some of the debt CCC+, meaning it was vulnerable to nonpayment within one year, and stated that Vanguard needed favorable economic conditions to meet its obligations. Vanguard will likely have to refinance, which is not so easy to do now when banks are not lending much. Its long-term survival depends on the credit markets' recovering and forgiving lenders. Going bankrupt would likely force many of its hospitals to shut down, further endangering the health care of entire communities. San Antonio Health Director Dr. Guerra said if Vanguard closed its hospitals "that would probably be devastating to the city."

Vice Chairman Pitts said he has a new long-term strategy. Vanguard in 2007 started offering its hospitals' CEOs bonuses for which only 50 percent of the grading is based on making an earnings threshold, 20 percent is for quality of care, 10 percent for employee satisfaction, 10 percent for physician satisfaction, and 10 percent for patient satisfaction.

Vanguard is not the first private-equity–controlled health-care institution headed toward bankruptcy where Pitts has worked. In the late 1990s, Leon Black's PE firm, Apollo Management, built the second-largest nursing-home chain in the country through acquisitions. In 1997 Apollo teamed with the publicly traded GranCare nursing-home chain to buy Living Centers of America, renaming it Paragon Health Networks and hiring Pitts as CEO. Paragon in 1998 acquired the Mariner Post-Acute chain, and soon the combined company, renamed Mariner, struggled to pay its debt. Pitts left in 1999 to start anew at Vanguard, while Mariner in 2001 filed for bankruptcy protection.

PE firms are continuing to invest in nursing homes as well as hospitals. The Carlyle Group in 2007 acquired HCR ManorCare, America's biggest operator, in a $5.8 billion buyout. State regulators prompted by a nurses' union questioned Carlyle about whether it would cut services. They had reason for doubt. Carlyle in 2005 hired Karen Bechtel from Morgan Stanley Capital Partners, where she created Vanguard, to head its health-care practice. Bechtel told regulators, "We are confident, because we have been doing this [buying health-care institutions] for 20 years, that we can provide quality products and services to people that is completely compatible with providing a return to investors." State regulators bought into the argument and approved the deal.

The PE track record in nursing homes may be even worse than in hospitals, however. In a 2007 investigative report, the *New York Times* found that private investment groups (including PE firms Carlyle and Warburg Pincus) owned six of the nation's ten largest nursing-home chains, representing 9 percent of all such facilities. The story said those acquired before 2006 scored worse than national rates in twelve of fourteen indicators that regulators use to track quality of care, including bedsores. Customer service at many of those homes fell after being acquired, the *Times* reported.

Anecdotal evidence at ManorCare's 142-bed York Township, Pennsylvania, home is painful. A ninety-year-old man in January 2008 hit his head during a fall, and the nursing-home staff did not promptly call the residents' physicians. He later died. The State Department of Health and Welfare investigated, putting the nursing home on a provisional license. Five months later, a woman, after taking medication that had potential serious side effects, complained of head and chest pain, and the staff did not call a physician. Five hours later she went into cardiac arrest and died. The state then gave the home an even more conditional operating license. None of the other 53 nursing homes in South Central Pennsylvania at that time were operating with that kind of provisional license.

Inspectors revisited the home in December 2008 and determined it had corrected its deficiencies.

Few in the PE industry like to discuss reducing customer service as a strategy, but it is a method often used to save money, and it is especially effective when a company's customers have few alternatives. Hospitals are just one industry in which customers' opportunities to shop around are limited.

Wired voice communications is another.

Many poor people living in rural areas of Arkansas, New Mexico, Oklahoma, and Texas in 1999 were fed up with the incumbent phone provider, GTE. The market wasn't very profitable, and GTE didn't want to spend the capital to improve services. It looked to sell its lines serving 520,000 homes and businesses in those markets.

"We know what we're dealing with with GTE, and it can't get any worse," said Monty Montgomery, executive director of the Development Corp. of Haskell Inc. at the time. "With GTE it's just been a total lack, it seems, of caring for the rural market, at least in Haskell [Texas]."

Federico Peña, a director at PE firm Vestar Capital Partners (and formerly the secretary of energy and secretary of transportation in the Clinton administration) took interest. Although it was a stagnant market, the lines seemed like a natural buyout candidate. PE firms do not need a company with a big growth curve ahead of it, but rather one that has consistent cash flow so it can pay its debt. Not only was there little competition, but 25 percent of GTE's revenue in the area came from the government-subsidized Universal Service Fund, that is, from the fees all users pay to ensure that rural telecom operators can offer affordable phone service.

Vestar teamed with two other private-equity firms—Welsh, Carson, Anderson & Stowe and Citicorp Venture Capital—and formed a syndicate of twelve well-heeled Hispanic investors to bid on the asset, touting a plan to create a Hispanic-run company serving Hispanic neighborhoods. In other words, Peña's team indicated, the group came from the community and wanted to improve the lives of its residents. The prominent investors who gave the claim credibility included former Clinton ambassador to Spain Edward Romero, New Mexico governor Toney Anaya, and former U.S. secretary of the interior Manuel Lujan, who served under President George H. W. Bush.

Reverend Jesse Jackson and the Hispanic Association on Corporate Responsibility successfully urged GTE to sell the lines to the PE investors.

The consortium in 2000 formed Valor Telecommunications just to buy the GTE lines in two leveraged buyouts totaling $1.7 billion. Vestar and Welsh Carson were the biggest investors, and each put down about $130 million in cash, while Citicorp Venture Capital put up less, and the company borrowed roughly $1.3 billion to fund the purchase. The PE firms controlled the board, which also included representatives of the twelve Hispanic investors.

Soon, unforeseen problems arose. MCI WorldCom went bankrupt in 2002. Valor had been receiving roughly 20 percent of its overall revenue from long-distance providers, including MCI, which it charged for access to its network so their customers could complete interstate and intrastate long-distance calls. Now MCI was not paying its bills.

Around this same time, it also became clear to Valor's new owners that the company's phone service infrastructure needed far more improvement than they'd realized. They might be forced to start investing more in modernizing its property, plants, and equipment. Between 2001 and 2003, Valor had dropped capital expenditures from $108 million to $70 million. (Generally, rural telecom companies spend between 14 percent and 18 percent of their revenue on capital expenditures; Valor was spending only 14 percent in 2003.)

The Texas Public Utility Commission (PUC) found itself besieged with complaints. In fact, outrage was so great that in April 2003 it held a public hearing in Texarkana, Texas, to address the matter. It was a standing-room-only session that lasted three hours. Angry customers rattled off complaints about static during rain, line noise, and service interruptions. The more the commission looked into the matter, the worse it got. Valor wasn't providing the PUC's 800 complaint-line number in its phone books, making it very difficult for customers to find. (It was, however, accidentally publishing the numbers of people who had requested that their numbers *not* be published in their phone books.) In winter 2003, owners of 31,000 phone lines started getting billed $1.50 per month for standard touch-tone service. When the commission paid a surprise visit to a local Valor retail office, it found customers waiting in long lines to pay bills, with no other option except dropping checks in a box, for which their accounts wouldn't be credited for five days.

When the State of Texas approved the buyout, it did so on the condition that Valor had to at least maintain GTE's level of customer service. In 2003 the Texas PUC concluded that Valor was offering worse service and should stop using its bad financial condition as an excuse. Valor had little choice but to comply.

Other complaints were mounting as well: There was no Hispanic employee at a level high enough to report to the company's president, although Valor was supposed to be about empowering Hispanics.

Valor decided the best way to raise money so it could pay debt and improve service was to sell shares on the New York Stock Exchange (NYSE). It told the investing public it hoped to raise $585 million, but it could raise only $410 million after expenses in 2005. The company was floundering. Less than eighteen months later, telephone company Windstream Communications bought Valor for $1.4 billion, $300 million less than the price the PE firms had paid for the business six years earlier.

But the PE firms still earned 1.6 times their money. Most of the profit was locked in, as Valor, at least through 2002, paid the owners a 21 percent annual dividend on $390 million in preferred stock, which guaranteed a good return as long as the company did not go bankrupt.

There is a pattern with private-equity firms and phone companies. The Carlyle Group in 2005 formed Hawaiian Telecom to buy Verizon's Hawaii landlines in a $1.65 billion buyout, and it also ran into trouble with regulators over reducing customer service. State regulators fined the business and ordered the company to provide detailed weekly reports on the time customers were spending on hold when calling with problems. Some customers fed up with the service switched to wireless providers.

Unlike the PE firms that owned Valor, Carlyle made little money from the deal, as Hawaiian Telecom in 2008 filed for bankruptcy protection.

Other PE-Owned Companies That Reduced Customer Service

PE Firm	Company	How It Reduced Costumer Service	Ownership Period
Clayton, Dubilier & Rice	Kinko's	The copy chain became the poster child for poor service. Comedian Dave Chappelle did a skit in 2003 in which he played the manager in	1996 through 2004

PE Firm	Company	How It Reduced Costumer Service	Ownership Period
		a training tape for a Popcopy store (which clearly looked like a Kinko's). He taught employees that whenever any customer asked for help, they should say the whole computer system was down for a few hours and they were busy.	
Strategic Investments and Holdings	Topps Meat Co. (maker of frozen hamburgers sold to schools and Walmart)	Topps had controls insufficient to eliminate or reduce *E. coli* bacteria, according to the USDA. In 2007, its burgers were linked to an *E. coli* outbreak, sickening customers and causing one of the nation's biggest beef recalls.	2003 through 2007
Hicks Muse Tate & Furst	AMFM (formerly Chancellor Media) which bought 465 radio stations through many different deals. It was the operator owning the most radio stations in the country before merging with Clear Channel.	Hicks Muse reduced staffs and took much of the independent feel out of its stations. For example, it converted Washington, D.C., political talk station WWRC to nationally syndicated Bloomberg Business News. Its actions made radio blander. Subsequently, radio listenership fell nationally throughout the 1990s.	1994 through 1999

Reducing customer service is at best a profitable short-term strategy. Over the long run, it drives away customers and weakens a company's finances. It also harms the reputation of a company: In the cases of HCR ManorCare, Valor, and Hawaiian Telecom, the government stepped in and forced them to improve their service. Once one gets tarnished with a bad reputation, however, it is hard to win back the trust of customers. The strategy of reducing customer service is just one of the reasons that many PE-owned companies will be going under in the coming years.

CHAPTER FOUR

Lifting Prices

In nine years, from 1998 through 2006, the price of beds sold to retailers in the United States rose 54 percent. This was twice the 26 percent inflation in the general economy, and it pushed name-brand mattresses out of the range of many Americans.

I sat with top executives at New York City–based bedding retailer Dial-A-Mattress in 2005 and asked about prices. They agreed to speak as long as their names were not used.

"How much do your customers expect to pay for a bedding set?" I asked.

"Almost sixty percent of consumers do not want to spend six hundred dollars or more," one of them replied.

"What is your most popular model?" I asked.

"It's a five ninety-nine private-label bed made in Canada; name brands start at six ninety-nine."

Sealy and Simmons, the two largest U.S. manufacturers at the time, they explained, had migrated to the high end of the market.

"The major brands target people earning fifty thousand dollars or more," one of the executives said. "This is like the car industry," added another. "They [the biggest manufacturers] now focus on SUVs, but how many of us really need SUVs?"

"Right," I said. "So Sealy and Simmons are only offering buyers more mattress than they want or need."

Yes and no, they said. While they are adding more features, they have cut their beds in half so are actually giving them less of a bed.

One executive said he thought the one-sided ("no-flip") bed was OK but the spring unit and padding were no better than the two-sided, despite manufacturers' claims. So the buyer was essentially getting half a bed and one that would need to be replaced sooner than a two-sided.

He also said, "What they should have done is taken the cost savings and put it in the top of the mattress."

Dial-A-Mattress CEO Neal Barragan invited me to stop by and rip open mattresses with him so we could see the difference among brands. On a brisk 2005 afternoon, we stood with several employees in one of his warehouses, with plastic-wrapped mattresses piled twenty feet high all around. Three beds were leaned against piles, a Sealy Posturepedic that sold for $899, a Simmons Beautyrest that sold for $799, and a private-label Canadian Nation's Pride that sold for $599. A worker with a sharp knife made four quick swipes with the blade, cutting deep into the top of the first mattress. Foam flew.

Inside the Sealy top was a layer of yellow foam that was resting on a piece of what looked to be chicken wire covering fourteen unbound coils. The Simmons mattress seemed even worse. "It's a balloon. There's nothing in there!" Barragan said when that one was cut open.

We measured foam thickness, which has become a more important issue since 2003 when Sealy and Simmons started making no-flip beds, ones with sleep surfaces on only one side. The Sealy had a 3.5-inch top and .75 inch of foam on the bottom, and the Simmons had a 1.5-inch top and .50 inch on the bottom.

The pressure that comes down on a bed through the springs needs to be cushioned, and without sufficient bottom padding, the bed wears out quickly. One of the Dial-A-Mattress executives noted that this specific Simmons bed seemed especially thin.

Next, we moved on to the private-label mattress. It was a harder bed, and sturdier. A border rod connected the ten-coil row, and a Cortex multifiber pad that was hard to rip was on the coils, with another pad on the back. I couldn't lift the mattress with one hand, as I had been able to do with the Sealy and the Simmons. But it had fewer coils than the others, so it probably wouldn't adjust as well to the sleeper's body.

In short, according to Barragan's standards, none of them were great options. Good bedding had become not just a luxury item, but also something that was hard to find. Why? What had happened in the mattress industry?

Think *private equity*.

The last chapter was about how PE firms boost their own profits by cutting costs and reducing the quality of the goods and services their companies sell. But in the mattress industry, the PE firms went that method one better. They compromised quality, and raised prices to boot. And they got away with it because they owned both of the two biggest U.S. mattress companies, Sealy and Simmons. As a result, they were able to raise prices for a long time because neither outfit cared about undercutting the other and gaining market share.

Between 1989 and 2004 three groups of PE firms bought and sold Sealy. All told, they put down roughly $410 million in cash and made $1.3 billion, a 3.2-times return. Between 1986 and 2004, four groups of PE firms bought and sold Simmons, putting down $278 million and collecting $1.03 billion, a 3.7-times return.

The mattress industry was not always this way. There was a time when it was highly competitive. Ohio Mattress, a publicly traded company, owned the Sealy brand in the 1980s. Bedding was a mature industry, so to show shareholders it was growing, the company competed for market share by keeping prices low.

Former Sealy executive Gary Fazio recalls a 1988 meeting at which Sealy regional managers were debating how to price a Posturepedic bed. CEO Ernie Wuliger walked into the meeting late.

"He said, 'Hi, boys. How are you doing today?' With his chin up in the air, he looks at the grease board with a thousand numbers. He points at the lowest number. He said, 'You're a little too high here to be competitive. See you, boys.'

"In total, he was in the room one and a half minutes. We realized we were pushing the price too high, and sure enough, we lowered the price," Fazio said. Sealy, with its low pricing, between 1980 and 1985 increased its market share by 66 percent and increased its lead over Simmons as the biggest mattress brand. In the late 1980s, Sealy had a 28 percent share of the U.S. mattress market based on the dollar value of beds and foundations sold.

While the business was doing well, Wuliger, who was in his mid-sixties, hadn't developed a deep leadership team. So when his right-hand man and likely successor, Ron Trzcinski, decided to leave, Ohio Mattress faced a leadership crisis. Trzcinski, who was twenty years younger, represented the future. The two men fought over such trifling matters as whether to open an office in West Cleveland or downtown Cleveland. The issues weren't always big, but Trzcinski began to look for another job. When the company's attorney, Thomas Cole, heard of this, he suggested that Ohio Mattress consider a sale. After all, LBO firms like Kohlberg Kravis Roberts were paying big prices.

Ohio Mattress tested the market, and LBO firm Gibbons, Green, van Amerongen in 1989 took the company private in a $980 million buyout—a price that exceeded the company's expectations. Gibbons Green put down $170 million, and Ohio Mattress borrowed the remaining $810 million.

Gibbons Green hired Malcolm Candlish, former Samsonite Corp. CEO, to run Ohio Mattress, though he had no mattress industry experience. While industrywide mattress and foundation sales fell in 1989 by 1.5 percent—because of a recession—Candlish focused on short-term gains and raised prices. He was interested in paying the company's debt, not on building the business. Wuliger, who'd made Sealy the market leader, soon found he had little influence in the company. When he expressed his dissatisfaction to LBO owner John Gibbons, he was told that that was the way it was. Wuliger left about a year after the sale.

An Ohio Mattress executive under Wuliger who remained for a short time when the PE firm took over said, "If we kept running Sealy, we would have beaten up Simmons. We would have been proud about being the best and the biggest...we would not have driven the price" in order to make interest payments.

By this time, Wesray, an LBO firm cofounded by former Nixon and Ford Treasury secretary William Simon, had owned Simmons for several years. Under Simon's Wesray, Simmons sold off foreign operations, as well as factories in the middle of cities like San Francisco. Simmons paid back almost all its debt thanks to the money generated this way.

Meanwhile, Candlish's Sealy strategy was backfiring. Higher prices were not compensating for lost sales. Sealy from December 1989 to May 1990 made $46.3 million in payments to lenders—while generating only $45.8 million in income before debt payments. It was losing money.

Simmons, which was almost debt free, had a chance to gain market share. It could have killed Sealy by beating it on price, but its PE own-ers chose to sell the business instead. As a company, Simmons lost out on a great opportunity. But Wesray made a nice profit.

Wesray took advantage of a law that its cofounder William Simon is said to have introduced when he was Treasury secretary. The law said Wesray could sell the company to an employee stock ownership plan (ESOP) and reinvest the proceeds without paying capital gains taxes—even if the new investment was unrelated. The owners set a $249 million valuation, despite having bought the company for $120 million only three years earlier and having sold assets since then. The 1989 deal resulted in Simmons borrowing $249 million from Chemi-cal Bank to fund the ESOP, about half of which went to Wesray after prior lenders and co-investors were paid.

Now Simmons and Sealy both had too much debt, and neither could risk lowering its prices.

Sealy maker Ohio Mattress's decision to raise prices during a reces-sion hurt sales so much it could no longer pay its debt, and lender First Boston in 1991 repossessed the business, though First Boston would have preferred to collect on the loans. Gibbons Green lost almost all its company shares. The bank then brought in another chief executive who had no mattress industry experience—John Beggs, former presi-dent of electric razor maker Norelco Consumer Products.

Beggs's initial strategy was to make higher quality products and sell more expensive beds. The pricier beds had larger profit margins and would make it easier to boost short-term earnings. He instructed Robert Wagner, who'd headed R & D since Wuliger's days, to design a dream bed.

When Wagner presented the specifications to his new boss, Beggs declared that the design—with sewn-on handles and steel spans in the foundations—would henceforth be *the* blueprint for *all* of Sealy's Posturepedic products. Wagner warned Beggs that adding these fea-tures would slow production. Nonetheless, Beggs decided to go ahead, but six months later production was dragging.

In 1993, First Boston sold what was renamed Sealy to a Sam Zell-managed fund for $250 million (much less than the $980 million that Gibbons paid in the 1989 LBO). Zell said, "Basically it was a very strong brand name with decent management. To a large extent, it was still a good company but bereft of ownership and direction."

Zell stuck with Beggs, who continued to focus on introducing more expensive mattresses. He began to make thicker beds, adding pillow tops even though Wagner said the thicker soft-top beds required expensive high-density foam, or else they would disintegrate quickly. "I think the product with thinner upholstery served better than plush," he said. But "because the sales people convinced marketing it was better, the pressure came on us to develop a thicker bed. I said, 'OK, thicker is better,' but it really wasn't."

Sealy kept increasing the price for its beds, even beyond what was required by the higher production costs, allowing its PE owners to make better returns at the expense of its customers.

One reason Sealy followed this path was that rival Simmons, facing the same debt pressure, was pursuing a similar strategy. Ron Hutchinson, who was VP of quality assurance at Simmons said, "They started piling on pillow tops and lots of stuff that made beds expensive—beyond what was necessary to get a good night's sleep."

He added, "It's just natural that when you have a commodity product and everyone is buying steel and materials from the same places, you try to come up with something that is unique."

A director at the PE firm Merrill Lynch Capital Partners, which bought Simmons in 1991 from the ESOP, said Simmons was trying to get people to pay much more for its beds. "Where Simmons was very focused was up-selling and having enough lower-priced promotional products to get people in the door, but to get people to pay the higher price points. We educated salespeople that our more expensive beds were superior."

Simmons in its 1996 annual report said it was generating most of its sales on beds retailing for more than $499, representing the top 40 percent of the bedding market.

David Judelson, who helped oversee Simmons in the 1970s and early 1980s when it was part of his public company, said, "I went to Bloomingdale's in the early 1990s to buy a mattress. There is one Simmons mattress, and it was under a designer name. It was two thousand dollars. That is what happened to Simmons. Some jerk thought that was how you transform Simmons. It was the same mattress."

Sealy stopped making its lower-priced basic models in the mid-1990s, even though they still represented 38 percent of revenue. Gary Fazio, then vice president of sales, recalls his reaction to these company directives. "We almost died."

Because they both increased prices, Sealy and Simmons did not win or lose market share against each other. Ron Jones, who took over from Beggs as Sealy CEO in 1996, said his goal was always to just stay ahead of Simmons by the same margin. The two were the market leaders, and consumers, for the most part, paid the higher prices.

In 1997, after boosting Sealy's profits, Zell decided to sell the business.

Bain Capital managing director Joshua Bekenstein learned of the opportunity and brought up the idea of buying Sealy at Bain's weekly partners' meeting. Mitt Romney, who was the owner of Bain Capital and would later become a Republican presidential candidate, ran those meetings.

"He'd listen very carefully...he did not dominate with his ego," a former Bain director said. "He would listen.... He used legal tactics. He was the type to constantly challenge partners about their ideas." The idea of buying Sealy held up under his questioning.

Bain Capital teamed with Charlesbank Capital Partners and bought Sealy for $791 million. The PE firms put down $140 million, and Sealy borrowed $651 million.

By the time Zell was handing over Sealy, Simmons had already been flipped again, giving it three different PE owners in ten years. Investcorp was the new acquirer. Because the goal of any PE firm is to quickly lift profits, Investcorp in 1997 raised the average bed price by 4.4 percent and cut production costs by 2.5 percent.

The intent always seemed to be to take more profit out of the businesses, not to build the companies by offering better products or growing market share.

Investcorp was soon ready to sell Simmons again. The buyer? Another PE firm: Fenway Partners. In 1998 Fenway paid roughly $550 million, which meant Investcorp collected $193 million from an $85 million investment over two years. Peter Lamm, Fenway Partners' cofounder, said, "Our thesis walking in was, here is a business...

[that] has been owned by six or seven firms over the last fifteen years, which means an average two- to two-and-a-half-year tenure. And in that two- to two-and-a-half-year tenure it takes time to acclimate to a new owner and six months to a year to sell the business. So there was seldom a focus on a long-term plan of What are operations? What is the potential? If we could have the mindset and financial structure in place to be longer-term investors, there was an opportunity to take advantage of some of the operations inside the company."

Lamm considered raising profits by opening Simmons retail stores so it could cut out the middleman, but its first few locations failed. He also looked at making international acquisitions. The right assets, though, were not available. He needed to come up with a new plan.

Over at Sealy, Bain, too, found it hard to quickly boost profits. After all, Sealy and Simmons had already added features to their beds, like pillow-tops, and were running out of reasons to raise prices. In 1999, two years after buying the company, Bain acquired one of Sealy's biggest retail customers, Mattress Discounters, for $212 million. Bain expanded Mattress Discounters while providing it with strong incentives to buy from Sealy. But Mattress Discounters was opening new locations while sales at its existing stores were not growing. The result: Mattress Discounters in October 2002 filed for bankruptcy protection.

After these failed attempts, the pressure from Bain and Fenway on Sealy and Simmons to raise earnings increased. Wagner, Sealy's head of R & D, designed the no-flip, or one-sided, bed. When Sealy made its mattresses thicker and heavier, they became hard to turn over, so he proposed eliminating the bottom cover, making the bottom simply a foundation. This would cut costs, though it would also shorten the life of the mattress.

Sealy did not put it on the market because it believed it cheapened the product, Wagner said. Simmons, though, had the same idea, and in 2000 it released the first no-flip bed.

Sealy responded saying it would never do such a thing. "The fact is, turning a Sealy mattress extends its Comfort Life because it gives the upholstery foam and filling time to rest and fluff back up," the company said on its Web site. "So to maximize the Comfort Life, you should rotate the mattress, much like rotating your tires for longer wear. And you'll need a mattress with two sides to do it. You'll need a Sealy."

Thanks to the cheaper to make and more expensive to buy no-flip, Simmons saw its EBITDA rise from 1999, the year before the no-flip, to 2002 by 48 percent while net sales increased only 22 percent. The profit margins had clearly improved.

Ron Hutchinson, who worked at Simmons from 1961 through 2002 and was vice president of quality assurance, said the no-flip can be a less durable bed. "There is no question if I owned a hotel, I would want a two-sided mattress. We made some mattresses uphol-stered on one side that would not last as long as a product with similar upholstery on two sides."

Continuing to offer two-sided beds, Sealy greatly increased its market-share lead over Simmons, but its PE owners noticed how Simmons was raising short-term profits. So the strategy changed. In February 2003, Sealy announced it was switching the flagship Pos-turepedic line to a no-flip design. Soon, both Sealy and Simmons sold *only* no-flip mattresses, and that is still the case today.

Ron Jones, Sealy CEO at that time, said if it was a public company, gaining market share would have mattered more.

Despite this radical reduction in costs, prices kept rising. The num-ber of mattress and foundation units sold industrywide in 2003 rose 2.4 percent while revenue increased 7.8 percent. In 2004, the volume rose a modest 3.2 percent while sales revenue increased 12.1 percent. The PE firms were still raising prices.

Bedding Price Boom

Year	Number of Mattresses and Foundations Shipped to Retailers	Price to Retailers	Average
1997	35.3 million	$3.6 billion	$101.98
2006	43.2 million	$6.8 billion	$157.00
TOTAL			54% rise

Inflation: One dollar in 1997 had the same buying power as $1.26 in 2006.

Based on data from International Sleep Products Association and Consumer Price Index.

While Sealy and Simmons were quickly improving earnings, competition came from unexpected corners. Tempur-Pedic started mass-producing foam mattresses, and newcomer Select Comfort introduced inflatable spring beds that allowed the consumer to adjust their firmness level. Companies with large debt payments, like Sealy and Simmons, could not allocate as big a percentage of revenue to research to develop new products as businesses with less debt. At first, these new specialty-bedding companies gave Sealy and Simmons an excuse to keep raising prices, because the new beds were expensive.

When the Tempur company's Swedish founders tried to sell out, most PE firms were not interested, because they believed Tempur was a risky proposition. One partner at a PE firm who considered buying Tempur said he believed Sealy and Simmons would soon start making their own foam beds and stop Tempur's advance. Kevin Landry, who runs TA Associates, one of the few PE groups seeking companies that are quickly growing revenue as opposed to those that generate a lot of surplus cash that can be used to pay debt, said, "The big PE firms buy more mature, what they consider safer, businesses and get their returns on the leverage; we get our returns from the growth." TA Associates and Friedman Fleischer & Lowe in late 2002 bought Tempur-Pedic for $390 million.

The problem for Sealy and Simmons was that Tempur's foam beds soon gained a reputation for being more comfortable and durable than *their* mattresses. In a June 2005 *Consumer Reports* magazine informal poll, three quarters of respondents were very or completely satisfied with their Tempur-Pedic beds, and two thirds were similarly happy with Select Comfort. Only half said the same about innerspring mattresses sold by the two industry leaders.

Over at Sealy and Simmons, it was time to flip the companies again. Legendary dealmaker Kohlberg Kravis Roberts took Sealy in a $1.5 billion 2004 LBO (almost four times what Tempur-Pedic attracted). KKR put down 29 percent, $436 million, and Sealy borrowed the rest. Simmons, meanwhile, was acquired that same year by PE firm Thomas H. Lee Partners for $1.1 billion. The sellers did quite well: Fenway collected $620 million on a roughly $148 million investment, plus 10 percent of Simmons; the Bain-led selling group received about $741 million for their $140 million Sealy outlay, a better than four-times return in seven years.

PE firms continued to find these bedding companies attractive because the nature of the business meant little needed to be spent on capital expenditures and there was a steady flow of customers. That usually made it easy for them to pay back their debt—especially when they both kept successfully pushing prices higher.

Months after Thomas H. Lee Partners bought Simmons, it had the company borrow an additional $163 million to pay its owners a dividend. Then a bedding industry executive said Simmons in early 2005 raised prices 11–12 percent, perhaps in part to help pay the debt. Meanwhile, KKR in April 2006 listed Sealy on the New York Stock Exchange, taking some proceeds from the stock sale but keeping enough shares to retain control over the business.

In December 2003, Tempur-Pedic listed its shares on the NYSE. Traders allegedly shorted the stock, believing Sealy and Simmons would introduce similar foam beds and stop Tempur's advance. But PE firms still owned the leading bed makers and Sealy did not start selling its own foam beds for another eighteen months, and both Sealy and Simmons continued to lift prices of innerspring models so they could more easily pay their debt. The number of innerspring mattresses across all manufacturers sold in 2005 rose 2.6 percent while revenue increased 7.2 percent.

This strategy worked when Sealy and Simmons were largely competing only with each other in the high-priced bedding market. But, now Tempur-Pedic was crashing the party.

Volume for innerspring makers the next year, 2006, fell 1.7 percent while they generated 6.1 percent revenue growth as they kept charging more even in a declining market. The arrogance of continually raising prices finally caught up with the mattress companies and their PE owners, as foam beds became more popular. The number of non-innerspring beds sold in 2005 rose 26 percent while innerspring grew only 3 percent, and noninnerspring by a much smaller margin outpaced innerspring again the next year. Sealy and Simmons after introducing their own foam beds had trouble penetrating the growing market.

Tempur-Pedic, which remained the dominant foam bed maker, in 2007 surpassed Sealy in enterprise value (shares plus debt). In October 2007, Tempur-Pedic was valued at $2.9 billion and Sealy only at $1.4 billion (privately held Simmons was behind them both).

Then Sealy and Simmons came up with a new product—expensive latex mattresses, which had been popular in Europe for decades. But by mid-2008, latex sales overall were only about one third the total of foam sales. There was limited opportunity for them in the high end of the U.S. bedding market, because the people willing to spend more than $1,500 were still often choosing Tempur foam beds.

Sealy and Simmons had to recapture some market share. The timing was not great. A housing crisis meant fewer people were buying homes—and beds. And while Sealy and Simmons had been raising prices, Serta, SpringAir, King Coil, and Restonic became bigger brands in the midprice range. Also, U.S. mattress makers International Bedding Corp., United Sleep Products, Corsicana, and Symbol Mattress Company filled the gap for beds that cost between $299 and $599, becoming the dominant low-end makers.

PE firms needed discounts to entice buyers. Sealy had some success selling midpriced beds retailing for between $799 and $1,299. Simmons had a harder time returning to lower price points.

After almost twenty years under PE ownership, raising prices and compromising quality had caught up with Sealy and Simmons. Sealy still sold the most U.S. mattresses, but its market share in 2008 eroded to roughly 20 percent from 28 percent when the first buyout happened. In order to save the company from collapsing, KKR in May 2009 lent Sealy money and engineered a debt restructuring. Simmons in July 2009 was in danger of collapsing after missing an interest payment.

The pressure to support huge debt burdens and to squeeze out big profits partially to pay hefty management fees often causes PE firms to overlook the realities of marketplace economics.

Other PE-Owned Companies That Raised Prices

PE Firm	Company	When It Raised Prices	Result
Kohlberg Kravis Roberts	Masonite (door manufacturer)	2006 during housing boom	Home Depot in 2007 moved most of its door business to a competitor. Masonite went bankrupt in March 2009.
Apollo Management	Vail Resorts (three ski resorts in Summit County, Colorado)	1997	More than doubled the price for seasonal lift tickets. Customers then flocked to its lone regional competitor. Apollo's resorts eventually dropped their prices.
Bain Capital, DLJ Merchant Banking Partners, and Oak Hill Capital Partners all separately bought and sold the business.	Duane Reade pharmacy chain	Raised prescription drug prices during the time PE firms controlled the chain (1992 through present)	Has a dominant 30 percent share of New York City pharmacy market, and raising drug prices has not significantly hurt business.

In the case of the mattress industry, the PE firms got away with ignoring competition for quite a while because the two biggest players in the market, Sealy and Simmons, were both PE owned and, therefore, not much interested in competing for market share. But eventually Tempur-Pedic moved in, and the PE firms that most recently bought Sealy and Simmons found that their unrealistic profit projections could not be met. Another case of unrealistic projections, this time about the New York City rent-controlled housing market, came back to bite its owners more quickly.

During the housing boom of the mid-2000s, Apollo Real Estate Advisors (founded by William Mack and Leon Black's PE firm Apollo

Global Management) partnered with the Vantage Group to buy more than ninety rent-regulated buildings in working-class New York neighborhoods in Washington Heights and Queens. The firm also partnered with Stellar Management and Taconic Investment Partners on other deals. After buying, Vantage, which bought some buildings without Apollo, allegedly intimidated tenants so they would leave and it could charge new tenants considerably higher rates.

New York City has a rent policy established in the 1940s to set aside many of its apartments for working-class people at affordable prices. Developers like Apollo Real Estate have bought buildings that own about 6 percent of the city's 1.2 million rent-stabilized units. While the buyers are not classic PE firms, the concept of the leveraged buyouts is the same. The buyer acquires a building by having it borrow most of the money to finance the buyout, causing pressure on the acquired property to increase earnings.

Developers told banks lending money to finance these buyouts that there would be turnover rates well above the city's 5 percent to 6 percent rent-controlled annual average, which would allow them to boost earnings. They secured loans for which debt repayment was possible only if rent rolls increased. Buildings were borrowing money equal to, say, $1,000 per apartment when their average rent was $750.

In a rent-stabilized apartment, the city allows a landlord to evict a tenant only for cause, which is usually when the tenant is not using the apartment as a primary residence or falls behind on the rent. Developers tried to buy out tenants or force them to leave by suing them repeatedly for lease-breaking violations, even when they had done nothing wrong.

Tenant groups fought back, and the turnover rates have been much lower than the PE firms expected. This has created a serious problem. For example, Apollo with Vantage Properties in 2007 bought eight Washington Heights apartment buildings with 455 units. In an SEC filing, it said it planned to empty as many as 30 percent of the rent-regulated apartments in the first year and 10 percent annually thereafter, well above the city average of 5.6 percent.

After more than one year net income covered only 46 percent of the annual mortgage payments.

United States Senator Charles Schumer of New York, who is trying to stop what he calls "predatory equity deals," said in a statement, "Developers, backed by private equity funds, have targeted rent-regulated and subsidized buildings to be purchased and then converted into market rate housing, often based on wildly unrealistic assumptions about operating costs, turnover rates, appreciation and future rent rolls."

In December 2008, Schumer asked federal regulators to help restructure unstable housing-complex loans. A housing advocate suggested that perhaps Treasury could provide TARP bailout money. Schumer considered it important because "when an owner defaults on financing, a property typically falls into physical distress. These distressed projects in turn depress the block in which they are located, and the neighborhoods in which they are concentrated."

In other types of businesses, such as mattress making, when bad management and unrealistic projections sink a PE-owned business, it is usually not considered a matter of national urgency. But when a lot of companies fail because of the short-term management strategies of PE firms, including raising prices to noncompetitive levels, it will become a matter of national urgency. We will find ourselves in the Next Great Credit Crisis.

CHAPTER FIVE

Starving Capital

Joseph Rice looks a bit annoyed. This is the second of two interviews we had during 2007, and we are getting down to the nuts and bolts of why he believes private-equity firms help businesses. He is chairman of one of the first PE firms, Clayton, Dubilier & Rice (CD&R), and has a strong reputation among the corporate elite—so strong that in 2001 he recruited former General Electric CEO Jack Welch to be a special partner. We are in a small conference room at his firm's Midtown Manhattan headquarters.

The aging former U.S. Marine lieutenant is holding in his famous temper, but Rice's arms are crossed as he answers what to him must be progressively more irritating questions.

I ask how the December 2005 buyout of Hertz is actually helping the business. CD&R, along with the Carlyle Group and Merrill Lynch Global Private Equity, bought the car rental agency by putting down $2.3 billion in a $15 billion LBO.

He explains that PE firms have made Hertz more profitable by getting out of off-airport locations where it did not have sufficient scale to beat rival Enterprise (he failed to mention that the company was less profitable when factoring in interest payments). Spending less on overhead, he said, had also boosted earnings.

In the first full year after the buyout, Hertz slashed the money it spent on cars by 8.2 percent, almost $1 billion, and in car-rental operations by 39 percent, an additional $100 million, often by outsourcing. After boosting the company's short-term earnings, the PE firms, in their first year of ownership, had Hertz borrow $1 billion to pay themselves a dividend *and* list 28 percent of its shares on the stock market, which generated enough money for the company to repay the $1 billion loan and to give the PE firms another $260 million. In total, the PE firms recouped more than half of their down payment.

"How do you think the cuts will help Hertz down the road?"

"Well, we certainly expect it's going to be a better business than it is today."

"What do you mean by better?"

Rice explained that being more profitable allowed it to invest more in marketing, locations, and people. "If you're not making money, you can't do those things."

I asked him if Hertz had been investing more in those areas. He said he was not sure, but the company's U.S. airport market share should give some indication. I never did get a clear, direct answer from anyone on whether Hertz had been taking any of its savings and using the money to invest more in marketing, locations, or people. But when I looked at Hertz's market share, I found that at U.S. airports it had *fallen* nearly 10 percent—from 29.2 percent in 2005, the year the buyout happened, to 26.9 percent in early 2009. If market share was the barometer, then Hertz's spending appeared to be lagging.

For an owner who doesn't care about building a sustainable business, one very effective way to boost profits in the short term is to starve a company of capital. Like reducing customer service and raising prices, starving a company of capital can deliver a short-term jolt of cash, but doing so has serious negative consequences over the longer term. Without the capital to compete, a company loses its customer base, its business dries up, and if it has big debts, as PE-owned companies do, it will often be unable to pay those debts when they come due. This is one of the reasons that in the next few years, many PE-owned firms are very likely to collapse.

While it is too early to say for certain that the PE firms have starved Hertz of enough capital to compete effectively, some PE-owned companies clearly have been malnourished.

PE firms Cerberus Capital Management and Sun Capital Partners, along with real-estate investors Lubert-Adler and Klaff Partners, in 2004 led a buyout of the Mervyn's discount retail chain for $1.26 billion. They saw value in Mervyn's real estate: both in the stores it owned and in its long-term leases, which allowed Mervyn's to pay below-market rents.

Upon closing the deal, they split Mervyn's into two separate companies. One held the real-estate assets; the other, the actual 257 Mervyn's stores. The newly formed company that held Mervyn's real estate borrowed $800 million to fund the LBO.

After the real estate was stripped away, the company holding Mervyn's retail stores was barely solvent. It had $674 million of assets and $664 million of liabilities. Mervyn's, according to its creditors, was even left with negative working capital (meaning it could not pay debts as they became due) of more than $22 million.

Then the Mervyn's property company increased the pressure. It started to charge the stores market-rate rents so it could more easily pay back the loans taken to finance the buyout. Annual rent expenses for the stores increased by approximately $80 million to $172 million. Competitors like Walmart often pay below-market rents, so the PE firms put Mervyn's at a competitive disadvantage by forcing it to pay market rents. The owners were profiting from the real estate by pressing the actual retail chain, an ongoing business that employed workers and served customers.

Mervyn's hired JCPenney CEO Vanessa Castagna to run the chain. Under her leadership, Mervyn's boosted profits by closing nearly 33 percent of its stores. This included exiting the unprofitable Michigan and Oklahoma regions so it could focus more on its core California market. She then tried unsuccessfully to get the property company to lower some of the increased lease payments it was charging the remaining stores. When her two-year employment contract expired, Castagna left. "It was a wonderful experience and I learned so much about private equity," she told *Women's Wear Daily*.

George Whalin, who runs California-based advisory firm Retail Management Consultants, said, "She saw the writing on the wall that you can't hamstring a retailer to that degree."

The recession soon started, and the retailer's profits fell. Now starving the business took its toll. Mervyn's was not able to spend the money needed on inventory, making it hard to restock popular items and to keep up with the latest styles by buying new products. Whalin said some of the stores began looking pretty lean.

Meanwhile, the PE firms took dividends and distributions from the real-estate company in excess of $400 million, roughly equal to the amount they put down in the buyout. Apparently none of that money went back into the Mervyn's retail stores to help them out during difficult times. In July 2008, the Mervyn's store company filed for bankruptcy, reporting that in the fiscal year ending February 2, 2008, it had lost $64 million, less than the extra money it was paying in rent. Mervyn's CEO John Goodman in October 2008 gathered employees in a meeting room and told them that the company was unable to find anyone willing to buy it out of bankruptcy and was shutting down—a victim of the recession and a competitive retail environment. The liquidation resulted in about eighteen thousand layoffs, with the workers receiving no severance or vacation pay.

Charlene Glafke, who began her career at Mervyn's thirty-five years before in the toy department and rose to an $80,000 marketing job, told the *Wall Street Journal*, "I gave my life to Mervyn's.... It's heartbreaking."

Whalin says the shame is that Mervyn's, as a discount retailer with its strong California roots, could have survived without the rent increases. "They were as well positioned as any company could have been to do well in a difficult economy," he said. Besides, before the buyout, it had valuable real estate that it could have sold to boost liquidity.

To Whalin the result was not a surprise. "You cannot starve a retail business for cash" because it needs a healthy stock of inventory. "We've seen this over the years. Every time a retailer is starved for cash, it essentially puts them out of business."

Mervyn's creditors in September 2008 filed a fraudulent transfer claim in the United States Bankruptcy Court for the District of Delaware against the PE firms, claiming they had profited by pressuring Mervyn's. The complaint says, "The result of the foregoing was to bleed Mervyn's dry in the years following the buyout."

Ironically, the other half of Mervyn's, which continued to own all the real-estate properties, might now be happy to have tenants paying below-market rents. Instead they are stuck with a bunch of vacant former Mervyn's stores in the middle of a recession.

I approached Rodger Krouse, the co-CEO of Sun Capital Partners, in person at a fall 2008 PE industry conference to ask about

Mervyn's after he had not returned several phone calls. Also, I wanted to see what his explanation was for what seemed to be the frequent Sun strategy of stripping assets out of the companies it owned. His firm had allegedly bankrupted trucking company Jevic so as to get at its valuable real estate, according to former Jevic workers who commented on the *New York Times* DealBook site; had bought CanGro Foods, the largest U.S. packager of frozen strawberries, and was selling off brands and closing sites; and was in the process of denuding apparel maker Kellwood of some labels. Krouse, who appeared to be socially awkward, said he understood my question and I should e-mail him. After doing so, his spokesperson called back and said Krouse declined comment.

In the mid-2000s, PE firms bought several iconic media companies and immediately set about boosting profits by cutting production. The competitive environment had changed; it had become harder to earn money from making new records or films, the PE firms said, so these businesses needed to be restructured to spend more prudently.

Scott Sperling, the man with the framed faked-up *Cash on Cash* album cover in his office featuring "Money for Nothing" as its final track, met me in 2007 to talk about his 2004 buyout of Warner Music.

Even though CD sales throughout the music industry were flat, Sperling said he found Warner Music appealing because most of its revenue came from rereleases, which made it an inexpensive company to operate. Indeed rereleases in 2004 accounted for 40 percent of Warner Music's sales. For example, Warner owned all the music written and recorded by the Eagles, an American rock group that reached its peak in the mid-1970s with the title song of their *Hotel California* album. Every few years, Warner could release an Eagles greatest hits album, and it would be a top-ten-selling CD, and yet the expenses for producing that album had been paid years before.

Then there were the huge profits from being a publisher—royalty fees non-Warner artists pay to cover Warner-owned songs and songs licensed for commercials. In 2003, publishing represented $100 million of its $270 million in earnings before interest, taxes, depreciation, and amortization.

But while Warner got the large majority of its revenue from rereleases and publishing, in 2003, it was also one of the largest producers of new records. These new records that it produced helped refresh its bank of material available for rerelease and publishing. Without new releases, the library would become increasingly stale and unattractive.

Sperling led a team of PE firms, including Bain Capital and Providence Equity Partners, that in March 2004 bought Warner Music in a $2.6 billion buyout. Their plan was to shift the company's focus away from producing new material to becoming more of a distributor. This new strategy would require less staff, and Sperling's goal was to make cost cuts that would save Warner $200 million a year.

Before the acquisition, Warner largely operated as three distinct labels—Warner, Elektra, and Atlantic. The Elektra label had one of the richest histories in the music industry. The Doors and Queen recorded for it, and the label popularized the hard-rock act Metallica. Atlantic too had a storied past, developing rhythm and blues and soul music. But while Elektra contributed to Warner's prestige and artist roster, it was no longer profitable. For the year ending November 2003, the label generated $170 million in revenue but lost $3 million in operating income before depreciation and amortization (OIBDA). So Sperling essentially eliminated it. He combined the two New York labels—Elektra and Atlantic—into one company, the Atlantic Records Group, the Los Angeles–based Warner label remaining independent.

Warner Music purged Elektra. Within one year of the buyout it fired sixteen hundred people companywide, about 30 percent of the staff, including almost all the senior-level Elektra executives. A morbid inside joke compared Warner's statement that it was merging Atlantic and Elektra to Germany's when it said it was merging with, instead of occupying, Poland during World War II. Jac Holzman, who founded Elektra and works with Warner Music, said Elektra was laid to rest.

Additionally, Warner told some Atlantic execs that they could retain their jobs only if they took pay cuts.

Besides gutting the Elektra label, Warner cut many artists, including the electronic-pop group Stereolab. Martin Pike, Stereolab's manager, told *Rolling Stone,* "We were told that our services are going to be dispensed with. We've been with Elektra since 1993. That company doesn't exist anymore."

Sperling said the purpose of these and later cuts "was not just to save costs. It was to come in and change the nature of a business that had become moribund and unable to respond to a changing environment." The environment was changing in part because of music piracy by consumers who downloaded songs and gave them to each other for free. This meant there was less revenue for each song produced.

But instead of investing to reposition Warner, Sperling and his PE fund investors used Warner Music as their personal till. Shortly after acquiring the business, Warner used the increased earnings from the cuts as the basis to borrow $202 million from Wall Street banks and give it to the PE firms as a dividend. In September 2004, Warner paid the owners another $350 million. Less than a year after the buyout, Sperling and co-investors had the music company with its increased earnings borrow an additional $681 million that they took as a dividend. The PE investment group through the three distributions quickly recovered substantially all of their down payment.

Former Elektra head Sylvia Rhone now heads Universal Music Group's Motown Records. Wearing a leopard-print shawl wrapped around her tall frame, she explained what Warner lost by firing her and her team: "What you want in the music business is as many sensibilities as you can afford. And so now, they have one creative vision coming out of the West Coast, and one coming out of the East Coast, and even under those umbrellas, there's not a lot of different views."

She added that Sony Music Entertainment (formerly Sony-BMG), like other music companies, also cut much of its staff during that time period but kept more major labels (Columbia, Epic, and Jive).

If the music industry had remained stable, Warner might have been able to make its cost-cutting strategy work. But U.S. industrywide record sales, which had been flat, started declining. They dropped 7.2 percent in 2005 and an additional 4.9 percent the next year.

Now Warner needed to boost revenue to pay its sizable debt. In good times, recycling old material might have been enough. Cassettes once replaced vinyl records, boosting music industry sales, and later CDs replaced cassettes. This often caused the consumer to buy the same album two or three times. But, there was no new technology that required the physical replacement of CDs.

Worse yet, legal music downloads were cutting into CD sales. Consumers were buying online from iTunes, which was becoming the biggest music retailer by selling songs for 99 cents each rather than entire albums that cost about $15. So the industry needed new hits—rather than library titles—to propel sales.

Warner did develop some of the newer acts that Elektra and its affiliates discovered shortly before the buyout—including James Blunt, Jason Mraz, and Staind. But for the most part, the PE firms turned off that pipeline of new supply, so Warner needed to find promising future acts from other sources.

It compensated by partnering more with independent labels. But that can be a risky strategy. Take the rock band Buckcherry. In 2006, Warner took a serious interest in signing the group, but because it had cut its budgets, it didn't have the money to risk signing many unproven acts. Warner ultimately did not make an offer, because it believed it was too much of a gamble. Buckcherry went instead with indie label Eleven Seven Music. The group hit it big with the album *15*, which Eleven Seven Music's head, Allen Kovac, promoted online, selling 104,000 copies in a week. Kovac said Warner quickly reached a partnership agreement in which it agreed to market the album for a 50 percent cut of sales. Warner says the agreement was actually far more favorable to Warner than Kovac said it was. In any case, partnering with Kovac proved to be a good decision, as the Buckcherry single "Crazy Bitch" went on to sell one million ring tones. Still, had Warner signed the band directly, it would have earned far more—more than 80 percent of profits minus royalties paid to the band and expenses, and it would have received exclusive rights to the group's next album.

In the end, Warner signed Buckcherry directly for its 2008 release, *Black Butterfly*, but the terms were almost certainly less favorable than if it had signed the band several years earlier.

Warner's partnership strategy became less effective as the company, Kovac said, continued to demand a big cut of sales while not delivering appreciable sales gains for the artists. He said in 2008 that he was now advising his acts not to partner with Warner. That includes Sixx:A.M., formed by Mötley Crüe founder Nikki Sixx, who in 2007 without Warner scored a U.S. mainstream rock number-two single with "Life Is Beautiful."

Kovac believes that, when promoting artists, Warner might boost sales by 20 percent, but that does not compensate for the cut Warner commands when marketing a record. By using YouTube and MySpace, he says he can create buzz. And since 2005, when New York Attorney General Eliot Spitzer forced music companies to stop paying radio station employees to promote artists, he has had just as good a chance to get radio airplay for his artists as a Warner does for its.

The old acts, too, started to fall away from Warner, also feeling they could make more money marketing records on their own.

Sperling talked about how he could rerelease Eagles albums every few years to boost sales, but he was unable to land them when the former Elektra act, which did not owe the label any more records, produced its first studio album in twenty-eight years. The Eagles recorded *Long Road out of Eden* on their own Eagles Recording Company and in 2007 distributed the CD in the United States exclusively through Walmart, and internationally through Warner rival Universal Music. The album debuted at number one on the U.S. *Billboard* album charts and became the fourth-biggest seller of the year. Eagles manager Irving Azoff said, "Walmart has tremendous resources that no label could afford to bring to the party [getting premium placement in the front of the store and at the registers] in addition to what they spent on TV, circulars, and radio advertising."

Considering that it killed off one of its three major labels, Warner held up well against its peers. It gained slightly against leading record company Universal Music Group, improving 5 percent in U.S. market share from 2004 through 2008, while Universal jumped 3.4 percent. Still, Warner's revenue has been flat since the buyout as industrywide record sales have dropped, and the trend is moving in the wrong direction. In the three months ending March 31, 2009, Warner's reported revenue slipped to $668 million compared to $800 million in the year-earlier period. It could not lose much more revenue and still pay its loans. The best hope for Warner may be to buy private-equity–owned rival EMI that is collapsing faster than Warner and then to combine labels and cut costs again.

To get more acts and boost its revenue now Warner changed tactics, and three years after closing Elektra to save money, in 2007, it bought the smaller, hard-rock label Roadrunner Records. Perhaps due to cash constraints, it could not hold on to Roadrunner's biggest act, Nickelback. After fulfilling its current obligations, Nickelback will be leaving for a more lucrative deal with Live Nation, the record company and concert promoter. Live Nation claims it is the largest producer of live concerts around the world and can help market artists in ways that a Warner cannot. Longtime Warner star Madonna also left for Live Nation.

Warner said the decision not to make deals with Madonna or Nickelback was simply based on its economic analysis, and any statement to the contrary was pure speculation. "What we're focused on are the newer artists and the mid-tier artist roster, not so much on the top tier of the artist roster where careers are already established. There is already a marketplace for that talent, and a market price for their services."

So the PE firms were essentially giving up the strategy that made Warner Music attractive to them in the first place. The record company of Ray Charles, Phil Collins, and Led Zeppelin is no longer interested in retaining top-tier artists. These are the performers who produce the albums that later generate earnings from rereleases and publishing. Without them, Warner will inevitably lose much of its remaining revenue base. But its PE owners have already earned their money back, plus significant fees. So what if Warner can't pay its debts and collapses? Don't worry about Scott Sperling and his partners, because as the song title on Sperling's fake framed album cover says, they will be "Leaving on a Private Jet Plane."

In 2001, Heartland Industrial Partners, a PE firm cofounded by Ronald Reagan's former budget director David Stockman, bought auto parts supplier Collins & Aikman from fellow PE firms, the Blackstone Group and Wasserstein Perella Capital Partners. The business made instrument panels and cockpit modules for all the big car makers, including General Motors and Ford.

Under the ownership of the PE firms, C&A trimmed its workforce while it aggressively sought new business. In 2003, the company won the contract to make door panels, instrument panels, and trunk systems for the Ford Fusion sedan. After winning the Ford contract that covered the Fusion and other models, Stockman said the project was the biggest in C&A's history and worth several billion dollars over the life of the program. C&A even built a special plant in Hermosillo, Mexico, for the project.

But according to a former C&A executive, C&A often did not allocate the engineering, design, and manpower resources it had promised on a program.

C&A, the former executive said, "committed to a certain number of people to Ford on the Fusion, but we had half as many as we said we did. Ford wanted regular meetings with us on the Fusion, so we'd send people to Dearborn who were managers that knew nothing about design or about the Fusion and tell Ford they were designers to make it look like we had X number of bodies for Ford. They were just placeholders. Had Ford asked them a question about the Fusion, it would have been ugly. It was outright deceit."

A different unidentified C&A executive, a former VP and general manager at a C&A facility in Troy, Michigan, who left the company in 2004, alleged in a lawsuit filed by a creditor against the company and the private-equity firm's partners that C&A cut back engineering, design, and manpower for auto-maker programs, even though it had promised certain levels of engineering or a certain number of people on a program.

For instance, the executive recounted occasions when Ford, which had required twenty-two designers and engineers to staff a project for the Mustang, called for meetings. At the direction of his superiors, the executive alleges in the lawsuit that he combed through the C&A organizational charts to dig up the required personnel. When he failed to find enough people, Heartland founder Stockman appeared at two meetings with Ford to explain why his supplier could not have all the personnel in attendance.

The creditor lawsuit was later dismissed.

By the summer of 2004, C&A's cutbacks caused production to

deteriorate so badly that it increasingly had bad launches of components and was frequently not able to pass inspection on a timely basis.
General Motors in early summer 2004 warned C&A, which already
had six "bad launches" of GM components, that one more bad launch
would automatically result in GM's putting the company on "new business hold."

C&A had another bad launch in October 2004, and it lost out on
two new contracts, the suit said. The company in May 2005 filed for
bankruptcy.

While other auto suppliers have struggled along with the rest of the
car industry, a source at one of the major auto makers, who handles
supplier relations, said C&A was the only one of its size forced into
bankruptcy because it was delivering inferior products. In 2007, after
selling some divisions, the company shut down.

A Heartland spokesperson was reached and declined to comment.

When faced with criticism that they eliminate jobs and starve companies of capital, PE firms often respond that they cut spending to
make businesses more profitable, and once the companies are more
profitable, they create new jobs. Unfortunately, that's not what usually
happens. The more common scenario is that PE owners starve their
businesses of both human and financial capital, and the weakened
companies suffer.

The American Enterprise Institute is a conservative think tank
whose twenty-four trustees include a number of partners at PE firms,
such as Marc Lipschultz of Kohlberg Kravis Roberts. In November
2007, it held a two-day conference on private equity, featuring speak-
ers who largely touted its merits. The most anticipated was perhaps
University of Chicago professor Steven Davis, who was presenting preliminary findings of the most comprehensive research ever done on
the impact of buyouts on employment.

The stakes were high.

Professor Davis looked a bit tense as he stood behind the podium
at AEI's conference center. He had written a book on job creation
patterns but was new to the buyout debate. The Kauffman Foundation, which focuses on entrepreneurship, had paid him to conduct the

study. Soon after starting his research, Davis teamed with Harvard professor Josh Lerner, who is seen as an authority on private equity and also friendly to the industry.

Jumping right into the findings, Davis described charts being projected onto an overhead screen. His words, however, did not match what everyone saw. The charts clearly showed that private-equity firms throughout different industries reduced employment at a much greater rate than competing companies. Davis explained this away by saying these were just preliminary numbers and did not factor in the jobs PE firms created.

His team soon released their finished report. They took the buyouts of U.S. companies from 1980 through 2000, looked at their 123,248 American establishments (factories, stores, etc.), and compared them to companies of similar industry, age, and size. Most companies reallocate jobs from older to new facilities, so existing establishments tend to lose jobs, but the study found that the losses were greater at PE-owned businesses. In the first two years after a buyout, they cut 17.7 percent of jobs, while their non-PE peers cut 10.9 percent. The difference between the two sets over five years grew to 10.3 percent.

The researchers then looked to see if these businesses were creating fewer jobs before being bought. The answer was yes, but the losses accelerated after the LBOs. Davis believes these businesses would have likely kept trimming jobs if they had not found buyers. But there is another theory. The study showed that those businesses were *adding* more jobs than their peers three to five years before the buyout and were creating fewer jobs only in the two years prior to the sale, which might mean that they decided to prepare for a sale and wanted to boost short-term earnings to attract a better price. Therefore, they may not have cut more jobs than their competitors if they had been intending to hold on to their businesses.

There were some more disturbing trends in the study. Job losses were much greater in the first three years after takeovers that were completed from 1995 through 2000, the last years the study covers, than in prior times. Davis said that could be because, in the 1980s and early 1990s, PE firms bought more manufacturers, among which there were no significant job losses compared to peers, and subsequently greatly broadened their scope. PE firms reduce employment most when buying retail, services, finance, insurance, and real-estate businesses.

A troubling sign for future employment was in data based on who sold the business to the PE firm. Losses were greatest when PE firms acquired businesses from other PE firms. Usually a PE firm makes all the obvious cost cuts it can to a company first, so by the time it resells, there are few areas left to slash except the workforce. Worse yet, these cuts that are made in later rounds are the most damaging to the business because they tend to hit core operations. With a glut of PE-owned companies and fewer attractive privately owned outfits left to purchase, there are likely to be deeper job cuts as more firms buy businesses from each other.

When Davis looked to see if the jobs PE firms created by opening new factories and stores offset the losses at existing establishments, he examined a sample of roughly a thousand PE-owned businesses and found that in the first two years after buying a business, PE firms drove a 14.9 percent increase in new-establishment "greenfield" jobs compared to 9 percent for peers. That helped reduce the net job loss to 3.6 percent over the first two years of ownership compared to their non-PE competitors.

CD&R's Rice, speaking to the *New York Times* about the study, said, "I thought the numbers would be more positive."

From 2000 through the first half of 2007, PE firms bought companies employing close to 10 percent of U.S. private-sector workers, about ten million people. (From 1980 to 1999, a much longer time period, they bought companies that employed fewer than five million Americans.)

Assuming that the job-destruction pattern continued, PE firms eliminated 360,000 more jobs in the companies they bought this decade than competitors during their first two years of ownership. That does not take into account the fact that the most job cuts happen in the third year after a buyout (Rice's CD&R, for example, in its third year of owning Hertz, eliminated 2,750 jobs, about 7 percent of its workforce), or the fact that we are in a deep recession, or the question of what will happen when many PE-owned companies go bankrupt.

Former Reagan and Bush Treasury secretary Nicholas Brady told me that PE firms, in fact, did cause job losses. "Some LBOs have put a lot of people out of work who probably would still have jobs if they [their companies] had not been subjected to such leverage. When you take eighty percent of the equity out of a business and replace it with debt, you have very very little margin for error."

In his report, Davis called PE firms catalysts for creative destruction, saying they reduce employment in inefficient lower-value segments and accelerate activity through greenfield jobs in new higher-value directions. Professor Davis told me, though, that he had not dug into the numbers to see what kinds of positions PE-owned companies were really creating. If he had, that is not the reality he would have found.

The jobs PE-owned companies retain and create are often those that pay less and have fewer benefits. This not only contributes to a bigger gap between the rich and the middle class, but also results in less disposable income, which reduces U.S. consumer spending and undermines the economy. Not to mention what it does to the people who suddenly find their standards of living slashed.

Needing a job in 1961, Memphis teen Joseph Irving Jr. thought about making furniture. He had taken woodworking classes. "I was fresh out of high school and just applied for the job" at Sealy licensee Slumber Products. "I applied for others too," he said. Slumber Products hired him for $1 an hour to bore holes for the chairs and sofas it was building.

The Haas family that owned Slumber Products "would try to take care of their own," Irving said. They even had a cook on staff who made food for the employees. The family was investing in its business. The Haas family in 1979 moved the plant from where it had been for years, a former Ford factory that leaked, to a better facility.

Over time, as he gained experience, Irving moved to more skilled jobs. In the early 1980s, he was a bed cutter. "I cut the fabric for the very top of mattresses. I used a roll of fabric, drew it out, cut it out, and then put it on stands for the women who sewed it on the box spring. It was like an assembly line," he said. "I was good at being a cutter because I took pride in my work."

But by the 1990s, Sealy had bought its licensees like Slumber Products and then sold out to PE firms. Bain Capital led a buyout of Sealy Mattress in 1997.

At the time, Irving had been at the company for nearly forty years and was earning the equivalent of about $20 an hour. His base salary was only $7.15 an hour, but he made most of his earnings from piecework, running close to 300 percent over his production quota.

"I could do my work quickly. I would start at seven, end at noon, and go home.... Others would leave at seven thirty to eight P.M."

Besides earning more, Irving had also risen to be chief steward for the Furniture Workers IUE, Local 282, which represented the Memphis hourly workers. That gave him increased responsibilities, and people to defend. He said Sealy around 1999 tried busting the union by hiring Hispanics who could not speak English. The idea was that the plant's new Spanish-speaking general manager would convince the workers not to join the union because he spoke their language and union representatives did not speak Spanish. If 50 percent of the hourly workers became nonunion, Bain could decertify the union. But Irving said eventually even the new workers joined.

"Sealy in 2000 had a meeting with us and wanted to enter into a partnership. They wanted the union and the company to partner where they would establish committees together for arbitration. The union said no," Irving said, explaining that it would have led to constant fighting.

Bain did not accept no for an answer.

According to Irving, Sealy started claiming that the work they were doing in Memphis was shabby, and he somewhat agreed with the criticism. "The quality was eighty-five percent of what it was in prior years. When I was first there, you still had people there twenty-five years who really knew how to make mattresses. The new people were not as efficient. I would spend two to three days showing new workers how to build; then they would make mistakes."

Under the pressure from Bain, he said, "the plant used to be a happy-go-lucky place, and it turned into a place where nobody cared."

As less material was sent to the plant, it made fewer products and became unprofitable. The plant at its peak was getting 1,600–1,800 pieces a day, but by 2002, Sealy was shipping it 400–500 pieces. Irving said it was all timed so that the plant would close when the union contract expired in April 2002.

In March 2001, Sealy announced it would shut down its Memphis factory and eliminate 147 jobs because it was not profitable. Production was moved to a nonunion Brenham, Texas, plant.

The Texas Department of Labor shows that in Washington County, Texas (where Brenham is the biggest town), the number of workers manufacturing furniture and related products rose from 288 in the first quarter of 2000 to 347 in the third quarter of 2001, a 59-person increase, which is equal to almost half the lost Memphis jobs.

The PE firms, as we learned to expect in the previous chapter, did not put much, if any, of the savings wrung out of Sealy into developing better products and as a result, soon after closing the Memphis plant, the company lost considerable market share to smaller competitors Select Comfort and Tempur-Pedic.

As far as creating jobs goes, when PE firms open new establishments, it is often just to replace shuttered ones. Four and a half years after buying the Alpha T-shirt distribution business from Ronald Berg, PE firm Linsalata resold the company in 2004 to Bain Capital-owned Broder Brothers, Alpha's chief competitor, making a sizable profit.

Bain then consolidated the combined company's seventeen distribution centers into seven mega-warehouses and one somewhat smaller facility. That would save on labor and allow it to better handle inventory. Bain planned to move centers to areas where via UPS they could reach the same number of customers with one-day shipping.

Broder CEO Thomas Myers closed the Philadelphia warehouse, moving distribution to a larger facility a hundred miles away near Harrisburg, Pennsylvania, despite the more than seventy-year history of Alpha in the city and despite the fact that some of its area customers liked to pick up orders in person. CEO Myers said Broder might have lost 5 percent to 10 percent of its Philadelphia-area business to competitors as a result of the move.

A former Broder worker says the company offered the Philadelphia workers less money for similar jobs in Harrisburg. CEO Myers said that may be true, but Harrisburg is a rural area that has a lower cost of living. He does acknowledge, though, that only 10 to 12 of the former 121 Philadelphia workers take company vans providing daily travel from Philadelphia to Harrisburg. Explaining why more workers did not stay with Broder, he said, "Would you travel two hours to make ten dollars an hour?"

Berg said the few former Alpha employees that are left at the company are pretty much in a demoralized state.

When Bain hired people at the Harrisburg facility, those were greenfield jobs, because the company was adding workers at a new establishment. Still, the positions were not like the ones Professor Davis said PE firms create in the pursuit of new higher-value business. The mega-warehouses were the same as the shuttered ones except they were bigger. And the salaries were lower.

Broder, in March 2009, in fact, announced it was hiring financial adviser Miller Buckfire to help restructure its debt so it could continue to meet its commitments when certain loans mature in October 2010.

Starving companies of operating and human capital makes it difficult for them to survive in good economic times. But as the overall economy sinks, more and more businesses will find themselves under intolerable stress, and those that were formerly strong enough to survive, like Mervyn's, will disappear as well.

CHAPTER SIX

Plunder and Profit

Standing behind a clear podium at the June 5, 2007, Republican presidential debate, candidate Mitt Romney was on the spot. With only 12 percent of voters in a *USA Today* poll saying they would choose him, and nine other candidates in the field, Romney had to make an impression.

Romney, sixty, was a former businessman, tall and handsome with black hair brushed back and to the right. But while good looks never hurt, Romney needed more than a full head of hair to become the nominee. Front-runner Rudolph Giuliani was pushing his reputation for "delivering results." Senator John McCain, as a former prisoner of war, embodied courage. Who would Romney, campaigning under the slogan "True Strength," be? So far, standing in a group of men who mostly were in dark suits and white button-down shirts, Romney was distinguished by a light blue silk tie and expensive-looking cufflinks.

CNN moderator Wolf Blitzer raised the topic of big money and oil. McCain said we should invest more in nuclear energy. The U.S. Navy had relied on it for sixty years to power submarines without incident, he said. Giuliani said the government should put the same effort into developing alternative fuel sources as it had in the 1960s when planning a mission to the moon.

Romney was next. This was his chance to push the image of himself as a successful businessman, as representative of "True Strength."

"What do you say to the audience who believes that there's too much of an alliance between the big oil companies and Republicans?" Blitzer asked.

"Big oil is making a lot of money right now," Romney said. "And I'd like to see them using that money to invest in refineries. Don't forget that when companies earn profit, that money is supposed to be reinvested in growth."

For people not familiar with Romney's background as the owner
of Bain Capital or with his relationships to other private-equity firms,
the irony of this advice might not have been immediately clear. PE
firms during the 2003–7 buyout boom often had their companies use
increased short-term earnings that came from reducing customer
service, raising prices, and starving them of capital—not to reinvest or
pay debt, but instead as the basis to borrow more money, which they
then gave to their PE owners through dividends. Many of these businesses are now stuck with enormous debt and falling earnings.

Fourteen of the largest American private-equity firms had more
than 40 percent of the North American companies they bought from
2002 until September 2006 borrow money to pay them dividends. In
thirty-two of the eighty-three cases, 38 percent, they took money out
in the first year.

Mitt Romney was a pioneer of this strategy. His private-equity
firm, Bain Capital, was the first large PE firm to make a serious portion of its money not from selling its companies or listing them on the
stock exchange, but rather by collecting distributions and dividends,
which in this context is the exact opposite of reinvesting in a company.
Bain Capital is notorious for its failure to plow profits back into its
businesses.

Romney's answer did not, however, come out of the blue. He had
already begun to distance himself from his past. In a *New York Times*
article a few days earlier, Romney said taking a big payment from a
business that ultimately failed would make him "sick, sick at heart."
Also, he told the *Times,* one should not take a dividend or a distribution from a business if it put that company at risk. And he also said he
had nothing to do with Bain Capital's decisions to take money from
two companies that later collapsed. Geoffrey Rehnert, who helped
start Bain Capital and is now co-CEO of the PE firm Audax Group,
told me Romney controlled Bain Capital between approximately 1992
and 2001. During that time the firm collected enormous distributions
from three companies (the *Times* did not mention the third) it drove
into bankruptcy. Romney, in a 2000 interview with *USA Today* about
being named CEO of the Winter Olympics, said, "The term manager
suggests that you manage. It doesn't mean you abdicate."

Bain Makes Fortunes by Hobbling Companies

Year Invested	Company	Investment	Return	Company Results After Bain Collects
1988	Stage Stores	$5m	$100m from stock offerings	Filed for bankruptcy in 2000
1990	Damon Corp.	$4m	$12m from selling the company	Pleaded guilty in 1996 to overbilling Medicare during the time of Bain's ownership and paid a $119m fine
1992	Ampad	$5m	$100m from dividends	Filed for bankruptcy in 2000
1993	GS Technologies (renamed GS Industries)	$60m	$65m from dividends	Filed for bankruptcy in 2001
1994	Dade Behring	°$85m	°$421m from dividends	Filed for bankruptcy in 2002
1997	Details (renamed DDi)	$46m	$93m from stock offerings	Filed for bankruptcy in 2003
2000	KB Toys	$18.5m	$85m from dividends	Filed for bankruptcy in 2004

°Including investment partners.

Traditionally, cash-rich public companies have paid dividends to lure and reward investors. They distribute some of the profits that they are not reinvesting as a way to say they have surplus funds and expect to have them in the future. These dividends generally amount to cents or a few dollars per share paid quarterly.

But when private-equity firms take distributions, they typically do not tap excess profits. Instead, they increase the pool of available funds by having their companies borrow money—on top of the original debt taken on to finance the LBO.

Mitt Romney used this strategy in the 1990s as part of his private-equity playbook, long before it became common practice during the 2003–7 buyout boom. The credit crisis that started in mid-2007 limited the practice, as it became difficult for companies to borrow funds to pay the dividends. But the scale back was purely a function of credit availability, not of any backing off by the PE firms. Just as venture capitalists rushed to get their businesses listed on the public markets in 1998 and 1999 to take advantage of the IPO frenzy, private-equity groups used dividend payments in this decade as a way to profit from the cheap-credit bubble. If Bain's experience is any indication, many of the companies that borrowed money to issue dividends will not be able to survive.

Mitt Romney's late father, George Romney, the American Motors chairman and Michigan governor, instilled in Mitt the idea of building financial independence so he was not beholden to anyone and then running for public office. He's clearly working on fulfilling the second half of his father's mandate. But in his earlier career, Romney was dedicated to pushing boundaries as the head of Bain Capital. In that role, he helped set what has become a dangerous standard for the whole private-equity industry.

After graduating from Harvard in 1975 with an MBA and a law degree, Romney worked at Boston Consulting Group alongside future Israeli prime minister Benjamin Netanyahu. In 1978, he left to become vice president at one of BCG's peers, Bain & Co.—joining Meg Whitman, who later became CEO of eBay and one of the national finance chairs of Romney's unsuccessful 2008 presidential campaign.

Bill Bain, who ran Bain & Co., felt the firm should invest its own money in companies as well as advise clients on their deals. To that end, he asked Romney and T. Coleman Andrews III in 1984 to head a new group, Bain Capital. Bain was the first consultancy to set up a private-equity shop, and the plan was both to buy businesses through LBOs and to make venture-capital investments. In 1992, Bill Bain gave Romney 100 percent ownership of Bain Capital in payment for taking time off from Bain Capital to help rescue Bain & Co. from bankruptcy (Andrews had left by that time and would eventually become CEO of South African Airways).

By the early 1990s Romney had turned Bain Capital almost exclusively into a private-equity firm, believing there was more money to be made in LBOs than small venture deals.

In 1994, medical equipment maker Baxter International sought a buyer for its testing division, which sold machines and reagents to labs. Romney's firm partnered with Goldman Sachs Capital Partners to buy the Baxter subsidiary for approximately $415 million, then named Scott Garrett, who had been running the division, as CEO.

Unlike competitors who were putting money into potentially lucrative but risky areas like DNA screening devices, Bain quickly reduced R & D spending from an average of $45 million annually in the three prior years to $27 million. The company focused on making equipment that would likely sell in the short term, said S. Michael Rumbin, who was vice president of technology management. "But the companies like Roche that did invest in long-range development obviously were able to make a quantum leap forward in terms of their position within the market."

Soon after Bain's purchase of Baxter's division, DuPont began seeking a buyer for its similar lab-equipment business. Bain was interested. When news of a possible sale got out, Robert Brightfelt, who ran the DuPont subsidiary, addressed employees in the first-floor auditorium at its Glasgow, Delaware, plant. It was an important speech because Brightfelt knew some of his scientists were thinking of leaving. "Don't worry," he told the crowd of four hundred people. "We're not going to sell you out to investment banks." He also made a point of reassuring the anxious audience that benefits would remain intact, according to one executive who attended the meeting.

The former Baxter business bought the DuPont division in 1996 for $582 million, more than what the PE firms had paid for Dade. A year later, it merged with Hoechst AG's Germany-based diagnostics subsidiary and renamed the combined company Dade Behring.

"Mitt was not that involved in Dade," former CEO Garrett said, "but he certainly was part of the process to approve the two big acquisitions that were made.... He was far more in tune with what was going on throughout his firm, and even the portfolio companies, than you might expect."

While lab-equipment manufacturers typically allocate between 10 percent and 15 percent of sales to R & D, Dade was spending only 6 percent to 7 percent—$61.7 million in 1997 and $88.2 million in 1998. For Bain the anemic R & D budget made sense. Often one sells medical equipment in three- to five-year deals—and Bain, like all private-equity firms, tries to exit businesses within five years. There was little upside three years into its investment to investing for the future because Bain was not planning to be part of it.

Garrett, the former CEO, believes that that analysis is oversimplifying the situation. "If there were two analyzers, one at DuPont in development and one at what was Baxter in development, you certainly didn't need to continue both. So I think throughout the early years of Dade the research and development investments were covering more opportunities each year rather then less opportunity. It was just a matter of the overlap creating the declining R & D expense in the financial statements."

In 1997 Garrett resigned, and Bain replaced him with one of its own, former Bain Capital executive vice president Steven Barnes. (Garrett declined to talk about why he left, and he later became CEO of the Dade peer Beckman Coulter.)

Four and a half years after its investment, in June 1999, Bain was thinking about how to get out. So Dade had financial people throughout the company make projections. Michael Johnson was one of them. "They were looking for us to be aggressive but realistic in our forecasts," said Johnson, who monitored the Miami, Florida, division that produced tests to detect Von Willebrand disease, a bleeding disorder.

While preparing these forecasts, Dade Behring changed the benefits it gave to the former DuPont workers—exactly what Brightfelt said wouldn't happen. The company froze their pensions and converted them from a defined-benefit plan, in which employees upon retiring were entitled to 75 percent of the average of their combined salary in their last three working years, to a cash-balance plan, in which they would get a lump sum equal to what they were owed in 1999. Former DuPont workers were furious at Brightfelt, who at the time was group president in Dade's Chicago office, far away from the affected Delaware employees.

Several former DuPont workers contacted Norman Stein, a University of Alabama professor and pension expert, to see if they had a legal case against Dade for converting the plan. After studying the situation, Stein said the move might well have been unlawful. But the employees never went forward with a lawsuit, fearing they would lose their jobs if they became named plaintiffs, Stein said, adding that Dade might have saved between $10 million and $40 million through the conversion.

The same month that Dade converted the pension, it used the projections of that very savings as part of the basis to borrow $421 million, which it then turned around and used to buy shares from its owners. The PE firms and Dade management took the whole distribution and still kept a 54 percent stake in Dade while giving merger partner Hoechst a bigger (46 percent) company stake. Bain and Goldman had only put $85 million down to buy the company, yet in June 1999 they received $365 million from the dividend, 4.3 times their money.

Dade borrowed so much to make this payment that its debt more than doubled to $871 million (68 percent of sales.) Standard & Poor's lowered Dade's credit rating from the BB to B category, believing it likely that the company with the added debt would be unable to pay its interest if it faced adverse business conditions.

A Dade executive, who requested anonymity, said he confronted CEO Barnes after a boardroom meeting within a week of the distribution.

"You really think it's a good idea to borrow, you know, one times sales?" he asked.

"Oh. Yeah. Yeah. You know, that's fine," Barnes reportedly responded. "You know, companies do that all the time."

The executive then told Barnes, "Well, that'd be like me going out and borrowing the amount of money I make in a year and then trying to pay it off and pay for my house and feed myself and everything else. That doesn't make sense." The executive said he let it drop after that.

Private-equity firms are often reckless when they have their companies declare dividends. Bain put Dade Behring in deep debt for the second time, after already wringing costs out of the business to pay back part of the loans taken to finance the initial buyout, forcing it to find new areas to cut. Now pretty much the only place left was the core of the business.

Dade controller Michael Johnson, who provided the Miami forecast and now is the chief financial officer at TPG-owned Fenwal Blood Technologies, said the company took chances in 1999 by not taking insurance against the euro, even though it had significant European operations through its merger with Hoechst's division. Instead, the PE firms had Dade borrow near the maximum it could and did not worry about what would happen afterward. Over the next two years, Dade paid for its cheapness: the euro fell in value and seriously affected sales of products within Europe. Dade's revenue fell from $1.29 billion in 1998 to $1.23 billion in 2001.

With so much debt and falling revenue, the company had little choice but to cut costs wherever it could. Rumbin, who had become vice president of international sales, was fired. He believes Dade let him go in 2000 because it needed money to pay the loan it took for the distribution. "There's no doubt there was a connection."

Meanwhile, Michael Johnson helped close down Dade's Miami office in 1999, consolidating operations with a similar division in Germany. There were 850 Miami employees. No amount of closing divisions or firing workers, though, could save the company from its crushing debt load. In August 2002, Dade Behring voluntarily filed for bankruptcy protection.

Dade's creditors took over the business, and Bain lost all its shares. But Bain and Goldman, after putting down only $85 million to buy Dade and receiving the $365 million, made a $280 million profit. After the bankruptcy, the creditors agreed to cut the company's debt by more than half for company shares. They were willing to do this because they saw that if Dade focused on growth and not paying debt, it had the potential to be a strong business. Dade began pumping money into R & D—more than 8 percent of revenue in 2003, 2004, and 2005. And by 2006, Dade's sales had risen 40 percent to $1.74 billion. The next year,

Siemens bought the company for $6.7 billion, five times more than its value at the time of the bankruptcy.

Bain generated very good returns by taking a distribution from Dade but could have done far better if it had built the business.

This was not an isolated incident in Bain's history.

Following a similar pattern, Bain in 1992 bought American Pad and Paper (Ampad) from Mead Corp. in a $56 million buyout. Just as with Dade, Bain's strategy was to build the company through acquisitions. In 1994, Ampad bought Smith Corona's Marion, Indiana, paper-pad and hanging-file-folder operations. On Independence Day weekend that year, the company dissolved the union that represented the Marion employees, laying off 320 workers—though it did offer to hire some of them back at lower wages and reduced benefits. (The union members went on strike.)

Meanwhile, Romney was the Republican senatorial candidate running against incumbent Massachusetts Senator Edward Kennedy. The challenger was gaining momentum by claiming he knew how to get Massachusetts out of the recession because he had helped create ten thousand jobs at Bain. Kennedy ran ads exposing the Marion layoffs, and it resonated with voters, costing Romney any chance of winning. In February 1995, after losing the election, Bain closed the Marion plant and moved its patented machines to Ampad's other factories.

Ampad was struggling. In 1994, the company lost $7.5 million, partly because of rising paper prices. Still, Bain kept expanding the business, believing the loss was temporary, and in 1995 Ampad borrowed money from Bankers Trust (now part of Deutsche Bank) to buy envelope manufacturer Williamhouse-Regency for approximately $300 million. Bain had projected that the combined business would have more pricing power with office-supply stores like Staples. Money-losing Ampad, at the same time it borrowed money to buy Williamhouse-Regency, also took out a $75 million loan to pay Bain a dividend.

Bain had put down less than $5 million in cash to buy Ampad and made roughly a twenty-times return. Although it may seem odd that Ampad could even get a loan for such a purpose, it's important to remember that the banks doing business with firms like Bain derived as much as 20 percent of their total profits during the buyout boom from PE-driven work (it was a lower percentage in 1995 but growing). Therefore it was in their interest to maintain good relationships with PE firms, even if a particular request might appear risky. Also, banks generally resell the loans they've made. This means another fee, and the risk of holding a questionable loan is sloughed off onto someone else. So banks had the incentive to make these kinds of loans, and there was not a lot of downside.

Lucky for Bain.

"Bain Capital had a business model that was intended to essentially transfer wealth from its holdings to itself," said current Ampad chief executive Don Meltzer, who was not involved with the business in 1995. "... [They did this] instead of building the wealth of the company that they owned and extracting gains through selling the company."

Romney's comments during the debate about good businesses reinvesting profits, in this light, seem hypocritical.

In 1996, Ampad went public on the New York Stock Exchange, diluting Bain's ownership to roughly a 40 percent stake, and used the $173 million in share proceeds to reduce some of its debt. At the time, big-box retailers were driving down the prices they paid for their products. Profits declined, and even with the share proceeds, it was a strain for Ampad to pay the money borrowed to finance the distributions and acquisition. While this was happening, CEO Charles Hanson was still telling analysts for months to keep expecting Ampad to achieve its growth objectives. In September 1997, when Ampad reported flat revenue and predicted a sharp decline in earnings, its share price fell from more than $24 to $11.50 in five trading sessions.

John Rodgers, who became Ampad senior vice president and general counsel in 1998, said the company started moving production to Mexico, but the situation was so dire that it couldn't finish. "By that time, it was too late to do anything," Rodgers said. "I mean, the company was focused on just staying alive." In 2000, Ampad's creditors forced the business to file for bankruptcy.

Current CEO Meltzer said Ampad has since spent under $20 million (much less than Bain's windfall) finishing the Mexican move. This has lowered manufacturing costs, and it now sells to retailers for prices that are competitive with its peers. Ampad's revenue, after selling several office-product divisions, is less than one third what it was under Bain but it has stayed relevant by making paper pads in forms ranging from high-end gold fiber pads to a creative expressions notebook, with artwork on the borders, for printing invitations.

So another Bain company that collapsed under the weight of debt became viable after bankruptcy when it again had enough capital to maintain and improve operations.

Bain's most aggressive debt-to-distribution play might have been the one it collected from KB Toys shortly after Romney left the firm to run the 2002 Winter Olympics.

In 2000, Michael Glazer was the president of retail conglomerate Big Lots Stores, which owned KB, America's fifth biggest toy retailer. Glazer was personally trying to buy KB from Big Lots—while also fulfilling his fiduciary duty (responsibility to the business) by shopping the retailer to other suitors, including Bain Capital. He said he did too good a sales job, and Bain in 2000 ended up outbidding him, acquiring KB Toys in a $303 million leveraged buyout. The PE firm hired Glazer as KB Toys chief executive.

Part of the reason Bain found KB attractive was that while it mostly sold the toys manufacturers pushed, 20 percent were lower-priced close-out items, which offered bigger profit margins. "I mean, for every Tickle Me Elmo, there are twenty-five toys that don't quite make it," Glazer said. "As a result, there are a lot of so-called close-outs or value propositions." In addition, the fact that most of its locations were in malls became an unexpected advantage.

After the September 11, 2001, terrorist attacks, mall owners started advertising that they were a safe place to shop, and traffic boomed. During the 2001 Christmas holiday season, KB saw same-store sales grow more than 15 percent compared to the prior year. While customers played with their new toys, Bain partners thought KB should borrow money to give *them* some Christmas cash—a dividend.

Although it had owned the business less than two years, Bain approached Glazer with the idea of arranging a payment.

It was KB's responsibility to determine how much it could give Bain. That was because the retailer had creditors and was not supposed to put them at risk. As is common among PE-owned companies, KB hired a valuation firm, Houlihan Lokey Howard & Zukin, to determine if the proposed dividend would leave the business legally solvent. A solvency opinion is created by getting an earnings forecast for the next five to seven years, comparing that to historical performance, and looking at competitors.

Bain wanted KB to borrow $67 million and to take nearly all of the company's $55 million in cash to buy some of its shares for more than $85 million and provide $31 million in bonuses for KB executives, including Glazer. This meant that Bain, on the $18 million it had put down to buy the business, would—in two years—be making a 4.7-times return. "Even with those kinds of numbers, we certainly at the end of the day thought KB would be safe," Glazer said, adding that he couldn't imagine the company's sales dropping more than five percent per year. Ten percent, maximum.

One might believe it would be hard to find a firm to provide a solvency opinion in such a situation. But once again, it's a matter of incentive. A source who writes solvency opinions for PE-owned companies and did not work on KB pointed out that he actually gets higher fees for analyzing these risky deals. After all, the work is more time-consuming, and the firm puts its reputation on the line. Just as there are incentives for banks to make the loans that get used as dividends, there are incentives for valuation firms to prepare difficult solvency opinions. In fact, according to the source, some are particularly motivated to reach positive conclusions because they only receive a full fee if the dividend is paid, having to settle for a smaller "break-up" fee if it never gets issued.

Houlihan Lokey was actually not so bullish. It found that KB, by borrowing $67 million and spending all its cash, would not pass three of its four solvency tests, a source said. However, in some states, such as Delaware, the only legal requirement before issuing a dividend is for the company to show that afterward its assets (valuation) will exceed liabilities. Having the actual ability to pay the debt is not a legal requirement.

Once a solvency opinion has been secured, a PE company's board of directors votes on whether to go through with the distribution. Board members who are also partners of the PE firm rarely disqualify themselves from voting, although they have an obvious conflict of interest. At KB there were four board members: Glazer and three Bain Capital partners—Joshua Bekenstein, Matthew Levin, and Robert White—all of whom likely stood to profit handsomely from the distribution. Glazer said the board voted unanimously to take the $119 million.

Soon after this, Glazer started pushing KB in new directions, selling toys in Sears, Safeway, and CVS stores and buying eToys's Web site for $15 million. But the company was not prepared for what came next.

During the 2002-holiday season, Walmart, the nation's biggest retailer, and Target, heavily discounted toys to get customers into its stores. "Sort of out of nowhere they started offering the hot toys, if you will, at prices that were certainly below what we were paying," Glazer said. "There were quite a few of them. It was devastating, because they sold them in some cases ten or fifteen dollars below our cost."

KB was not only losing sales but also had to sell toys at cost. The company wasn't even making a profit on the sales it did make. "We did quite a few things trying to get ourselves in position for the next holiday season without even imagining that they were going to do this again in '03," Glazer said. "When they did it again with the same aggressiveness, we just couldn't withstand that" (so much for his worst-case scenarios of a 5 percent to 10 percent drop in sales). KB filed for bankruptcy January 14, 2004, less than two years after Bain and management collected $67 million by having the company borrow money to pay them. The retailer in the nineteen months it was in bankruptcy closed about six hundred stores and fired five thousand workers.

Big Lots Stores (which became a KB creditor) filed a lawsuit against Bain for unjust enrichment and fraud when collecting its money and settled in bankruptcy court for a confidential amount, said a source close to the case.

For his part, Glazer said there are simply no profits for toy retailers as long as Walmart is willing to sell toys at below cost. He points to Prentice Capital, which bought KB out of bankruptcy and failed to turn it around, and competitor FAO Schwarz, which in 2003 also filed for bankruptcy.

But this less than rosy outlook for the retail toy business didn't keep Bain away. In 2005, it co-led a $7.3 billion buyout of Toys "R" Us. How was it expecting to recoup and make a profit on its $450 million down payment? Surely not just by selling toys.

Dividend destruction became possible for Bain and its followers in the 1970s after the courts ruled that companies had the right to use the fair-market value of their businesses minus liabilities and paid-in capital to determine the pool of money from which they could declare dividends. Previously, only hard assets, minus liabilities and paid-in capital, determined the size of the potential dividend pool. Expanding the definition to base it on fair-market value potentially adds to the amount the company can borrow.

A lawyer who advises PE firms on dividends said, "The only flaw in that, of course, is, well, the market goes up and down. So, the appreciated value that you're returning (to shareholders) today may not exist tomorrow." That was particularly a problem from 2004 through 2007, when PE firms had their companies borrow more than they could likely repay based on the belief that they could refinance the debt a few years later.

Other PE Companies Destroyed Through Dividends

Company	Year Issued Dividend(s)	Total	To Whom	Number of Employees	Year Declared Bankruptcy
Buffets (Old Country and HomeTown Buffet restaurant chains), Eagan, MN	2002 and 2004	$225m	Caxton-Iseman Capital and Sentinel Capital	37,000	2008

Company	Year Issued Dividend(s)	Total	To Whom	Number of Employees	Year Declared Bankruptcy
Maax Corp. (tubs, spas, and showers), Lachine, Quebec, Canada	2005	$110m	JW Childs, Borealis Capital, and Ontario Municipal Pension	2,034	2008
Nellson Nutraceutical (diet bars and shakes), Irwindale, CA	2004	$100m	Fremont Partners	1,500	2006

The lawyer said he advised clients during the credit boom to consider whether their companies could use the money they borrowed to pay dividends, even when it was not a legal requirement in the states in which their companies were incorporated.

He said he suggested to PE firms that they take several months to consider if their companies could take the dividend strain but that the PE firms tended to underestimate the risks. After a bank agreed to make the loan and they got a solvency opinion, company boards sometimes made the decision to borrow money to fund a dividend in a perfunctory director's meeting that took place by phone and lasted maybe twenty minutes, the lawyer said.

PE firms, even though they may have already collected from their companies, are not required to help them if they later struggle. And often, as has been the experience at many Bain holdings, they don't.

Geoffrey Rehnert, the Bain Capital founder who in 1999 formed a Boston PE firm, the Audax Group, spoke about why Bain might have decided not to reinvest in its companies when they ran into difficulties. He drew a parallel with a homeowner who struggles to pay a second mortgage.

"If you think it's worth sticking the money back in because that house is going to be worth more, you stick the money back in," Rehnert said. "If you think you have nothing to gain and the house is way under water, you let the bank have it, and you walk away. Most sophisticated players always have plenty of capital to put back in if it's worth doing," he said. "Anybody who's in this business on a real basis—who's really got a fund and a real firm—they never let a company get taken over by the creditors that's worth saving. That's irresponsible business."

Indeed, it's curious that Bain didn't bother to reinvest in Dade Behring—which five years after emerging from bankruptcy was sold for $6.7 billion. Romney and other members of the firm had earned four times their money from the debt-financed distribution, but Dade later proved to be a solid business, so why didn't they save it?

As Rehnert points out, a second mortgage does not inherently hurt a house, but an irresponsible homeowner can if he takes the money out and neglects the upkeep.

CHAPTER SEVEN

Leaving Little to Chance

Henry Kravis loves the word *entrepreneur.*

He is on the board of Columbia University's Business School's Board of Overseers and recalls speaking to a student audience.

"How many of you want to be entrepreneurs?" he asked.

Hands flew up.

"OK, you explain to me, what does that mean?"

"Well, I'd like to go to work at IBM," one student responded.

Kravis said, "You just failed."

"Well, I'd like to work at Procter & Gamble," said the next student, and Kravis again responded, "You failed."

"A real entrepreneur," he explained, "is somebody who has no safety net underneath them."

The irony of Kravis painting himself as a swashbuckling entrepreneur is that he helped create a deal-making system in which PE firms reap big profits while assuming almost no risk. This may seem impossible. But those actually shouldering the risk in most PE deals aren't the rich PE barons who put them together, but the everyday people whose pension plans invest in PE funds. PE firms are so clever in structuring deals and levying fees as to almost eradicate any real chance of losing money themselves.

Let's take a look, for example, at the 2006 acquisition of the HCA hospital chain by Kohlberg Kravis Roberts & Co. (KKR), Bain Capital, and Merrill Lynch. With a $33 billion price tag, the deal was the biggest LBO up to that time.

The three PE firms and coinvestors together put 12 percent down, $3.78 billion, with the three firms each getting 25 percent of the company's shares. Following only Bain's finances, we find that the deal succeeds even if HCA fails. Had we examined the other buyers, we wouldn't find them to be much different.

Bain's partners didn't actually put down the firm's $1.02 billion share. The money came from two funds Bain Capital raised in 2006 from its investors. But because Bain only committed to funding roughly 6.3 percent of those funds, Bain itself only invested $64 million. The remaining 93.7 percent came from limited partners, such as the Pennsylvania retirement system, the California teachers' pension fund, and endowments. This is typical, and actually Bain contributes a larger percentage to its funds than most PE firms do.

In fact, during the 2004–7 buyout boom, the PE partners who did put up the small amount the firms do contribute to their buyout funds often borrowed even those stakes from banks. So it wasn't always their money that they were putting at risk: It was the banks'. The banks were willing to make these loans because they knew the PE firms would make enough on fees to easily pay back any loans even if their funds lost money.

PE firms historically have their buyout funds put down about 30 percent of the money in their deals and have the companies they buy borrow the money to finance the rest (in HCA they put down only 12 percent). Then they cover their own small portion of their fund's down payment by charging exorbitant management fees to the companies they have just taken over.

For example, Bain and its partners charged HCA a $175 million transaction fee for putting together the deal. Bain got one third, $58 million, which it kept for itself. Bain took the fee even though it only put up 6.3 percent of the buyout fund, according to a fund participant who requested anonymity.

The PE firms also started charging HCA a $15 million annual management fee (also called a monitoring fee). The ten-year management contract calls for the amount to increase by the percentage by which EBITDA rises every year. So even if EBITDA rises only slightly, this would be $20 million annually, or $200 million over the life of the contract (the PE firms will likely be able to charge HCA management fees for the whole ten years, even if they sell it long before then). Bain's share would be $67 million, or one third of the total, all of which it keeps for itself without sharing with its fund investors.

The charging of management fees is common among PE firms, but not among other businesses. In fact, a source said the 2002 Sarbanes-Oxley Act prevented those who sat on a public company board, like PE directors, from collecting management fees from that company. Venture capitalists too don't generally charge fees to the companies they own, and nor does Warren Buffett's Berkshire Hathaway. Sony CEO Howard Stringer told *Fortune* magazine in 2008, "Those of us in regular business tend to think of private equity as having the mentality, 'What's mine is mine, and what's yours is mine.'"

Also, the PE firms will collect a 1 percent fee when they sell HCA. This means that even if they sell it for the same $33 billion price they paid, they will have another $330 million in profit. In Bain's case, it might keep half of the $110 million, and give fund investors the rest.

The result for Bain overall would be that for buying, managing, and selling HCA at the same price they paid for it, it would collect $235 million in fees. Even after sharing some of that with investors, it would retain 76 percent, or $180 million. That is almost three times more than what they risked in the HCA buyout. Because Bain does not disclose its expenses, there is no way of knowing how much, or how little, they actually spent for the services they provided and how much was pure profit. Bain declined comment.

In addition to the fees it collects from HCA, Bain also charges the buyout fund an annual 2 percent management fee for monitoring HCA that will be reduced after five years by the money it returns to investors from HCA, and that could be another $96 million.

For an investment of $64 million, Bain is almost guaranteed to get $276 million *in fees alone*. This is before factoring in the 30 percent commission that it will take on any gains that the fund makes from reselling the business, listing shares on the stock market, or taking dividends. (While most PE firms keep 20 percent of gains and give 80 percent to investors, Bain retains 30 percent.) When buying HCA, the PE firms predicted they would double the money their buyout funds put down in five years by reselling HCA, listing its shares, or taking money out through dividends. If HCA meets these projections, Bain will end up collecting $691 million on the $64 million it put down, almost eleven times its money.

So for all their talk about taking risks, the PE firms take practically none. They put very little money into their deals, and then they arrange to get it all back in the fees they charge to the companies and to their investors. Raymond Held, cofounder of pension adviser Abbott Capital Management, said in 2007, "There has been a misalignment probably more so than ever between the firm and the investor."

What if HCA goes bankrupt in 2013 when much of its $27 billion in debt comes due? Bain would still collect $58 million for the initial transaction fee; the management fees it charged HCA for seven years, $47 million; plus about $125 million in management fees it charged fund investors for the HCA buyout. It would lose out on the lucrative transaction fees for selling the company, but the total, $230 million, would still more than cover the $64 million it risked in its buyout fund to make the investment that they might lose in the bankruptcy.

If HCA goes bankrupt, the outlook would not be so rosy for the other fund investors, who would stand to lose all of their $956 million.

Many PE firms take half of the transaction fee when a deal goes through, unlike Bain, so you might expect that they would be responsible for half of the penalty when they break a deal agreement. But that would, of course, be wrong. In one way or another, the fund investors almost always end up paying. PE firms canceled deals for roughly 130 companies when buyout financing evaporated in mid-2007.

In July 2007, Hexion Specialty Chemicals, which is owned by the PE firm Apollo, beat out Dutch company Basell in a bidding war to buy publicly traded Huntsman Corp., signing a $10.6 billion agreement. The credit crisis hit before the deal closed, so Hexion filed a lawsuit alleging that the transaction with Huntsman was no longer viable. But Huntsman, with its share price falling, sued Apollo partners Leon Black, Josh Harris, and their firm for damages. The Delaware Court of Chancery in 2008 ruled that the PE firm had knowingly and intentionally breached the merger agreement and needed to make its best efforts to close the buyout, according to the *New York Times* DealBook.

This put Black in a bind because Hexion could not afford to buy Huntsman without debt financing. And because of the credit crisis,

Hexion could not borrow much money. (Credit Suisse and Deutsche Bank had already agreed to fund the deal but allegedly backed out.) If the deal didn't go through, Huntsman said it wanted more than $3 billion in damages. Black (with a net worth of $3.5 billion, according to *Forbes*) and Harris ($2 billion) faced personal exposure for much of that amount. So in December 2008, Black and Harris met with Huntsman founding-family members Peter and Jon Huntsman to hammer out a settlement. After several days of haggling, they agreed that Apollo would pay Huntsman $750 million, plus lend Huntsman $250 million in notes paying 7 percent interest that could be converted into stock at $7.857 per share at any time. Black now needed to get the money.

He raised the $250 million for the Huntsman loan largely from the 2005 Apollo buyout fund that was going to put down most of the cash to help Hexion buy Huntsman. It wasn't a bad deal for this Apollo fund's investors.

Apollo, the firm, was expected to provide $200 million that Black hoped would be partially covered by insurance policies. This left $550 million. So, he spread it around.

Black got Credit Suisse and Deutsche Bank, which had agreed to fund the Huntsman buyout before the credit crisis, to loan Hexion $325 million to pay part of the settlement. That was much cheaper for them than being forced to finance the buyout at anything close to its original terms, as the loan would then have traded at a big discount, forcing the banks to mark down its value by much more than $325 million and to write down the loss against earnings. Then Black charged investors in two much earlier Apollo funds, which were not going to put down much, if any, money to buy Huntsman, for the rest, on the grounds that they had bought chemical businesses that became part of Hexion, and Hexion had agreed to buy Huntsman. An Apollo fund raised in 1998 was charged $70 million of the settlement, and a fund raised in 2002 was charged $155 million. Even though the investors in these earlier funds might have received a very small percentage of the transaction fee if the deal had been completed, they were responsible for a significant part of the damages now that it had fallen through.

An investor in the 1998 Apollo fund complained, "In order to get Leon and Josh Harris off the hook for their personal liability, they charged us a fee. We were innocent bystanders. We had nothing to do with this." Black and Harris may pay close to nothing.

PE firms have not only created a system in which they are guaranteed to make money, but also one that assures access to more money, even during a recession. One of the pitfalls of investing in PE firms' buyout funds is that investors may be called upon to deliver money to the fund for up to six years after they agree to make the investment. The way the funds work is, the PE firm lines up commitments from investors for a specific amount that will be invested across perhaps ten buyouts, but the investors don't actually deliver money until the firm identifies an investment and is ready to do the deal. This means that even if an investor's finances or goals change, it is still obligated to deliver the money and make the investment when the PE firms call on them.

Why did their investors, many of which were investing public money, agree to these terms? It was the allure of big returns when they desperately needed them.

David Rubenstein, the Carlyle Group's cofounder, pointed out in December 2007 that funds generating returns in the top 25 percent had done quite well, producing a 20 percent return for five years after fees, compared to NASDAQ's 12 percent and the Standard & Poor's 500 stock market index fund's 9 percent. He did not talk about average fund returns. The pitch was appealing to pension managers who were starting to pay out more benefits to retiring Baby Boomers. In 2006, fifty-one of sixty-four state pensions were underfunded, compared with only twenty-five in 2000.

From 1997 through 2007, the $24 billion Employees Retirement System of Texas had seen a 17 percent fall in active members and an 85 percent rise in retirees. So in 2007, Texas started to build a private-equity program to boost returns. The average Texas plan member who was earning $35,000 contributed 6 percent of that income, $2,100, annually to the trust. The pension's aim was over years to invest 7 percent to 8 percent of its fund in private equity, of which 60 percent would go into LBOs. That means that each active employee would be allocating about $100 annually to firms like Bain Capital and KKR if the trust was only using contributions to fund investments.

It was not too hard for PE firms to get new investors to commit to their funds. In 2000 Kevin Albert was Merrill Lynch's placement agent who helped Kohlberg Kravis Roberts raise capital for a fund that ended up investing in the HCA buyout. Since the 1980s, the Oregon and Washington state pensions contributed the most money to KKR, and together committed $2.5 billion while Albert hit the road to find other investors.

Albert describes a first sales meeting with a potential new investor. Henry Kravis (who in 2008 was worth $6.5 billion) might fly to visit a pension office on his private plane. He would deliver an hour-long presentation, turning on all his charm to talk about strategy and the firm's senior staff, and to make the case for what separated KKR from its competitors. The pension managers usually didn't ask many questions, especially ones who had never invested with PE firms before. "They can be easily dazzled by senior people coming in to visit them initially," Albert said. "You can blow a lot of stuff by them." The goal was convincing the pension manager to visit KKR's opulent New York headquarters where Kravis could close the deal.

Investors this decade didn't fight for better terms, as there was a huge pool of investment money competing for opportunities. With the collapse of the dot-com bubble and in the wake of the big corporate accounting scandals, the stock markets were lackluster, and there were not many other places to invest if you wanted, or needed, the potential of big returns. Pensions were scrambling for high-yielding investments, and they were besieging the PE firms to take their money. They knew that if they didn't agree to the terms that the PE firms set, the PE firms could simply raise the money elsewhere. Indeed, U.S.-based groups were raising record amounts. In 2007, they attracted $228 billion, 29 percent more than in 2006, and almost nine times greater than the 2003 level.

A partner at a PE firm who raised a fund during the buyout boom said, "It was the LPs [investors] who were flooding the buyout business with money, and driving the business. The buyout guys were standing out there with the money raining down on their heads. We just had to turn our umbrellas upside down."

Ten Biggest PE Fund-raisers 1/1/03–4/15/08

PE Firm	Located	Capital Raised (billions)
Carlyle Group	Washington, DC	$52
Goldman Sachs	New York	$49
Texas Pacific Group (TPG)	Fort Worth, TX	$49
Kohlberg Kravis Roberts	New York	$40
CVC Capital Partners	London	$37
Apollo Management	New York	$33
Bain Capital	Boston	$32
Permira	London	$25
Apax Partners	London	$25
Blackstone Group	New York	$23

Source: PEI Media.

By the time some investors began to realize that they might have committed too much money to PE funds, it was too late.

When an investor commits money to a ten-year buyout fund (five years to invest and five to exit), the money is contractually locked in for the life of the fund. The firm will only ask the investor to put up money on an as-needed basis. Nevertheless, the investor needs to have the money available.

Investors can get out of their commitments by selling their stakes in the funds to other investors, but in a down market, they have to discount the price and take a loss to do it. The way it works is that the original investor, who may have invested $50 million so far and have a commitment to invest a further $50 million, may sell both his stake in the assets already acquired and the commitment to pay the added $50 million to the new investor. The new investor, however, in early 2009 was paying as little as 50 cents on the dollar. David de Weese, who leads the team at Paul Capital Partners that buys interests in PE funds from fund investors, told *BusinessWeek* in November 2008 that from 2004 to 2007, PE investors resold about $7 billion of their PE fund commitments annually. He estimated that PE investors now were looking to resell $130 billion in commitments. "At the moment there are lots of motivated sellers," he said, adding that secondary buyers like his firm only have $10 billion to

$12 billion available to spend. He believes the main reason PE fund investors are trying to sell is that they need liquidity during these challenging economic times. But some of the rush is also the fear that certain PE funds may not end up making much money and may even lose part of the original stake—a "negative return."

Guy Hands, who heads the large London PE firm Terra Firma Capital Partners, said at a November 2008 industry conference, "I am afraid returns in private equity for the vast majority of firms are coming down, not only for the deals already done at high prices in 2006 and 2007, but also for future deals." He said returns on the hundreds of billions of dollars invested at the peak of the private-equity boom in 2006 and 2007 would be "negative, very negative."

Besides the difficulty in finding a buyer, there is another hurdle in reselling a PE-fund position: The PE firm has to approve the transfer. And if capital representing more than 2 percent of a buyout fund trades in a year, the fund may lose the tax benefits of being a limited partnership. For the most part, PE investors are stuck.

Pensions have only themselves to blame, according to Weil, Gotshal Manges lawyer Ira Millstein, an expert on corporate governance.

"I suspect many pension funds were not properly assessing risk. My point is it might well be fine to invest in known organizations such as KKR, provided the fund used the needed expertise to do the risk assessment and considered how that risk fit its obligations to its beneficiaries."

He added that pensions may have not fully appreciated that while they could do well by investing in buyout funds, they could also do very poorly.

California Public Employees Retirement System (CalPERS), the country's largest pension fund, in the year ended June 30, 2009, marked down the value of its private-equity investments by 31 percent, worse than the underfunded pension's overall 23 percent loss.

TPG founder David Bonderman, at a November 2008 conference, seemed cavalier about the problems of investors when speaking to his peers. "Private equity all has long-term lockups. So you may like our performance, you may not like our performance, but you're my partner for the next twelve years [he then makes a smooching sound]. At a hedge fund, you're my partner for the next forty-five days until you can give me notice and get the hell out. So you have a situation where a trillion dollars have come out of hedge funds, which is a third of all the capital they had, and virtually no money coming out of private equity."

Bonderman and his peers seemed uninterested in helping their investors, and the truth was they did not have to. Private-equity firms globally in early 2009 had more than $450 billion they could invest by calling down money from their investors. The Boston Consulting Group in December 2008 reported that the average PE fund raised in the prior five years had only invested about 44 percent of its committed capital.

Some investors have started pushing back. CalPERS had roughly 14 percent of its market value allocated to alternative investments as of January 1, 2009, and about half of the alternatives was dedicated to private equity. The looming problem is that that does not include about an equal amount of money in unfunded commitments that had not yet been drawn down. If the uninvested money CalPERS has committed to private equity *is* called down and the rest of the CalPERS market value stays the same, in a few years, the pension fund could have more than 20 percent of its market value tied into alternative investments.

While saying that it continued to honor capital calls, CalPERS urged PE firms to slow down their investment pace. CalPERS committed almost $1 billion to a fund TPG raised in 2008, and a source said one reason TPG, a month after Bonderman's cavalier comment, agreed to reduce pledges made in 2008 by 10 percent was pressure by CalPERS managers. TPG also agreed to cut its fund management fees by 10 percent.

How Much the Largest Pensions Have Invested and Committed to Alternative Assets (Much of Which Is in Private Equity)

Pension	Invested (billions)	% of Assets Invested	Committed and Not Invested (billions)
TIAA-CREF (teachers, medical)	$6.1	1.5%	$5.0
°California Public Employees Retirement System	$23.1	12.2%	$23.9
Florida State Board of Administration	N/A	N/A	$9.0

Pension	Invested (billions)	% of Assets Invested	Committed and Not Invested (billions)
New York State Common Retirement Fund	$10.3	6.7%	$12.6
California State Teachers' Retirement System	$8.2	5.6%	$19.8

Source: Dow Jones' 2009 Directory of Alternative Investment Programs.

°Based on third quarter 2008 CalPERS press release.

London PE firm Permira has been the first to let investors completely out of their future fund commitments—for a price. The firm was managing an €11.1 billion buyout fund in which it had spent about half the money. One of its biggest investors, SVG Capital, was a publicly traded vehicle whose purpose was to sell stock to smaller investors so they could invest in private-equity funds. When SVG's share price collapsed in 2008, it suddenly did not have the money to meet capital calls. Permira—which has to treat all fund investors equally—in November 2008 told investors that any of them by the end of the year could break their remaining fund commitments. But they would have to pay the annual 1.35 percent fund management fee on all the money they originally committed to invest over the life of the ten-year fund even if they chose to end that commitment. Investors representing about 30 percent of the unfunded money accepted the terms and canceled their commitments. By making sure it still collected its management fees, Permira essentially guaranteed that it would continue to make money, regardless of how its funds performed.

Although PE firms like to talk about the big returns they get for investors, the reality is that they have always charged enormous fees that have cut into the profits. Gross annual compound returns for U.S. funds raised based on investment adviser Cambridge Associates' database, as of June 30, 2007, were 21.8 percent, and net returns to investors were 16.1 percent, a 26 percent difference.

Steven Kaplan, a University of Chicago professor of entrepreneurship and finance, says a study he co-wrote shows that PE firms between 1980 and 2001 produced returns—after fees—that were roughly on par with the Standard & Poor's 500 stock market index fund. While PE firms generated earnings from buying and selling companies and dividends above the S&P 500, Kaplan says, their fees wiped out those gains for most investors. Although the study ended with 2001, Kaplan at a November 2007 conference said he hadn't seen anything to make him think much had changed.

Furthermore, returns in the Kaplan study do not factor in the reality that investors need to put aside the money they have committed to private equity, which often goes into low-paying Treasury notes. PE firms invest about half their fund's money in the first three years. If one calculates returns from the point of fund commitment instead of when the money is drawn down, returns are much lower.

But PE firms, when selling new funds often say they will outperform their peers, and potential investors should just look at how the top 25 percent of fund performers did over a given year, because they will be among that group. "The reason everybody focuses on top quartile [25 percent] is because if you are on the high end of the second quartile you might as well buy bonds," said David Thomas, managing partner of PE firm Court Square Capital Partners. "And if you are in the middle or low end of the second quartile, you might as well be in a CD. And anything below that [the top 50 percent of funds] and you're losing money."

Any realistic pension manager admits that identifying which funds will be in the top quartile is hard. A firm delivering good returns through one fund may not do it all the time. Take KKR. In the early and mid-1980s, it did very well. A 1983 vehicle generated 40 percent annual returns; a 1984 fund, 29 percent; and a 1986 fund, 26 percent—all after fees. But, the 1987 partnership bought RJR Nabisco and eked out a 9 percent return, one of the worst-performing funds raised that year. The next vehicle, first invested in 1993, produced a below-average 16.7 percent when compared to its peers, slightly underperforming the stock market. Yet, with its 1997 and 2002 funds, KKR delivered top quartile performances.

Another group that generally doesn't come out as well as the PE firms claim is the public shareholders in the companies that they buy. While PE barons manage to stay technically on the right side of the law, their ability to give public company CEOs outsized compensation to support a sale helps them to arrange buyouts at artificially low prices. The 2003 acquisition of Nortek by Kelso shows how a PE firm was able to muscle out its competitors by locking in the support of the CEO with a nice financial package. Nortek CEO Richard Bready hired investment adviser Daroth Capital to see if he could find a PE partner to help him buy his publicly listed building products company. Daroth CEO and president Peter Rothschild said he wasn't sure that the Nortek board of directors knew Bready was shopping the company. "I wouldn't be surprised if Rick waited until there was something to talk about."

Bready believed Nortek should have been trading at a higher earnings multiple, and he told the PE firms about a plan he had to sell some of its three divisions, like the Ply Gem windows, doors, and vinyl siding business, which would raise the company's value. "There were certain pieces that he thought it would be better to sell, but to do that [while Nortek was publicly traded] was going to be difficult," Rothschild said, because Nortek would have had to report losses on the businesses it sold, which would temporarily deflate earnings and the share price. Write-downs have little impact on a private company because they do not affect long-term earnings.

After a number of months, PE firm Kelso & Co. made an offer to buy the business and take it private. Kelso guaranteed Bready a five-year employment agreement that better than doubled his annual salary to more than $2.5 million. It also agreed to pay him $17 million while not diluting his 16 percent ownership stake. Normally, CEOs of selling companies receive payouts equal to about three times their annual pay. The buyer offers this to compensate the selling CEOs for essentially replacing them. Kelso was giving Bready close to the typical compensation for a soon-to-be-fired CEO, while offering continued employment.

It also awarded Bready options to acquire an additional 4.3 percent of the business. Rothschild, who has worked on several similar deals, said generally a CEO's cash compensation does not rise after an LBO, but usually there is the potential to increase that person's stake in the business for little additional money.

In addition to the Kelso offer, Bready also stood to receive a $73 million retirement package that Nortek had agreed in 1996 to give Bready if the company was sold, even if he stuck with the business.

But while the Kelso offer would make Bready much wealthier, the PE firm suggested paying only $40 a share for Nortek, less than a 10 percent premium over the stock price. From 1980 to 2005, PE firms on average paid a 28 percent premium for public companies, while listed companies in all-cash deals for other public companies offered a much higher 47 percent average premium. Still, Rothschild said the offer was fair because "We talked to more than one party, so we knew where a transaction could happen."

The board considered the $40-a-share, $1.43 billion proposal, and in April 2002, appointed a special committee of directors not involved in the proposed buyout to review this and other potential bids. The directors hired Morgan Stanley to advise them on the process.

Mario Gabelli, whose firm owned 16 percent of the shares, threatened to retain his own independent expert to analyze the Kelso offer. Other private-equity firms soon started showing interest in buying Nortek, but Bready made it clear he would work only with Kelso. "When you are going into a marriage, you want to make sure you are marrying a particular person, not just any girl," Rothschild said.

Because it was working with Bready, Kelso had a decided advantage in the developing auction. It did not need to pay off existing Nortek lenders, because their deal would be considered a recapitalization and not trigger a change-of-control clause. Other PE firms, which were working without Bready, would need to spend $50 million to $100 million, $4.50 to $9 a share, in additional finance expenses, Rothschild said.

Morgan Stanley contacted approximately twenty potential Nortek suitors and asked them to sign confidentiality agreements if they wanted detailed financial information. Half the parties returned signed agreements. Three soon submitted nonbinding offers ranging between $42 and $48 a share, contingent on visiting the company and doing more homework. Morgan Stanley told the board how the auction was developing.

On June 14, 2002, Kelso requested a meeting with Morgan Stanley and met later that day. There, Kelso raised its offer by 13 percent to $45 a share. Kelso also made a threat. It stated that if the special committee was not prepared to recommend an agreement with them at the raised price, it intended to withdraw its proposal, and understood that Bready would also stop attempting to buy the company, with Kelso or anyone else.

Competing bidders who were already suggesting they would offer as much as Kelso, if they had a chance to partner with Bready, would also have saved the financing fees, enabling them to pay $49 to $53 a share. But Bready didn't seem interested.

Within several days, the special committee got Kelso to raise its bid another dollar to $46 a share and inked a $1.6 billion merger agreement without seeing what it could attract from competing suitors. A partner at one of the competing PE firms said, "It [$46] was not a terrible price, but they could have done better in a full sales process."

Rothschild said he originally anticipated that Nortek would sell for more than $40 a share but was surprised it got to $46. Kelso in the end paid a 23 percent premium to the price weeks before the initial takeover announcement, a level close to the normal premium PE firms pay for public companies.

After the buyout, Bready followed through with his plans, quickly selling Nortek's Ply Gem windows, doors, and vinyl siding business, representing roughly one quarter of sales, for $570 million. Then— less than eighteen months after Kelso bought Nortek—Kelso started an auction to resell the rest of Nortek. But, this time it was a more open, competitive process. Fellow PE firm Thomas H. Lee Partners bought Nortek for $1.75 billion, paying a higher 7.4-times-EBITDA multiple than the 6.8-times multiple Kelso had paid. The $1.75 billion for Nortek minus Ply Gem was more than Kelso spent for the whole company.

Bready and his management team received roughly $250 million for their shares, which had better than doubled in value since the Kelso buyout. The options Kelso awarded Bready also proved to be worth more than $50 million, for which Bready likely pocketed at least a $30 million profit.

The Nortek deal may have been particularly lucrative for Bready and his management colleagues, but inside deals similar to this are not rare. In four of this decade's five biggest buyouts, management partnered with a PE buyer before the board had the opportunity to consider other proposals. On one of those occasions, Harrah's, the board stood up to the PE buyers and created a competitive auction. Shareholder activist Carl Icahn, who often buys stakes in companies with languishing stock prices and then agitates for change, in March 2007 explained the difference between him and private-equity firms. He said he tried to get businesses to make moves that increased their share price, while PE firms instead bought at low premiums and then made improvements that only benefited themselves.

Private-equity firms pay little compared to public acquirers for listed companies, according to a study by University of Pittsburgh professors Leonce Bargeron, Frederik Schlingemann, and Chad Zutter, and Ohio State's René Stulz. Looking at the 1,667 completed cash acquisitions between 1980 and 2005 for U.S.-listed companies (of which PE-led buyouts represented 14 percent), publicly traded acquirers paid premiums that were on average 63 percent higher than private-equity firms paid.

Some reasons for the difference in premiums have little to do with conflict of interest. PE firms targeted companies that grew at slower rates than those bought by public companies. Listed companies, too, were typically buying businesses similar to themselves and so could cut costs by combining operations, enabling them to pay more. There was also evidence of another kind of conflict of interest, however. CEOs of public companies often get compensated based on the size of their businesses and therefore have an incentive to make acquisitions no matter the price. But these may not be the only explanations. The study says, "It would not be surprising if private bidders could convince managers of public firms to be acquired in exchange for keeping their jobs and receiving a share of the payout when the acquired firm goes [back] public."

PE firms basically guarantee themselves profits by skimming from the companies they buy, their own investors, and the selling shareholders.

No wonder seventeen of the four hundred richest Americans are PE barons. Some of the barons spend their money buying sports franchises like Bain Capital Managing Director Stephen Pagliuca, who in 2002 became a principal owner of the Boston Celtics basketball team.

Leon Black prefers the arts, having given away, or committed, more than $150 million to educational, health-care, and cultural institutions. He has been a trustee of the Museum of Modern Art, Mt. Sinai Hospital, the Lincoln Center for the Performing Arts, Prep for Prep, the Jewish Museum, Cardozo School of Law, the Asia Society, Spence School, and the Vail Valley Foundation.

Kravis is a past chairman of New York City's public television station and is on the board of the Metropolitan Museum of Art, and like Black, he is a Mt. Sinai Hospital trustee. Black told the *New York Times* in 2008, "Art and literature are what differentiate us from barbarians."

CHAPTER EIGHT

A Different Approach

Hal Krisbergh thought he knew what to expect in 1990 when he entered the Four Seasons Manhattan restaurant. General Instrument, the company for which he was a division head, had just been taken over in a heavily leveraged buyout by one of the private-equity industry's biggest players, Forstmann Little & Co. This was his first meeting with the new bosses.

As Krisbergh traveled to the Four Seasons, which was ninety miles from Horsham, Pennsylvania, where his cable television set-top box division was based, he ruminated on the upcoming meeting. Although the Four Seasons wasn't his usual territory, he figured it would be a typical new management get-together: questions about operations, projects in development, suggestions he had for the future.

At the table sat Forstmann Little's chief, Ted Forstmann—a fifty-year-old former hockey player with a chiseled build and a reputation for being an obnoxious know-it-all, and his athletic-looking partner Steven Klinsky, who was significantly taller and younger. There too would be a few other General Instrument executives who'd made it through the buyout (the CEO was already gone).

"I'll never forget it," said Krisbergh, known for being a creative manager who would always be coming up with new product ideas. "Forstmann turned to the group and said, 'OK, why don't all of us write down on a piece of paper what we think the price will be when we do the IPO.' This is the first meeting of us sitting together, introducing ourselves. We had just got acquired, and his question is 'What will be the price of the IPO?'"

Ted Forstmann, speaking through his spokesperson, said if he did say something like that, though he doesn't recall, he would have said it jokingly.

Krisbergh said Forstmann then laid out his plans for the business.

He explained that he would sell off several of GI's divisions and use the proceeds to pay down the money the company had just borrowed. And also, Forstmann said, the executives should decide how much they wanted to reinvest in General Instrument.

The handful of GI executives at that table, Krisbergh included, had just made millions from selling shares in the LBO. But still, it seemed odd that the new owners assumed they were going to turn around and put much of that money right back in the company—especially when the PE firm took little risk itself. "It was like we were all going to do it and that was just part of the deal," Krisbergh said. "I don't know if I had said no what would have happened. It almost wasn't an option."

Although Krisbergh was surprised, PE firms often make the request. It's an attempt to keep the goals of a company's top executives aligned with their own: quick profits rather than long-term growth.

"I remember walking out of that meeting thinking, *Well, they don't even give a damn about what our business is,*" Krisbergh recalls.... "Here these guys are coming in saying, 'How do we rip this thing apart and just strip it down, dress it up, and sell it?' That was clearly their intent from day one. Absolutely nothing else."

Fortune magazine in 1993 called the buyout of General Instrument one of the biggest LBO moneymakers ever. Peeling back the folds of the story reveals the usual PE scenario of Forstmann Little making a fortune by shedding assets and cutting costs. Not investing much in research and development imperiled at least one major technological breakthrough, digitizing TV signals so cable companies could fit many more channels in their boxes. But what happened after 1993 is what separates General Instrument from most other successful LBOs.

After taking the company public, Forstmann Little had trouble selling its remaining shares. Like many PE firms today, they were stuck owning a business they had hoped to sell. But rather than walk away, Forstmann Little took a more active interest in the business. It changed tactics and turned General Instrument into a high-tech champ.

The story offers a hopeful example of what can happen if a PE firm chooses, or is forced by circumstance, to abandon its short-term strategy and to stick with an investment for a longer period of time. As we have seen, when PE firms cut costs too deeply and starve a company of human and financial capital, the crippled company is often too weak to survive. But the General Instrument example shows that if the initial phases of PE-driven cost cutting are followed by judicious investment, the result can be a lean and powerful company. We can only hope that PE firms will take note of the General Instrument experience and try to save more companies rather than walking away when the weakening economy makes selling them impossible.

Back in 1967, New York attorney Moses Shapiro built the foundation of General Instrument by buying companies that made cable TV boxes and electronic betting systems. GI eventually became the dominant player in these markets. How this flourishing entrepreneurial venture ended up in the hands of Forstmann Little twenty-three years later is a story filled with missteps and double-dealing.

The trouble started when it came time for Shapiro to name a successor. He passed over his son Robert Shapiro, who was in his thirties and running the General Instrument legal department. Anxious to chart his own path, Robert left to run a division for pharmaceutical company G. D. Searle and eventually became CEO of Monsanto.

He also did not groom the openly ambitious head of the cable-box business, John Malone. This was the same John Malone who went on to become owner of Liberty Media and possibly the biggest name in the cable industry.

Moses Shapiro felt a bond with the unpolished and tough Frank Hickey, who was moving up through the sales department. For a time, Hickey looked like a good fit. He became president in 1975, and under his management, GI expanded its gaming business—supplying 80 percent of the North American horse racetrack tote boards and a good-size chunk of the state lottery wagering systems.

The company's semiconductor business also boomed in the late 1970s when video-game makers Atari and Intellivision emerged and needed their chips. And he expanded the cable division. In 1986, GI acquired M/A-Com's cable television equipment operations, which focused on making scrambling decoders that allowed people to watch HBO and other pay television stations.

At the same time, GI was building smaller businesses in areas as diverse as defense electronics, miniature lighting, and remittance credit-card processing. Hickey's management strategy was largely to let the division heads run their own operations. For some divisions, this hands-off approach worked well, but others began to drift and lose money.

In the mid-1980s, Hickey, according to another senior executive, became increasingly reclusive, spending most days at his Arizona ranch. GI, as a result, got sloppy. The company stopped tracking inventory closely and waited too long to collect receivables. There were other, strategic problems, as well. The gaming division's VP of sales left around 1984 to a competitor, taking clients with him, precipitating a decline in that business. A plan to offer satellite dishes to homeowners in rural areas proved to be a bust.

In this rudderless state, GI was a perfect target for a leveraged buyout. Several of GI's divisions—cable set-top boxes, cable wires, TV satellite equipment, and semiconductor chips—still held number-one market-share positions and were highly profitable. GI in 1990 even had $650 million of cash on its balance sheet.

Hickey didn't know what to do with the company. It had the top market positions in three of the four industries mentioned above and had run out of companies to buy, but it had a lot of cash, so he thought about using it as a down payment in a management buyout. This is where Forstmann Little entered the picture.

Hickey started working with investment bank Lazard Frères & Co. to see if he could do a management buyout. To his surprise, Lazard suggested that instead of buying the business, he should sell it to Forstmann Little, Krisbergh said. Hickey soon felt Lazard was pushing the issue. Finally, frustrated, he asked them for whom they were working—Forstmann or him.

Lazard told him it was working for Forstmann, Krisbergh said. To be working like this for both sides in a potential deal was at best a conflict of interest. Considering, however, that banks like Lazard can earn 20 percent of their annual revenue from PE firms, it isn't surprising that Lazard helped Forstmann Little. In any event, what this meant for Hickey was that he'd lost precious time in trying to put together an LBO, while Forstmann had been laying the groundwork for one.

Forstmann also had another big advantage. Ted Forstmann was one of the few PE Barons who had raised money from investors to lend to the companies he bought. He was both buyer and banker. So in 1990, when, like today, the credit markets froze because of a real-estate crash and recession, Forstmann Little had the money to make a down payment and to issue GI a loan to finance much of the buyout. The offer it made was about 20 percent above GI's stock price. It would have been hard for others to get banks to finance a similar deal. Soon the buyer and seller negotiated.

The GI Board was not enthusiastic about selling to Forstmann but viewed it as a way out of the absentee CEO problem. They also knew it might be their only chance to sell at a premium. So in July 1990, the PE firm reached a deal with the board to buy the business for $1.5 billion. Hickey never got the financing in place to make a rival bid.

A source close to Forstmann Little tells a somewhat different version of events. He says the firm initiated the buyout by calling Lazard's Felix Rohatyn to express its interest in acquiring General Instrument and that Rohatyn arranged an introduction with the company's management. Rohatyn eventually became a GI board member. He did not respond to an e-mailed request for comment.

About a month after the buyout closed, Forstmann hosted his annual event at the Hotel Jerome in Aspen, Colorado, where top executives of his various companies mingle with political heavyweights. (Forstmann himself was a major contributor to the Republican Party and George H. W. Bush's presidential campaign).

The big talk at this particular 1990 gathering was that Forstmann wanted to bring in Donald Rumsfeld as the new CEO of General Instrument. Rumsfeld was already on Forstmann Little's advisory board and was known mainly for his political credentials as a four-term congressman, former president Ford's chief of staff, and later defense secretary.

The buzz at the Hotel Jerome was that Rumsfeld wasn't going to accept. Indeed, it was a strange match. Rumsfeld had no cable or telecom experience but rather had made his mark in the business world with a seven-year stint as head of pharmaceutical company G. D. Searle (the maker of Metamucil), the same company at which the GI founder's son had worked. Probably more to his credit, he was a big name politician who could help market an initial public offering and talk with Washington telecom regulators. Krisbergh, of the cable division, recalls everyone's surprise when, a month after the Aspen gathering, Rumsfeld took the position. "The word was they just made him an offer he couldn't refuse," Krisbergh said.

General Instrument with Rumsfeld at the helm quickly shed assets. During this time, GI sold its defense electronics business and the race-track and lottery systems division. What remained were cable boxes, satellite TV equipment, cable wires, and semiconductors. All told, it shed operations that generated about 30 percent of its $1.4 billion in annual sales.

Rumsfeld also added more disciplined management.

"There was all sorts of dysfunction among the managers," the source close to Forstmann Little said. "I mean, the satellite business was in conflict with the cable business because some people in the cable industry thought satellite was their competitor and used to call it the death star. So there was no unity on the team. And Don Rumsfeld was considered a disciplined professional executive who could bring order" to central senior management of a diversified company. For example, he asked the people who were used to giving the most optimistic numbers in their budgets and projections, to provide numbers that had as much potential downside as upside. "He executed a plan. He didn't come up with a strategy for the investment, but he helped oversee the execution."

Even though Forstmann and Rumsfeld were successfully transforming a business in need of help, they were also making some careless cuts.

As soon as Rumsfeld was put in charge, he began firing workers. It may be a good idea to get rid of unnecessary employees, but PE firms like Forstmann Little often go too far. The new CEO moved the headquarters to Chicago from New York, though GI had no operations near there, so he could be close to home and more easily clean out the staff. He fired two thirds of the people working at the New York office. GI, overall, cut $65 million in overhead. Marching orders were given to division heads to reduce staff as well. Through his spokesman, Rumsfeld declined to be interviewed.

Krisbergh remained as head of the cable-box division and focused on slimming down his Pennsylvania-based operations, which employed 1,500 people. One particular layoff speaks volumes about the PE-ownership style. Krisbergh fired Dr. David Huber, a reclusive PhD working on fiber optics. In Krisbergh's mind, fiber optics had nothing to do with cable television, so Dr. Huber was expendable. Dr. Huber was developing ways to run more data through fiber-optic cables for the telecom industry. After being fired, Huber stopped by Krisbergh's office.

"He says, 'Look, I'm thinking of starting a company,'" Krisbergh remembers. "I said, 'Well, that's great.' And he says, 'But I'd like to use the patents that I've gotten here while I was at GI.' And I said, 'That's fine with me. I'll tell you what. We'll make a deal here. I'll help you out. I'll get behind you. I'll go on the board; give GI ten percent of the company.'"

Huber agreed. He founded Ciena Corporation in November 1992. Those former GI patents became the underpinning for a business that sold wavelength-division multiplexing, a technique of sending signals of several different wavelengths of light into a fiber simultaneously, to Sprint. Ciena launched a February 1997 IPO and, after the stock ran up, ended its first trading day with a $3.4 billion market capitalization. One could argue that GI essentially gave away patents that proved, with resources put behind them, in 1997 to be worth more than GI. Krisbergh said GI for its 10 percent stake in Ciena got a $250 million check.

"I'm thinking to myself, $250 million for air [not doing anything] was unbelievable to me. Yet you could spin it by the fact that it turned into this huge successful business."

A GI executive who worked under Forstmann Little and requested anonymity was highly critical of the giveaway. He said if he was in charge he would at least have hired an outside consultant like Bell Labs to determine the patents' real worth. The former GI executive also knows Dr. Huber and believes he understood full well when taking those patents from GI that they were very valuable. Dr. Huber did not return calls.

Ted Forstmann, through a spokesperson, said, "If that is what Don did, Don believed it was the right thing to do at the time."

The source close to Forstmann Little said the company did not underspend in research and development, pointing out that GI increased R & D spending from where it was before the buyout and maintained funding for the digital compression of video signals, although the PE firm was not counting on it to generate profits.

During the early 1990s recession, cable television companies had a harder time borrowing money to expand and were buying fewer set-top boxes. As a result, Forstmann Little was having some difficulty improving GI's sales. GI in 1992 posted a $53 million loss. However, Forstmann had turned the business into a much more focused cable and satellite TV company, making GI an easier company for stock analysts to understand.

Forstmann in early 1992, less than two years after taking the company private, had GI file an initial public offering to sell shares on the NYSE. Rumsfeld believed that, with the business losing money, it was not the right time to be pushing a public sale. But Forstmann was the boss.

"There was not a good feeling between Rumsfeld and Forstmann about the timing and what needed to be done to sell the IPO," Krisbergh said. "I think it was very clear Forstmann felt that Rumsfeld just wasn't playing the game that he wanted to play to maximize his investment."

Still, they crafted a story about earnings growth.

"Here's what the future looks like, here's all the stuff that's going on. I mean, it was the standard story," Krisbergh said. "There was nothing inaccurate about it. It was how enthusiastic Rumsfeld was in presenting it that was the key issue."

Despite Rumsfeld's reluctance, they persuaded analysts to recommend the stock.

GI's IPO in June 1992 was a qualified success, with the shares in the first day of trading closing at $15, 14 percent below the expectations GI had a few months earlier. Still Forstmann Little's cost basis when buying the business was $5.23 a share. The PE firm sold shares that diluted its holdings to a 53 percent stake in the company, and GI used the $307 million in proceeds to pay down debt.

Meanwhile, three to five scientists in the San Diego–based satellite division were successfully pioneering digital compression, using a method that today is the standard for high definition television (HDTV).

The scientists were unique in pursuing this path; other companies, like Zenith, were working on compressing *analog* transmission of HDTV. Compressing the actual digital transmission was much easier and efficient. The problem with this amazing breakthrough was that there was little commercial value in developing HDTV when there were no compatible television sets that could receive digital signals. Krisbergh looked into adapting the digital technology to compress the number of analog channels it could get into its cable boxes.

He then made the highly questionable decision of telling John Malone, who by this time was running the cable company TCI and was one of GI's biggest set-top customers, that it was developing a way to make digital cable boxes that could access five hundred analog channels as opposed to the boxes common at the time, which could get only eighty to ninety channels. Malone was so excited that in December 1992, he announced publicly that within two years Tele-Communications Inc. would be selling GI's digital boxes in one million American homes, and signed a letter of intent to buy them.

GI's stock rose on the news, and within months GI held a secondary offering of stock that sold for $30.50 a share (double the IPO price from less than a year earlier).

Soon, GI released more news about future growth.

General Instrument announced in April 1993 that it had joined with two other companies, Microsoft and Intel, to develop a cable box that combined the functions of a cable converter and a computer, allowing for interactive television. The company held another stock offering in September of that year (the third share offering in fifteen months), selling stock for $51 a share.

Through the three offerings, Forstmann Little collected $850 million while still holding a 30 percent stake in the business worth an additional $1 billion. Not bad for $182 million down and a three-year investment.

This is where things started to go awry. GI had not actually finished designing the digital set-top boxes for which Malone was waiting. Krisbergh said, "I'm thinking this is two years away. I mean this technology is not going to happen that quickly...it wasn't just a matter of putting it in a box. There was a lot of work to be done to make chips and special chips and redesign the chips...it was a major project."

Yet the whole company's future was at stake. What if some competitor—now alerted to the technological advance—made a digital box first? Sure enough, Scientific-Atlantic, AT&T, Sony, and Thomson's RCA all started working on digital cable boxes too. There was a risk that if GI, which controlled 60 percent of the cable-box market, fell behind technologically, it would lose its leading market position. GI increased R & D spending in 1993 by 28 percent to $74 million, which represented 5.3 percent of sales. That may sound like a lot, but to put the number in context, the smaller competitor Scientific-Atlantic increased R & D spending by 15 percent to $60 million, 8.2 percent of its sales.

But Krisbergh did not use all the R & D money allotted to his division for digital boxes. Ed Breen, the cable division's senior VP of sales at the time, said, "I think Hal thought that digital was going to happen, but Hal was never convinced that digital was going to happen in the time frame, for instance, that TCI wanted. So Hal continued to spend a lot of R & D money on the analog set-top boxes." The Forstmann Little source defended the decision, saying that analog set-top sales doubled during the early 1990s.

Krisbergh, the tinkerer, was also dabbling in projects that actually put General Instrument in direct head-to-head competition with its most important customer, Malone's TCI. He began partnering with cable companies Time Warner and Comcast to develop channels that could carry music—even as TCI's engineers were working on the same thing. Obviously TCI was less than pleased that its vendor had teamed with its rivals. So TCI offered to partner with GI on its music project. Krisbergh refused.

Malone was upset not only over the music channels but also because it was becoming clear that General Instrument wasn't going to make its delivery date for the digital boxes.

J. C. Sparkman, TCI's chief operations officer, told Rumsfeld he would pull all of his business if Krisbergh wasn't replaced. But Rumsfeld is a strangely stubborn man—to the point of appearing *incapable* of changing direction. Here he was faced with losing GI's most important account, and he failed to act. Instead, he took Sparkman to a Washington, D.C., dinner and attempted to impress him with introductions to people like General Electric's Jack Welch, as well as some politicians. Sparkman recalls that when they discussed Krisbergh, Rumsfeld did not take a stand. By this time, Rumsfeld had become quite chummy with Krisbergh, exchanging their thoughts on politics. Krisbergh said Rumsfeld let him run his division with little interference as long as he was hitting his financial targets. Soon TCI began to deal only with Sales Director Ed Breen instead of Breen's boss, Krisbergh.

Ted Forstmann, having already made a fantastic return on GI, had some unexpected decisions to make. He may have wanted to exit the business, but his firm could not easily sell its remaining stake. Motorola around this time is said to have expressed interest in buying GI, but it didn't want to make an offer until GI finished developing digital cable boxes. In addition, GI's share price was no longer soaring, so it was not easy for Forstmann Little to sell its stock on the NYSE without causing the price to fall. So, in a sense, Forstmann was stuck. He would have to keep his GI stake and figure out how to manage it. More PE firms may soon be facing similar questions: What is the best way to manage a business from which you have already reaped profits but which you are now unable to sell?

Forstmann decided to change management. He was already irritated with Rumsfeld, first for spending too much time analyzing the Gulf War on CNN instead of running the business, and then for not enthusiastically premarketing the 1992 IPO to analysts, whom he called ankle biters. In 1993, according to one source, he ousted Rumsfeld. Forstmann, through a spokesperson, said to me, "Don was hired to clean up the company, and he did, and when that was done, I felt it was time for him to move on, and he did."

The whole thing went over without a murmur from the press. Rumsfeld told the media his resignation had been in the works for months and he had asked GI's board to start looking for a replacement. The explanation was not challenged.

Rumsfeld left a richer man. His salary included 913,690 GI shares at $3.02 per share. He had sold 26 percent of the stock for $29.28, earning $6 million, while holding another $28 million in shares.

Forstmann replaced Rumsfeld with a top telecom/cable executive: Daniel Akerson, former president of MCI, who had just been passed over for its top position. The high-level GI source said Akerson asked Rumsfeld, who was still on the board, how far behind the company was on filling the TCI order, and Rumsfeld told him not to worry about Malone. A frustrated Akerson soon asked Rumsfeld to leave GI's board. Krisbergh he fired outright (Krisbergh said he resigned after a falling out). There is no way to overemphasize in what jeopardy Rumsfeld and Krisbergh had placed General Instrument by their handling of the TCI account.

As for the publicly announced plan to develop interactive television with Microsoft, which had lifted the company's stock, there was little business-plan writing and a lot of dreaming, Krisbergh said.

The company was at a tipping point.

Breen said much of the delay in filling Malone's digital cable-box order was the semiconductor chips. "It was really getting it integrated down into a small box, if I could summarize it for you. Instead of having three PC boards with all kinds of components on it, we needed to get it down to one chip."

There was reason to be nervous.

At the annual industry cable show, John Malone marched right past the General Instrument booth to rival Scientific-Atlanta's table and sat down for two hours. Sparkman, the TCI COO, said Malone could have gotten out of the GI contract and that even after Krisbergh left, he was seriously considering making a switch.

Under Akerson, GI increased research-and-development spending so it could finish redesigning the boxes. In 1994 GI boosted R & D by 50 percent to $111 million—though this still represented less than 6 percent of total sales.

But the troubles continued. A joint venture between Bell Atlantic, Nynex, and Pacific Telesis in 1995 chose Thomson Consumer Electronics over General Instrument when preordering $1 billion in digital cable boxes because, though neither company was ready to deliver the boxes, it did not believe in GI's technology. In July 1995, Akerson resigned and soon became CEO of cellular phone company Nextel Communications. Forstmann then tapped president and Chief Operating Officer Rick Friedland, who helped engineer the 1992 public offering, to run the business. Breen points out that what GI needed at the time more than anything was someone who had good relationships with the big cable players—not a financial wizard.

By 1996, GI's stock price was floundering. The company had announced yet again a delay in shipping its digital set-top boxes to TCI. The satellite division lost customers, as DirecTV, which was not using GI equipment, overtook GI customer Primestar as the biggest satellite TV business. GI's share price during Friedland's first few months dropped 35 percent. To raise overall value, he split the business into three independent stocks—General Instrument (the cable and satellite business), CommScope (cable wires), and General Semiconductor. GI's peers were trading at much higher multiples to earnings, and Friedland believed separating the cable piece would raise GI's overall valuation. Apparently Forstmann was less than pleased with the results, because two senior executives said he fired Friedland two months after he split the company in three (the company said he resigned). He then made Ed Breen CEO of GI, its fourth in seven years.

Forstmann Little did what it needed to do to turn the company around. During this time, it increased R & D spending from 5.4 percent of sales in 1994 to 9 percent in 1995, 11 percent in 1996, and 12 percent the next year. Other changes started happening as well. Forstmann Little's lead partner on the investment, Steven Klinsky, started talking to new CEO Breen every other day. To better focus the business, GI also moved its headquarters from Chicago (where Rumsfeld had relocated it though, that was nowhere near the operations) to Horsham, Pennsylvania, where the cable TV division was located.

Work on the digital boxes continued through 1997. Breen said, "I think Malone was very frustrated it was taking this long, but he's also a very smart technology guy. He was getting weekly updates on where this was, and he could see we were going to get there." TCI stuck with GI. COO Sparkman said, "We were in it with GI and had made a monetary commitment to the project, and there was no one else on time with delivery either."

Late that year, General Instrument finally came out with the first digital set-top box, although it was so expensive to make ($500) that it was hard to sell. "So everyone's scratching their heads saying, 'Well, this is great technology. We can't put five hundred dollars in every home.' So that was the issue, where can you get this thing priced?" Breen said.

He came up with a creative way to entice cable providers to buy the digital boxes. GI would offer them warrants to buy shares in GI potentially worth, in all, 12 percent of the company, based proportionally on the number of boxes they ordered. John Malone liked the proposal because the more boxes ordered, the more power GI would have with its suppliers to lower prices.

With Malone convinced, he and Breen needed to sell Forstmann, because giving up that much stock would mean diluting his firm's roughly 20 percent stake in the business. Breen and Malone met with Forstmann in his New York office to discuss the plan. "A guy like Ted needed a little bit of convincing at first, because everyone was getting diluted," Breen said. "But I have to tell you, Ted's light bulb went off and he was like 'I like this.'" Forstmann adapted to the situation.

Soon GI locked up orders with eight of the ten biggest cable providers for 15 million digital boxes, and with those orders in hand, got breaks from its suppliers so it could sell the boxes for less. GI was back on track. Forstmann Little sold the last of its shares around 1999.

PE firms in the twenty-first century have mostly made fortunes by hobbling their companies. Their businesses have reduced customer service, raised prices for their goods, starved their companies of capital, and then used increased short-term earnings to borrow money to pay themselves rapacious dividends. Now, though, with fewer buyers acquiring companies and a dormant IPO market, it will be hard for them to exit their businesses before they start imploding. What they have going for them is time, because many of their businesses took out loans with few performance requirements and will remain solvent until principal is due, which often is between 2012 and 2015. What they'll need is the awareness to see that averting the Next Great Credit Crisis will require them to run companies in a different manner.

PART THREE

WHAT NOW?

CHAPTER NINE

The Next Great European Credit Crisis

"How many industries can you think of right now where America is the dominant player in the world?" asked Carlyle Group cofounder David Rubenstein of a friendly audience at the conservative American Enterprise Institute think tank in November 2007.

Rubenstein, tall and wearing a dark blue pinstripe suit, was explaining why he believed the government should encourage private equity. "There are very few industries now where without question we are the dominant player in the world. Maybe entertainment in some ways. Maybe some Silicon Valley software-type companies. One of those where we do dominate the global economy in is private equity."

And nowhere has the influence of American private-equity firms been more notable than in England. In the 1980s and early 1990s, several English firms were doing LBOs and other private-equity deals, but they were relatively small. Then, in the late 1990s, the Americans invaded with their much larger deals and aggressive tactics, and the rules of the game changed. By 2008, private equity was more pervasive in England than America, and had expanded to the rest of Europe. Now the companies they bought are facing the same huge debt burdens and likely defaults as those looming in the United States.

As Peter Taylor, managing partner at London's Duke Street Capital, describes the situation in Britain, "I started in private equity in the 1980s at a time when, actually, the term *private equity* didn't exist. We weren't really doing venture capital, but that's what we called it. And, of course, nobody had any money. We had to club together to do all our deals." In 1988, his previous firm, Bridgepoint, partnered with three other firms to buy Focus, a do-it-yourself retailer and gardening center, for £10 million. At the same time, U.S. firm Kohlberg Kravis Roberts (KKR) was buying RJR Nabisco for $25 billion. The occasional

£100 million deals were getting done in the United Kingdom, but it was nothing like what was happening in America.

During the 1990s, British PE firms started to buy companies on their own. Then in 1998, the British government, led by Chancellor of the Exchequer Gordon Brown (later to become prime minister), cut the capital gains tax from 40 percent to 10 percent. This meant that people buying and selling businesses could keep much more of their money. At the same time, taxes were imposed on those collecting options from public companies. Brown wanted to promote entrepreneurship and in the process opened the floodgates. "Suddenly, the step change happened in the very late 90s," Taylor said.

These changes in British tax laws occurred just as the rich valuations of the dot-com boom had put many public companies in the United States beyond the reach of PE firms. The U.S. PE firms, that had more than $90 billion in unspent capital, sensed opportunity and quickly allocated 25 percent of that, $22.5 billion, to buying European businesses. Heavyweights Apollo Management; Clayton, Dubilier & Rice; Hicks, Muse, Tate & Furst; KKR; and TPG all opened London offices from 1997 to 1999. So did Rubenstein, who in 1998 hired former British prime minister John Major to help him find local businesses to buy.

The private-equity model that the Americans brought to England is far different from the British version. In England, it is often the management teams who execute their own buyouts of growing companies and then run their businesses for several years before thinking of reselling. In contrast, U.S. PE firms sometimes get rid of existing management almost immediately. They often bring in their own teams, who have little emotional attachment to the acquired companies, to slash budgets and fire workers.

Unlike the British, the Americans liked to buy divisions from sprawling British businesses, as well as public companies. During the 1980s, U.S. PE firms had made fortunes acquiring divisions from U.S. conglomerates, but by the late 1990s, most of the domestic conglomerates had broken up. Along with the American PE firms also came the U.S. and international banks that introduced junk bonds. This gave local companies the ability to borrow more money to finance buyouts. And

American pensions that invested in buyout funds also got in the spirit and soon started funding both U.S. firms expanding into England and UK PE firms, which allowed them to raise larger pools of money.

United States PE firms were much more aggressive when buying companies than their British counterparts. In 1999 TPG bought the Punch taverns chain from Hugh Osmond and simultaneously considered bidding for Allied Domecq's larger pubs business, although Allied was already in exclusive talks to sell its bars to publicly traded brewer Whitbread.

On May 25, 1999, Allied signed a deal to sell its pubs to Whitbread for £2.36 billion ($3.8 billion) in stock and said it would not share confidential information about the business with anyone else until August 2, by which time the deal was expected to close. The purpose was to effectively stop rival offers.

That did not deter TPG. Only weeks later, the PE firm had Punch make a £2.7 billion counterbid. TPG's Punch also told Allied that if it did not respond, it would appeal directly to Allied shareholders ahead of the upcoming annual meeting where the Whitbread proposal would be voted on. The press closely covered the unfolding drama and portrayed it as Punch CEO Osmond versus Whitbread and Allied Domecq, but it was really TPG who was behind Osmond.

Allied responded by saying it recognized that Punch had made a serious offer but the potential for growth that shareholders would receive by selling to Whitbread made its lower stock bid a superior proposal.

TPG then went hostile. Punch ran ads aimed at Allied shareholders saying, "How many pints do you have to drink to think the Whitbread offer is more attractive?" It did not wait for Whitbread to counter. The firm instead kept the pressure on, increasing its rejected bid three days before the July 2, 1999, shareholder vote by 6 percent to £2.85 billion. Allied Domecq postponed the vote.

Whitbread then increased its offer by more than 25 percent to nearly £3 billion and reached what seemed to be a revised final deal with Allied for the pubs.

But the UK Department of Trade and Industry one week later said the Whitbread deal raised antitrust concerns because Whitbread brewed the country's top-selling premium lager, Stella Artois, and would be making money from both supplying beer to the Allied chain and then reselling the beer. It referred the matter to the Competition Commission for further review. When Whitbread then dropped its increasingly expensive offer, TPG's Punch pounced. The firm, now allied with Bass PLC, lowered its rejected proposal to £2.75 billion. Allied signed a sales agreement within days. After that, Taylor said, the British corporate establishment started taking the PE industry much more seriously.

In little time, American-style private equity took off in England. PE firms backed companies that employed about 20 percent of the private sector and by 2008 had resold many of those businesses. In 2008 they owned 349 UK companies that employed 1.1 million British workers, or 6 percent of the private sector. Using the United Kingdom as a beachhead, U.S. and British PE firms raised more money from investors and expanded throughout Europe. Carlyle's Rubenstein, who had hired former British prime minister Major to help find UK businesses, soon named him chairman of its European operations.

The expansion into Continental Europe, for the most part, succeeded. During the 2004–7 buyout boom, European companies borrowed $740 billion to finance buyouts, more than the $701 billion that American businesses borrowed. The American gross domestic product and Western Europe's are about the same, so the level of borrowing shows that PE became as prevalent overseas as stateside. As a result, the credit crisis that is going to hit the United States around 2012 will also hit Europe. It may even happen there sooner, because more of the loans supporting European buyouts include covenants that force businesses to keep debt ratios within certain levels to remain in compliance. If the companies can't meet those ratios, they will be in default even before the due date of the loan.

Prospects for PE-owned companies in Europe could, in fact, be even worse than for American businesses. PE firms paid more to buy them, and it appears that they may have done even less homework on their financials. Buyers paid an average multiple of EBITDA for a British company from 2001 to 2007 that was 11 percent higher than for an American business. Duke Street's Taylor said that because it was possible to borrow more in England, PE firms could commonly outbid competitors in auctions.

Jon Moulton from London PE firm Alchemy Partners also says that buyers were not very careful in checking to see if private companies were reporting accurate numbers. He says there was even less financial information provided to buyers of European companies than American businesses, and that meant that buyers in a rush to do deals were often paying purchase multiples based on very inflated earnings.

Jack Dromey, deputy general secretary of the British Transport and General Workers' Union, said in December 2008, "We could be staring at a fresh financial meltdown. Private equity used cheap credit in the good times to swoop on vulnerable companies, but now the banks are not lending, [and] those debts are looking very hard to sustain.... [This] has the potential to be another subprime scandal that shakes our banking system."

The societal risks in England are huge, bigger than anywhere in Europe. With private-equity firms buying UK companies over the last twelve years that employ 20 percent of the private sector, many people will be directly and indirectly affected.

Lenders will be less likely to force PE-owned British companies into bankruptcy than American companies because they have a smaller chance at recovering their loans through bankruptcy. (British companies forced into receivership must liquidate, while American businesses often operate in bankruptcy and improve enough over time to pay much of their loans). British companies, therefore, tend to make deals with their lenders when they can't pay their loans. This can involve selling off pieces of themselves to pay debt. As a result, Moulton predicts that some PE-owned British companies in five to ten years will be a lot smaller, some will be a lot less healthy, and a few will manage to do quite well.

Besides weakening companies, PE firms in England are also accused of starving their company pensions. The GMB, Britain's General Union (meaning anyone can join), in June 2007 named fifty-eight businesses with private-equity links that had insolvent pension funds and were in the government's Financial Assistance Scheme. That represented roughly 10 percent of the failed Financial Services Authority pensions. Paul Kenny, GMB general secretary, asserted, "Private investors, hiding under a cloak of secrecy and pretending to be interested in building

up the UK economy, are taking the taxpayer for a ride, while destroy-
ing jobs and leaving in their wake thousands of workers who saved for
their pensions without a pension and dependent on the state."

Few in England seemed to notice PE's growing influence until
May 2006 when the GMB launched a campaign criticizing London
PE firm Permira for firing thousands of its workers at AA, the road-
side assistance company (similar to America's AAA). The union's tactics included turning up outside Permira chairman Damon Buffini's
church with a camel. The protesters, with the media watching, put a
sash on the animal that said it was easier for a camel to go through the
eye of a needle than for a rich man, Buffini, to enter heaven.

They failed to attract significant allies, though, until three PE firms—
Blackstone, CVC Capital Partners, and KKR—announced they were
interested in teaming to buy English supermarket chain J Sainsbury in
what would have been a record-breaking £10 billion deal, six times larger
than any British LBO during the buyout boom. Sainsbury employed
150,000 people and handled 18 percent of the nation's food supply. Now
some people who had heard GMB's claims became concerned.

At the same time, John Prescott was resigning as Labor Party
deputy leader leaving a contest to replace him. Alan Johnson and Jon
Cruddas, who both wanted the post, recognized they could champion
the union cause and voiced concern about the impact of private equity.
The House of Commons scheduled June 2007 hearings.

Meanwhile, KKR launched an equally large offer for pharmacy
chain Alliance Boots, teaming with Stefano Pessina, the company's
executive deputy chairman and largest shareholder. They tried to
buy the company for £10 per share, £9.7 billion ($18.74 billion), and
then after being forced to raise their bid, agreed to a £10.9 per share,
£10.6 billion, buyout weeks before the hearings.

Sainsbury, on the other hand, rejected the buyout offer that was
made to it and remained a publicly traded company.

Emotions ran high when the House of Commons Treasury Select
Committee began the hearings. There was a public uproar about
the way private-equity firms seemed to be treating their companies
and workers, and Parliament, specifically the ruling Labor Party, was

expected to rein them in. Meanwhile, Conservative Party Member of Parliament Brooks Newmark was in an awkward position. Newmark was a partner at Leon Black's PE firm, Apollo Management, before becoming a politician. He called Apollo a venture-capital group on his Web site, though while at Apollo he tried unsuccessfully to acquire British supermarket chain Somerfield PLC in a leveraged buyout. A few months before the hearings, Apollo bought England's biggest realtor, Countrywide, in a £1.05 billion ($1.94 billion) LBO.

The first day of questioning included Peter Linthwaite, the head of the British Private Equity and Venture Capital Association (BVCA), whose members included most of the biggest PE firms. Linthwaite and his staff maintained that PE-owned companies in many cases paid more in tax than independent private businesses, but provided few specifics. However, when one of Linthwaite's associates, Jeremy Hand, argued that the companies paid more taxes because they did not receive research-and-development tax credits, he seemed to imply that they cut R & D spending. The BVCA accepted Linthwaite's resignation before the next session.

There was great public expectation for the second day of hearings, as the powerful PE barons would appear as witnesses. Hundreds waited on lines that wound around Portcullis House, a Parliament annex, to see the expected grilling in a hot room that only held fifty to sixty visitors. Mostly the public wanted to see the PE overlords exposed and brought down to size.

"Is taper relief presently being used as intended?" Chairman John McFall asked, referring to the law that allows individuals to reduce their capital gains tax after holding an asset for only two years.

Permira's Buffini said, "I think it is. We are generating business investment and creating jobs in the UK."

The chairman continued the line of questioning, turning to KKR's Dominic Murphy. "This committee is interested to find out how much capital gains tax goes to the Treasury from private equity. I have not yet got that figure. Can you help me?"

"I do not know that figure."

"You do not know that figure for your company?"

"No, I do not."

"Mr. Buffini, do you know the figure for your company?"

"I do not know."

"You do not know how much CGT you pay?"

"No."

"You guys are the really bright ones and are masters of the universe. I ask you how much you pay in capital gains tax and you cannot tell me. There is something flawed here."

KKR's Murphy then said, "Our passion is value creation." For the PE industry, it was another public-relations disaster.

The looming threat from the committee was that it could recommend changes such as ending the corporate tax deduction on interest and raising the capital gains taxes individual partners paid. Duke Street's Taylor was a scheduled witness for the next session.

Taylor said the prospect of appearing was scary. "The advice we had, which was good advice, was, 'Look, just show a human face of the industry. That's the biggest thing that's needed here. And be prepared to admit mistakes.'"

Parliament members questioned Taylor about Duke Street's 1988 investment in do-it-yourself retailer Focus. The firm made a good return over the years by expanding the chain through acquisitions. Then in 2005, it sold off Focus's 172 Wickes branded building-materials stores, which represented about half its locations. But by early 2007, Focus could not pay its debt. Months before the hearings, Duke Street sold Focus to Cerberus Capital Management for one pound. Despite this final nominal sale, Duke Street made a good profit on its Focus investment.

Labor MP Andrew Love asked, "Can you tell us what the return has been to you from selling off Focus?"

"For an investment of just under three hundred million euros, our investors received total proceeds of around eight hundred million euros, which was a very successful deal."

"I understand there were a series of leveraged recapitalizations [dividends] from which you earned money?"

"We did one leveraged recap in 2003, which returned some cash to our investors, but the largest return of cash came from the sale of Wickes."

Former Apollo principal Newmark pressed Taylor: "My question to you is, is their any relationship between the amount of debt raised during your ownership of Focus and its subsequent difficulties? In simple language, did you raise too much debt?

"Initially, no.... Two years ago we successfully sold the largest part of the Group, which was Wickes, and we used the proceeds to repay the majority of the borrowings and to return a profit to the shareholders.... We took the borrowings down lower than was required by the banks at the time but none of us could foresee the downturn in the DIY [do-it-yourself] market that then followed and affected everybody in the industry. So with hindsight, to answer your question directly, yes."

"In the meantime, did people end up losing their jobs as you tried to restructure the business?"

"No. The employment in Focus has remained stable or growing throughout."

While this may have been true, Cerberus, after buying the chain, announced plans to close or sell 20 percent of the stores, which would result in hundreds of layoffs.

British media made the testimony big news. The *Daily Mail* in its regular "Hero and Zero" column chose Taylor the loser of the day. And the *Sun* ran a lead story with the headline "Private Equity Boss Admits DIY Botch Job." Taylor became something of a celebrity.

At the end of the day, the PE industry association BVCA managed to preempt the committee's findings by having Sir David Walker, a Morgan Stanley senior adviser, craft a voluntary code to improve disclosure in PE-owned companies. The idea was that PE firms would not reduce customer service, raise prices, or starve companies of capital if they knew their actions would be exposed. So the argument went that there was no need to change the tax code as that would only discourage PE activity, which from that point forward would always be aimed at helping businesses. The code, as presented to the committee, applied only to businesses that at the time of the buyout fit all of the following: were worth more than £500 million (or if public the shares were acquired for more than £300 million), generated half their revenue in the United Kingdom, and had more than one thousand full-time employees. Walker recommended that PE firms have these businesses publish midyear and annual reports.

Several months after the hearings, Colin Breed, a Liberal Democrat MP on the Treasury Select Committee, spoke about the Walker Report in the large atrium at Parliament's Portcullis House. "I believe very strongly in professional self-regulation, and I would be prepared to give the David Walker recommendations fair weight. And then review the situation in eighteen months' time. Now if they had not seemed to fulfill the expectations that we have of them, we could then revisit and make other recommendations. It's very difficult to legislate and then go back. It's much better to put recommendations and self-regulations forward and give it the opportunity to succeed before you then move into a legislative mode."

The PE industry, by convincing Parliament members like Breed to give them a chance, did an end run around the committee and continued to buy up British companies. The government did raise taxes on the profits PE partners collected from their funds from 10 percent to 18 percent, but that in itself was hardly going to slow down the buyout train.

PE firms, for the most part, ignored the Walker code. Only a mere thirty-two of the British Private Equity and Venture Capital Association's two hundred members were covered by the transparency guidelines and fifty-six of the country's thirteen hundred PE-owned companies.

Though PE firms largely refused to be transparent in England, the results of their actions in other European countries became increasingly clear. Take Denmark, for example.

A group of mostly American PE firms—Apax Partners, Blackstone Group, KKR, Permira, and Providence Equity Partners—in February 2006 bought Denmark's wire-line phone company, TDC (formerly Tele Danmark), for €10.2 billion ($13.9 billion) in what was Europe's largest LBO up to that time.

Denmark's government had privatized the company in 1998, and its shares were listed on the stock market. TDC's management team supported the sale to be taken private.

The new owners funded the deal by having TDC borrow money from Barclays, Credit Suisse, Deutsche Bank, JPMorgan, and Royal Bank of Scotland equal to roughly 80 percent of the transaction price.

Denmark's tax law regarding the deductibility of interest payments was similar to the law in the United States, England, and the rest of the world. TDC, which was tripling its debt, could deduct the interest it was paying from taxes. This would have a huge impact on the Danish Government, as TDC was its biggest corporate taxpayer. There was hope, though, that the buyout might help the Danish economy overall if the new owners pushed the somewhat sleepy TDC aggressively into new areas. At the time, TDC generated about two thirds of its domestic revenue from a slowing wire-line services business that was losing customers to wireless. The company did have a mobile-phone division that faced competition and a smaller cable-television operation, but they were not growing rapidly.

"The buyers were extremely vague, if not evasive, about their future plans for TDC," said William Melody, a guest professor at the Technical University of Denmark.

Weeks after the deal, TDC, which might have had as many customers outside Denmark as within the country, started selling many of its international holdings, including stakes in German, Lithuanian, and Polish cellular-phone companies. Disposing of these assets generated money but also caused the company to fall from being the world's thirtieth-biggest telecom company to being between forty-fifth and fiftieth.

In addition, TDC said it would fire 5 percent of TDC's Danish staff, 720 workers, and the same percentage in its smaller TDC Switzerland division, 145 workers. There was another 5 percent reduction in the Danish staff planned for 2007. Meanwhile, spending on capital projects stayed roughly the same or dropped off slightly, an analyst who follows the company and requested anonymity said. Much of the money generated from asset sales and layoffs was instead used to reduce debt taken on to finance the buyout. A PE firm's equity rises with each dollar paid back if the value of the company remains the same.

In TDC the PE firms seemingly found a perfect target to slim down, as it was the dominant wire-line player in Denmark, guaranteed steady, if slowly declining, revenue, regardless of the stewardship. TDC could also sell valuable international assets without hurting the underlying domestic business.

Blackstone had executed a similar telecom strategy before. It had held a large stake in U.S. cellular-phone company Centennial Communications (see the appendix) that it shrank by selling or shutting down operations outside its core Fort Wayne, Indiana, market. It then took out a dividend and later sold the business, making a good return. Milking and stripping TDC to pay back foreign lenders on an almost tax-free basis was coming at someone's expense—the Danish taxpayer.

When politicians looked at the situation, it was easy to comprehend because TDC was such a large part of the tax base. Denmark's Ministry of Taxation estimated it was losing 2 billion kroner ($390 million) annually from highly leveraged companies deducting the interest they were paying from taxes. In 2006, that represented about 3 percent of collected corporate tax. The ministry projected that the loss, if unchecked, could rise to about 15 billion kroner ($2.9 billion).

On June 1, 2007, the Danish Parliament enacted Bill L 213, which reduced corporate deductible interest expenses annually to 20 million kroner ($4 million), provided other provisions were met and made the law retroactive. TDC now had to pay about €100 million ($145 million) more in annual taxes, the analyst said. As a result, TDC in December 2008 was generating only about €230 million ($321 million) in annual free cash flow and still carried €6.25 billion ($8.74 billion) in debt. At that rate and with revenue declining, TDC will take twenty-seven years to pay its principal. Yet the first big loans are due in 2014. By that time, the company's best hopes for survival are to sell shares on the stock market; to refinance, if the credit markets recover; or to sell the business to another telecom operator.

Poul Nyrup Rasmussen, the Danish prime minister at the time of the TDC buyout and later a member of the European Parliament, in September 2008 called for more regulation of PE firms. "For the sake of our pensions, our jobs, our savings, and our welfare . . . the sooner we take action the better."

There is some irony here as the European countries that the World Bank praised in 2004 for having the fewest regulatory burdens on businesses—England, the Netherlands, Sweden, and Denmark—are the four where PE firms have had the greatest influence and will soon do the most damage when their actions drive many companies into bankruptcy. If you look at companies bought through buyouts, add up the equity PE firms put down, and then divide that by the gross domestic product (GDP) of each country, private equity in 2007 had the most influence on Sweden (1.195 percent), followed by the United Kingdom (1.033 percent), Netherlands (1.027 percent), and Denmark (0.751 percent). For the United States, the number was only 0.663 percent.

Governments with more regulations were less affected. PE investment as a percentage of GDP in France during 2007 was 0.635 percent, less than in the most business-friendly European countries or the United States. In Germany, it was much less (0.437 percent), while PE had an even smaller impact on Ireland (0.300 percent), Italy (0.206 percent), and Greece (0.193 percent).

PE Down Payments for Buyouts in the Following
Countries as a Percentage of GDP, 2007

Country	Percentage
Sweden	1.195
United Kingdom	1.033
Netherlands	1.027
Denmark	0.751
Belgium	0.641
United States	0.663
France	0.635
Finland	0.605
Europe	0.571
Norway	0.543
Hungary	0.487
Germany	0.437
Switzerland	0.421
Spain	0.403
Romania	0.389
Austria	0.314
Ireland	0.300
Poland	0.243

Country	Percentage
Italy	0.206
Greece	0.193
Czech Republic	0.158
Portugal	0.104

Source: European Venture Capital Association and PEREP_Analytics.

The attitude in Germany was reflected by ruling Social Democratic Party chairman Franz Muentefering in 2005 when he compared PE firms to locusts, saying they graze on underpriced businesses, lay off employees, and move on.

Although many family businesses are going through generational changes in Germany, Europe's biggest economy, few have sold out to foreign PE firms. Dominique Mégret, chairman and CEO of Paris-based PE firm PAI partners, suggests that in Germany "many founders of businesses believe that the future of their firms may be better served by the succession of a son or daughter. Those who wish to sell may prefer a strategic buyer to a PE firm."

PAI has a Munich office, and in early 2008, two of the fifteen companies it owned were Germany-based. The largest was Monier, the former German roofing business of Lafarge; PAI acquired Monier in a February 2007 €2.4 billion buyout. The most willing sellers of German businesses have been industrial conglomerates shedding unwanted divisions.

In 2006 Blackstone borrowed money to buy a 4.5 percent stake in publicly traded Deutsche Telekom AG, one of the country's most venerable businesses, for €2.7 billion. The firm has one seat on the supervisory board and little say in operations, leading at least one PE partner to question the logic of the purchase.

Things could open up if Germany goes through a prolonged recession. The legacy of cross-shareholding in public companies, by which banks, insurers, and leading industrial companies own shares to protect businesses from hostile takeovers, is ending as the government has lowered taxes on sales of these stakes. If some cross-shareholders find themselves needing to raise money, they may sell their shares.

The French private-equity market, while not like England's, has been more active than Germany's. But local PE firms have been landing many of the deals. French President Nicolas Sarkozy in January 2008 pledged to defend companies from the assault of foreign investment funds. "In the face of the increasing power of speculative funds, which are extremely aggressive...there's no reason for France not to react. France must protect its companies." His government created a fund to invest in strategic French businesses whose share prices have fallen, to protect them from being bought by foreigners. PAI has €11 billion of funds under management and owns companies (including yogurt maker Yoplait) that employ more than a hundred thousand people in all. "France is probably the only [European] country where a local PE player has such a strong position as PAI," Mégret said. The profit PAI Partners generates, though, often goes to American investors, who contribute 32 percent of the money in its buyout funds, while French investors represent only 25 percent.

Mégret, who almost shrugs when he talks, says he is different from many of his counterparts in that he tends to own his businesses for a longer time because he has a strong operational focus. United States PE firms would have trouble buying businesses considered key to the national interest in France, but they sometimes win auctions for other French businesses by paying much higher prices than local groups.

Henry Kravis has taken a particular interest in France. He and his wife, Canadian Marie-Josée Kravis, who used to sit on Vivendi's supervisory board, have a Paris home. In 2006 his firm, KKR, made an unsuccessful $51 billion bid for media giant Vivendi that would have rocked the country's establishment had it gone further. KKR has bought Legrand Holdings (electrical-systems provider for offices and homes), PagesJaunes Group (the country's phone-directories business), and Tarkett (flooring products) in billion-dollar buyouts.

Carlyle's Rubenstein in spring 2008 hired the French prime minister's half-brother, Oliver Sarkozy, to help find banks and other financial-services companies to buy.

Italy, with the world's sixth largest market economy, is perhaps the most frustrating to PE firms. Italian designer Giorgio Armani in November 2007 said he was open to a tie-up with a wealthy "fashion lover" or another investor—but not private-equity firms, which he described as exploitative. "These funds borrow money from banks, they merge two companies, and then they go on the stock market to get back their money immediately, leaving the organization adrift."

U.S. Ambassador to Italy Ronald Spogli in a 2006 speech appealed to locals to see PE in a new light. "Many of the corporations that create Italy's GDP are unlisted—privately held—fertile ground for private equity.... Simply put, Italy has never had the level of private equity investment that its European peers have.... While other countries are using private equity to help companies grow, Italy is missing out."

Naturally Spogli feels this way: He cofounded Los Angeles PE firm Freeman Spogli & Co. During his address, Spogli didn't mention one of his group's few European forays, a 1989 buyout of Austria-based Head/Tyrolia/Mares (HTM), the makers of Head skis and rackets. This was at the height of the 1980s buyout boom, and the investment, like many made from 2004 to 2007, was done at a high price that put too much debt on the acquired company. His firm had HTM borrow about 85 percent of the money needed to fund the $335 million buyout. HTM during the 1990s recession had trouble paying the loan and was losing money. Freeman Spogli sold HTM in 1993 to Austria Tabakwerke, the state-owned tobacco monopoly, for $240 million, which injected money into the business to protect local jobs. After one of HTM's lenders called in a loan, Tabakwerke resold the business in 1995 to a group led by Swedish investor Johan Eliasch for just assuming its debts.

The more recent American invasion of Britain now is taking its toll on the country's businesses. TPG, which bought Punch Taverns and orchestrated the acquisition spree that made it Britain's biggest pubs chain, walked away from its investment in 2003, making $400 million, nearly three times its money. Punch, now a publicly traded company, is struggling. Fewer consumers have the extra money to go out drinking, and some of its operators who rent their pubs from Punch are having difficulty paying rent. The problem is, Punch still has a tremendous amount of debt. Charlie Winston, an analyst at Redburn Partners, predicted in 2008 that the chain would likely default on its loans due December 2010.

Meanwhile, Apollo Management changed tactics and as of spring 2009 was raising a €1.5 billion fund to buy underperforming European corporate loans, including debt in its own Countrywide, the British real-estate brokerage, which was subsequently taken over by creditors. The plan is to make money when companies improve or to have borrowers give them ownership stakes in return for loan forgiveness.

Apollo bought 20 percent of the debt in Mégret's struggling German company, Monier. Mégret proposed to lenders that his firm could put some much-needed money into Monier and give them shares in the business in exchange for some loan forgiveness. Apollo, which was not willing to invest in Monier, rejected the offer. Black's firm instead repossessed the business while not greatly reducing the loans. This was better for Black but not necessarily for Monier.

Monier believed the Apollo plan would put its capital investment and growth program at risk, but a source close to the situation told *The Deal* that "the management wants [a structure with] more equity, but they don't have much bargaining power."

Soon Rubenstein may have to stop crowing about how America dominates the PE industry.

CHAPTER TEN

What's Next?

With all the major economies in recession and worldwide credit markets frozen, PE firms in late 2008 found themselves in a pinch. They had plenty of money to invest, an estimated $450 billion in commitments they could call in at any time from investors. But the banks weren't lending and the credit markets weren't functioning, so they couldn't get the big loans required to complete deals. They needed a new investment strategy and found what appeared to be a golden opportunity in the faltering banking system itself.

Fortress Investment Group is a publicly traded company that is in the business of raising and investing private-equity and hedge funds. It isn't a typical PE firm, but it is part of the chain of investors and lenders who make up the private-equity industry.

When William Doniger, who heads the part of Fortress's business that makes private-equity investments, appeared on a panel of experts at an industry conference in January 2009, he talked about the situation:

"I've looked at a lot of banks trying to figure out how to invest in the space, and you can do due diligence on fifty banks and come to the same conclusion, which is they have a lot of problem assets [loans], and it is hard to understand where it is going to go." Nonetheless, he said Fortress was seeking to buy the smallest bank it could with enough infrastructure to allow it to invest in assets that "should represent the best investment opportunity in our lifetime." The potential upside of the assets would more than offset the future losses the bank might incur from existing loans.

Government officials who were trying to shore up ailing banks and restart the financial system at the time welcomed private equity's interest in the banking sector. In fact, they made the securing of private equity a prerequisite for some banks before agreeing to provide government bailout funds. The fact that government regulators would encourage private-equity takeovers of struggling banks was a sign of their desperation. It was also a troubling development, because there really was little in the track record of the private-equity industry to indicate they would make the banks any stronger, and there was much to suggest they would find ways to siphon even more money out of them.

William Doniger didn't say exactly what assets Fortress intended to buy, but afterward one of the experts on the panel with him said that he interpreted Doniger's words as meaning he was going to buy a bank and then use it to buy existing loans at discount prices.

Buying a bank would give Fortress (via the bank) access to the very cheap loans the Federal Reserve was making to banks to encourage lending. But instead of lending that money out, the Fortress-owned bank could use the money to buy mortgages and corporate debt from other financial institutions at deep discounts from their face value. In essence, Fortress would "rescue" a bank that had collapsed from making bad loans and then use taxpayer money to have it buy more bad loans, which would put the bank at risk again.

Once the private-equity group owned the bank, banking guidelines would allow it to create a portfolio of loans valued at roughly ten times the size of its deposit base. The PE group, for example, might buy a bank with $1 billion in deposits that had $10 billion of loans outstanding but which has marked down the value of those loans to $5 billion. The bank then has the freedom to acquire or issue loans valued at $5 billion more. What Fortress's Doniger outlined appeared to be a plan that would use federal loans to build a big portfolio of the risky loans that had already been made and that could be purchased at big discounts.

Because of the leverage, only a slight recovery in the economy could raise the value of the loan portfolio enough to give Fortress a huge profit. If the gamble paid off, it could win big. If it didn't, the bank might collapse again and Fortress would lose the fairly small amount it spent to buy the bank. From the bank's (and Fortress's) perspective, if it made a new $100 million loan to a financially sound customer, it would make some money on the fees and interest charges, but the loan would never be worth much more than $100 million in the near-term. But if it used the same assets to buy existing bad loans that had been discounted by 50 percent, there was the potential that it could get as much as another $100 million fairly quickly.

Unfortunately, when it came to dealing with the failing banks, the government had no good options. The $700 billion Troubled Assets Relief Program (TARP) did not provide nearly enough money to save them. Theoretically, it could nationalize banks that fell into receivership, but that would be an expensive administrative and political nightmare, and if they let them collapse, the government would still have to make good on their depositor guarantees.

Instead the government sought to provide incentives to outside investors to rescue banks. The most logical buyers, though, couldn't or wouldn't provide much assistance. Foreign governments, through their sovereign wealth funds, had helped in 2007, but they lost so much money investing in U.S. banks that they were now not anxious to reinvest. Hedge funds, which often buy stocks, bonds, and currency, were running out of money, and large banks that had bought smaller peers in the past now couldn't afford many acquisitions.

That left private-equity firms. So, despite reservations, the government began to seek their help. Theoretically, it might make some sense to try to tap into the $450 billion of ready-to-invest assets that the private-equity firms were sitting on. It was a huge pool of money that was available at a time when financing was tight. But the strategy was very much a long shot, and while it might have been difficult to weaken U.S. banks from where they were in early 2009, the chances that private-equity ownership was going to make them stronger were quite slim.

In order to acquire banks in or heading for receivership, PE firms needed to get around the Bank Holding Company Act, which prevents buyers that have commercial interests (nonfinancial corporations) from owning more than one third of the voting shares in a bank. This is to protect depositors from having their money diverted to unrelated businesses. It presented a problem, though, because the rules prevent almost all PE firms from buying a majority stake in a bank, and most do not want to buy a bank they cannot control. So government regulators bent the Bank Holding Company Act to get them engaged.

The first big deal to result from the rule bending was the March 2009 acquisition by a group of seven PE firms, hedge funds, and financiers of IndyMac Federal Bank, one of the nation's largest savings and loans. They put $1.55 billion down in the $16 billion buyout, with the government reportedly financing much of the deal. None of the investors likely owns more than a 33 percent stake, but as a group they control IndyMac. Soon after, the government sold similarly sized BankUnited to a group of PE firms. Fortress, weeks after the January conference, led a trio of investors that bought shares of Florida's First Southern Bancorp.

To allow the acquisition, the Federal Deposit Insurance Corporation (FDIC) and the Office of Thrift Supervision (OTS) softened their position on simultaneous investments—different groups providing capital at the same time. In the past, government agencies might have believed a bidding consortium was acting in concert and barred it from buying a bank. Fortress's Doniger said he had been to Washington, D.C., many times to work on the issue and was looking to buy a bank by teaming with a few investors.

Besides allowing PE firms to bid in groups to get around the Bank Holding Company Act, government regulators also began to let them acquire controlling stakes and then give shares to fund investors to get over the 33 percent ownership limit. In January 2009, for example, the OTS approved PE firm MatlinPatterson's acquisition of shares in Flagstar Bancorp, one of the largest originators of residential mortgages, that gave it and its investors a majority stake and the right to designate more than half of the board. Money that was committed to the firm's PE fund was used to buy Flagstar, but the investment was structured slightly differently from a typical fund investment. MatlinPatterson has management control over fund investments, so if the fund bought the bank directly, as it had acquired other companies, MatlinPatterson would have violated the Bank Holding Company Act. Still, Fortress's Doniger believed the fund essentially bought the bank, and MatlinPatterson would be managing the investment, like the rest of its holdings.

The Treasury wanted PE firms to buy banks so badly that it persuaded Flagstar Bancorp, with $14 billion in assets, to secure private capital first, before it would provide TARP funding. When MatlinPatterson agreed to invest $250 million in Flagstar, TARP invested alongside the PE firm, buying $266 million of preferred Flagstar shares.

Carlyle Managing Director Randal Quarles, the former undersecretary of the Treasury under President George W. Bush who directed the Treasury's financial-sector policy, predicts that by the end of the recession, PE firms will have significant holdings of smaller and regional community banks that have between $1 billion and $10 billion in assets. In some cases, he believes the government will share future bank losses to encourage investment.

PE firms will also be buying banks in Europe, where regulators in a number of jurisdictions are seeking private capital. "There will be a lot of private equity investing in the European financial sector just as in the U.S.," Quarles said.

If PE firms own banks, then the question becomes How closely will the banks be regulated?

The FDIC, which monitors banks, became concerned and in the summer of 2009 went against the wishes of the regulatory agencies proposing that banks PE firms bought out of receivership should keep much more money in reserve than their peers. After getting feedback from PE firms, the FDIC signaled it would back off.

Bill Isaac, chairman of the FDIC from 1981 to 1985, said he didn't believe the FDIC would tolerate a firm like Fortress using a bank to buy junky loans. At the time, he was raising several billion dollars to buy banks himself in partnership with London's Oceanview Capital Management. But he had a different approach. Unlike Fortress, he was raising one fund to buy banks and a separate fund to acquire troubled loans.

Isaac said he believed most PE firms really were interested in managing banks, and not acquiring them as a way to borrow money from the government so that they could buy loans cheaply. "I think PE wants to buy banks inexpensively, get them stabilized, get them turned around, create some attractive franchises, and then get out." But even if Isaac was correct in his view that it was the PE firms' intention to manage the banks prudently and put them on sound footing, the temptation to gamble on junk loans and other risky plays was there. And reliance on the moderation and self-regulation of Wall Street played a big role in getting the banks in such bad shape to begin with.

The last time PE firms bought a sizable bank before the current credit crisis was the 2000 buyout of Long-Term Credit Bank of Japan. The story is not a pretty one.

In 1998, the Japanese government nationalized Long-Term Credit Bank, which had collapsed due to low-interest corporate loans and real-estate mortgages. The Japanese government took over some loans and hired investment bank Goldman Sachs to find a buyer for the bank.

Meanwhile, former Goldman Sachs partner Chris Flowers in 1998 formed what would become PE firm J.C. Flowers to buy struggling banks and insurance companies. At the time, there were few American or European financial services businesses in trouble, so he targeted Japan, even though he had no expertise in the region. To bid on Long-Term Credit, he partnered with New York PE firm Ripplewood Holdings, whose board included the chairman of Mitsubishi, and with former Fed chairman Paul Volcker (who later headed President Obama's Economic Recovery Advisory Board).

Japan wanted to sell Long-Term Credit to a local bank, but the Flowers team was the most serious suitor. The bidders were concerned that many of the bank's outstanding loans might not be repaid. The Flowers/Ripplewood buying group wanted a provision that would require the government for three years to buy any loans that were worth significantly less than what the government was claiming. It wanted the government to pay the original book value of those loans (minus the set reserves against those losses).

The Japanese government was very reluctant to give the guarantee, but it soon became clear if it didn't agree, it wouldn't be able to sell the bank to the Flowers team. Japan then stipulated that the buyers could only sell back a loan after they had exercised all remedies against a borrower, including bankruptcy. But the government also required the PE firms to meet the proper finance needs of borrowers and not collect loans abruptly. It was a very mixed message.

For the buyers, the big question after getting the guarantee was whether the Japanese courts would uphold their contract if the government later decided they did not want to make good on the guarantee. Flowers brought in coinvestors, including Gap's controlling Fisher family, AIG, Mellon Bank, and UBS, who believed the legality of the purchase agreement would be upheld and that this would give them real downside protection. The PE-led buying group acquired Long-Term Credit in March 2000 for ¥121 billion ($1.1 billion), which was one third of book value (book value is essentially a bank's assets minus liabilities). The buying group put down the whole $1.1 billion.

The bank was renamed Shinsei Bank, and the new owners hired the retired CEO of Citibank Japan, Masamoto Yashiro, as CEO to work quickly on assessing the bank's loans. Yashiro in 2004 told an audience at Columbia University Business School, "I vividly recall that in the first week of April 2000, Sogo [a major Japanese retailer] came to see us and asked us to forgive a large amount of money. I said, 'What do you mean, *forgive?*' I had never heard the word.... Loan forgiveness was not in my vocabulary. I asked, 'Why?' They said, 'Well, because this is done in Japan.' I asked them how much they wanted forgiven. They said about $1 billion of the $2 billion loan. I said, 'Absolutely not.'"

In its first year of PE ownership, Shinsei Bank forced Sogo, consumer credit firm Life Co. Ltd., the Dai-ichi Hotel, and others into bankruptcy. Because the PE firms had paid only one third of book value, they could do well by bankrupting companies and putting loans back to the government at net book value.

The government was surprised it was forced to buy $10 billion of loans, a source with direct knowledge of the situation said, adding that Shinsei put back practically every loan that had fallen enough in value to trigger the warranty. A major Tokyo bank executive told the *Yomiuri Shimbun* newspaper, "Shinsei Bank is the only bank in the world that benefits from wrecking its business partners."

Over the next few years, the Japanese Parliament brought CEO Yashiro in front of them several times to answer questions like Why didn't the bank refinance loans and charge higher interest rates instead of forcing businesses into bankruptcy? Yashiro said Shinsei had to foreclose on clients to survive.

Quarles, who in 2000 was advising JPMorgan about possibly buying Long-Term Credit, said it flatly: "The Shinsei deal worked because of the government backstop."

Despite the criticism, the PE firms stayed the course. By September 2007, the bank's assets had been reduced by 40 percent, from $150 billion to $90 billion, by not rolling over loans and then foreclosing on delinquent borrowers. A smaller Shinsei expanded by buying consumer-finance businesses that loaned money to people with poor credit. By 2004 Shinsei seemed like a success, earning a $626 million profit. The PE-led owners listed the bank on the Tokyo Stock Exchange. They had bought in at ¥89 a share, and the stock opened at ¥525, giving them almost a six-times return on their $1.1 billion investment.

Within a few years, the government capped the interest rates on consumer loans, which hurt Shinsei's credit card business. As a result, Shinsei in 2007, three years after the IPO, reported a full-year loss, and its stock sank to under ¥350 a share.

Flowers in January 2008 thought he saw a bargain and bought Shinsei stock, after selling shares several years earlier, raising his firm's stake in Shinsei from 6 percent to 33 percent.

But Shinsei soon suffered more blows when foreign investments, including loans to Lehman Brothers and a coinvestment alongside J.C. Flowers in German commercial real-estate lender Hypo Real Estate Holding AG, soured. Shinsei CEO Yashiro, who had retired from the bank in 2005, came back as CEO in November 2008 at seventy-nine years of age, saying he felt a responsibility to fix Shinsei, which was at best breaking even.

The PE firms made a bad impression. A Japanese book written on Ripplewood and Shinsei was titled *The Day the Vulture Laughed*. A popular TV series called *Vulture* was about a Japanese company that comes under assault by U.S. investors. In September 2007, the Japanese Parliament enacted the Financial Instruments and Exchange Law, which required greater transparency and taxation of foreign investment funds operating in Japan.

As the current credit crisis deepened, Quarles said he was anticipating more Shinsei-like deals, with governments around the world agreeing to sell insolvent banks to PE firms and then backstopping future losses.

Flowers, who engineered the Shinsei deal, was part of the team that bought IndyMac out of receivership. That didn't seem to bother the Office of Thrift Supervision, which reviews buyers who do not already own American thrifts when they apply to buy one. OTS approved the IndyMac deal even after examining the character, integrity, financial and managerial resources, and general business plan of the buyers.

While the U.S. government didn't provide incentives to the Indy-Mac buyers to foreclose on borrowers, it did take on much of the risk. The buyers invested only $1.55 billion, with the government reportedly providing loans to finance the rest of the $16.9 billion IndyMac buyout. In addition, the government agreed to assume some of the losses on the single-family residential portfolio. Flowers quipped at an investor forum, "The government has all the downside and we have all the upside."

Government backing to protect PE firms against future losses is probably a necessary incentive if the government wants them to invest. This became truer after PE firm TPG in 2008 invested $1.35 billion for shares in Washington Mutual and saw that money wiped out in five months after unexpected losses caused the bank to file for bankruptcy.

The most hassle-free way for PE firms to profit from the financial wreckage is to directly buy mortgages and loans trading at deep discounts.

Lone Star Funds, a private-equity firm that specializes in buying financial assets trading at distressed prices, in a 2008 deal that wasn't government assisted, bought $31 billion in CDOs (repackaged mortgages), from Merrill Lynch for $6.7 billion. It paid Merrill only one quarter of the $6.7 billion purchase price and faced no further exposure if the loans fell deeper in value.

The Blackstone Group has tried taking an active role in increasing the value of loans it buys at discount prices. In 2008 it allocated $1.25 billion to invest alongside mortgage-finance company Bayview Financial to buy packages of mortgages from banks. They would pay an average price of, say, 50 cents on the dollar, and then ask the actual homeowners, who never approved the transfers, if they would like to buy back their mortgages for, say, 75 cents on the dollar to avoid foreclosure. It became a very profitable endeavor, said a source close to the team.

When Blackstone, Carlyle and coinvestors bought Florida's Bank-United in 2009, they tried the same approach on a bigger scale. They bought its $12.3 billion in loans, much of it toxic mortgages, at less than 50 cents on the dollar, when factoring in the government guarantee they received for loans that failed. Sources close to the buying team predicted they would make multiples of the $900 million they put down on the buyout. They got the sweetheart deal because the government, which had just taken over the collapsed bank, was anxious to sell so it did not have to service loans and make the politically unpopular move of foreclosing on homeowners.

Meanwhile, some PE firms have tried to make money buying leveraged loans. Citigroup, Deutsche Bank, and other lenders in early 2008 resold more than $30 billion of leveraged loans to PE firms. Many of these loans financed LBOs of companies like Harrah's Entertainment, First Data, and TXU. Banks were willing to sell them at a discount, in some cases, to the same PE firms that engineered those buyouts.

PE firms bought these loans in a manner similar to the way they bought companies. They put 20 percent down to buy a loan for 80 cents on the dollar. The bank that was reselling the loan would continue to hold the rest on its books, perhaps charging a nominal interest rate on that money. A PE buyer might stand to make all the upside on the full amount of the loan if its value recovered. So if they put down $200 million to buy a $1 billion loan for $800 million and resold the loan in five years for $900 million, the PE firm would make a $100 million profit. Beyond that, they could collect the interest on the entire loan.

What the banks received in return was a cushion against further losses. Citigroup, for example, in spring 2008 likely sold to PE firms loans with a $12.5 billion face value for $2.5 billion and got the security of knowing that if those loans fell another $2.5 billion in value, from 80 cents on the dollar to 60 cents, it would not take the hit. The PE firm would absorb those losses. In some cases, PE firms also agreed that if the value of the loan fell to, say, 50 cents in eighteen to twenty-four months, it would put up more capital, covering that shortfall. But they would not cover losses beyond that point. "The flavor of the day is buying your own debt at below face value," said Carlyle cofounder David Rubenstein in a May 2008 *Fortune* interview. "I'm buying bank debt in my deal with leverage from the bank that made me that deal."

A possibility exists that in the deepening recession PE firms may end up having to make good on the agreement to put up more capital if the loan values fall to 50 cents. Still they are looking to buy more loans, especially for those that were made to finance their own buyouts.

They are interested now, though, in buying debt to keep their businesses from collapsing and are less concerned about making money on the debt purchases. PE firms pushed hard to get the U.S. Senate to include a provision in the 2009 stimulus bill that allowed companies to buy their own debt back at discount prices and defer paying taxes on the profit from lowering their debt. In the past if a company like Clear Channel Communications used $500 million to buy $2 billion in debt at 25 percent of face value, it would have to pay taxes on the $1.5 billion gain. Now that this bill became law companies that buy back their own debt at less than face value can delay paying taxes on the profit for five years.

While the buyers of these loans hoped the loans would regain value, there are PE firms who are trying to make money by buying loans in businesses they believe will fail, so that through their debt positions, they can repossess the companies.

KKR and a team of lenders in November 2008 repossessed Real Mex Restaurants, which owns the Chevy's casual Mexican food dining chain, after Real Mex could not repay the money borrowed to finance a 2006 Sun Capital Partners LBO. It is unclear if they originally lent the money thinking this was a likely outcome. The lending team left PE firm Sun Capital Partners with a 15 percent stake. Jeffrey Schwartz, a lawyer at Dechert LLP, told the *Wall Street Journal,* "Many companies with debt that's maturing or in default will be handed over to the debt holders."

Most PE firms' top priority was saving their companies or buying financial assets, which they hope will recover in value. But those opportunities, to a degree, are limited, and eventually some will take the road blazed in the early 1990s by Leon Black's Apollo.

Black, who had engineered some of the biggest buyouts in the 1980s as head of mergers and acquisitions at Drexel Burnham Lambert, was one of the first to see the opportunity in buying existing loans to gain control of collapsing companies. He made a fortune in the early 1990s repossessing businesses Drexel had essentially forced into bankruptcy.

For example, in 1988 Drexel financed the Rales brothers when they made a surprise offer for publicly traded Interco, a mini-conglomerate that owned Ethan Allen furniture, Converse sneakers, and Florsheim shoes brands. Interco had a shareholder rights plan, a poison pill, which gave it the ability to prevent the Raleses from acquiring beyond a certain number of shares. However, the Delaware Chancery Court ruled that Interco should dismantle its poison pill because it prevented shareholders from choosing to accept the hostile offer. Interco appealed to the Delaware Supreme Court. There was time to mount a defense, but Interco couldn't just rely on the courts.

Interco, working with banker Bruce Wasserstein, borrowed about $1.9 billion to pay shareholders a big dividend. That appeased shareholders and ended the takeover battle, but Interco was then left with a tremendous amount of debt.

The company's plan was to sell some of its diverse assets to repay the loans, but the recession hit, and Interco could not raise the money it needed. Lynn Chipperfield, a company lawyer, said, "We sold all the companies we could afford to sell and still had $1.1 billion in debt," adding that there was no way it could meet its obligations. Interco filed for bankruptcy in 1991, and received financing from lenders so it could keep operating.

Black, who formed PE firm Apollo Advisors in 1990, started buying pieces of the loans Interco had taken to defend itself against the Rales brothers. Chipperfield said, "My guess is a number of banks had written much of it off and were looking to sell what was on the books at the value they held it," which was a deep discount to par.

Apollo soon owned most of the bank debt. By mid-1992, the recession was ending, and Black reached a deal with the remaining creditors to buy Interco out of bankruptcy, converting his debt into a 66 percent stake in the business. Right off the bat, it looked as though he would make a fortune. He bought debt for $338 million that was worth about double that amount when he quickly listed the company's shares on the New York Stock Exchange.

Black ran Interco in the same way PE firms usually do, employing short-term strategies that cripple businesses over time. A cycle of driving the company into bankruptcy, rescuing it, and then driving it again into the ground began.

"They just tried to maximize sales and earnings," Chipperfield, who remained with the company, said. In 1994 Interco created two independent companies—Florsheim and Converse—and distributed stock in those companies to Interco shareholders. Interco retained its furniture business, renaming it Furniture Brands International. The theory was that analysts would better understand and appreciate the value of each individual business than when they were part of the same company.

Florsheim, which was an upscale brand, started selling shoes in more discount stores like Mervyn's to boost revenue. That cheapened the brand's image. "There was an urgency to expand its market reach," Chipperfield said.

Converse, meanwhile, was faring well as its own company, but needed to raise more cash. It had a decision to make. It could either borrow money or sell stock. Of course, Converse took on more debt, said the then-CEO of Furniture Brands, Richard Loynd. That was a mistake, he said now.

By 2000 Apollo had sold almost all its stock in the three companies (Furniture Brands, Florsheim, and Converse) more than doubling its money, generating about a $370 million profit, a 25 percent annual return. Then the shoe companies paid the price for its actions. After losing money for four years, Florsheim in 2002 filed for bankruptcy protection. Thomas Florsheim Jr., the great-grandson of the company's founder who now runs the business, said he manages the company with more of a long-term perspective than Black's Apollo.

Converse also collapsed. "It hit a down market and ran out of cash," Loynd said. "They were strapped." Meanwhile, Nike had the money to pay colleges millions of dollars so athletes would wear their shoes, and it gained market share. Converse, whose name had been changed to CVEO Corp. in 2001, filed for bankruptcy protection. Nike ended up buying and reinvigorating Converse. Loynd, who ran Converse before becoming CEO of Furniture Brands, said if Converse had not gone bankrupt, it would have been a major player but now was only a significant brand.

Meanwhile, many of the companies Black subsequently bought in the 2000s, like Claire's Stores, were struggling, so he went back to acquiring leveraged loans in companies that will likely collapse. In a December 2008 *New York Times* feature, he said his firm had just raised $20 billion in new money that would go, in part, toward buying corporate loans. Big money over the next few years, he said, would be made in the vast restructurings companies need to make if they hope to survive the recession.

There is an argument to be made that 2009 was actually a good time for PE firms to invest. PE firms have historically generated the best returns during recessions, even though there is little financing for buyouts. The funds they raised in 2001 did better than those raised in any other year, generating a 31 percent annual return to investors. Those raised in 1991, when a recession started, posted the second-best results. Funds from the following year, 1992, are not far behind.

Because periods of economic growth followed those short recessions, it stands to reason that most investments made at the bottom of the economic cycles turned out well. The current recession is deeper than anything in recent memory, but eventually the economy will revive, and when it does, if history repeats itself, PE firms will emerge with big gains and a new lease on life.

CHAPTER ELEVEN

Handling the Fallout

In the fall of 2008, auto lender and mortgage provider GMAC was losing billions of dollars. Two years earlier, PE firm Cerberus Capital Management had led a group that acquired 51 percent of GMAC from General Motors. Now Cerberus was saying GMAC, which provided loans to GM buyers, might have to file for bankruptcy by year-end. It argued that the government should step in with help because if GMAC failed, it might bring down GM. GMAC in 2007 provided financing for about half of GM cars sold in the United States. Also, GMAC was one of the ten largest producers of residential mortgages in both the United States and England.

Cerberus worked on several fronts: In September it started talking to the Federal Reserve about converting GMAC into a bank. This, it argued, would allow it to borrow money from the Fed at low rates so it could make new auto loans. But banks are supposed to have diversified risks, so arguing that it needed to loan more to car buyers seemed to be in conflict with the application for bank holding-company status. If it succeeded in getting bank status from the Fed, Cerberus then wanted bailout money from the Treasury Department Rescue Fund because GMAC was running out of cash, as its losses mounted to almost $8 billion over fifteen months.

For the first time in many years, the U.S. government was faced with the question of whether to save a sizable PE-owned company and, if so, how to go about it. The way it handled the problem would set a precedent. From 2012 to 2015, as the huge loans taken on by PE-owned firms come due, it is likely that more of them will turn to the government for bailouts. How the government deals with collapsing PE-owned companies and whether it enacts tax-law changes to discourage new buyouts will help determine the future of the PE industry. So far, the picture is not promising, as the government appears unprepared, and at least one powerful PE firm has gamed the system.

When Cerberus began its campaign, the PE firm had on hand the right man to work Washington—John Snow. Snow was U.S. Treasury secretary in 2006 when Cerberus agreed to buy GMAC, and now he was chairman of Cerberus. Bill Isaac, a former chairman of the Federal Deposit Insurance Corporation, commented: "What he [Snow] could do is go in and get a full hearing and lots of attention from the right people. And they may have heard a case they may have not otherwise have heard, because he was making the case." Isaac described the arrangement as "very awkward."

While lobbying in Washington, Cerberus was also working another front. It was negotiating with GMAC bondholders and asking them to exchange their debt for new GMAC debt that had a smaller face value, and shares that were worth less. The argument was that GMAC needed $30 billion in capital to qualify as a bank, and it had to reduce debt. To meet the regulatory bank requirement, bondholders who held 75 percent of the GMAC bonds would have to exchange their notes for paper worth less money.

At the same time, General Motors and other automakers were lobbying Congress for a bailout of their own. But as the weeks passed and Congress did not act on an auto rescue bill, it became harder to justify using public money to shore up GMAC if Congress wouldn't shore up GM itself. In addition, one of GMAC's largest bondholders, Pacific Investment Management Company (PIMCO), said it would not exchange its notes.

With time running out, President Bush on December 19, 2008, approved using the bailout fund that the Treasury had received to rescue banks to help the car makers. This gave Cerberus an opening. It could make the case that even though GM had secured funding, it still might collapse if GMAC couldn't make loans to its customers.

The government still had options: It could allow GMAC to file for bankruptcy and then either buy its auto-financing division or just create a fund to make auto loans. But on December 24, the U.S. Federal Reserve approved GMAC's application to be a bank holding company, even though it had not gotten 75 percent of its bondholders to trade in their debt for stock. It said GMAC was given this status on an emergency, expedited basis.

To qualify GMAC as a bank, Cerberus agreed to reduce holdings in GMAC to no more than a 33 percent stake, giving the rest of its shares to its investors. GM, which had held a 49 percent stake, reduced its holdings to less than 10 percent, contributing excess equity to two blind trusts.

The Treasury then on December 29 agreed to invest up to $6 billion in GMAC. In exchange for $5 billion, it received preferred shares paying 8 percent interest (that if they were converted to common shares would give it about a 25 percent stake in GMAC) and the right to buy more shares. It loaned General Motors up to another $1 billion so GM could help GMAC become a bank. Like all companies receiving government rescue money, GMAC agreed to limit executives' pay, but it was not capping the profit Cerberus might still make on its investment.

The government did force Cerberus to reduce control, allowing the PE firm only one of four GMAC board seats, although the CEO, whom Cerberus had hired, would also get one seat. Treasury would create a trust that chose the other two members, and then the four directors planned to name three new independent members to fill out a seven-member GMAC board. Cerberus, overall, got the bailout money for GMAC while maintaining a meaningful role in the business.

Treasury spokesperson Brookly McLaughlin said, "The decision to invest in GMAC was part of a broad program to make the auto industry viable," and said Cerberus did not get preferential treatment because its chairman was former Treasury Secretary John Snow.

Former FDIC chairman Isaac, however, says that he is very troubled that GMAC was allowed to become a bank. "It goes against the grain of everything we have thought about in bank supervision. You have got a financial institution that has a very limited purpose—automobile loans—it is not a diversified financial institution,...I would tell you if five years ago GMAC came to the Fed and said we wanted to be an FDIC insured bank and...their primary mission was to make sweet deals to people to induce them to buy GM cars; I think that application would have been summarily turned down.

"I don't know how we stuff this genie back in the bottle when we allow something that is structured the way GMAC is to become a bank holding company, because it really does violate some pretty fundamental principles of bank regulation.... When you try to make exceptions for policies when you are in difficult times, you can wind up creating consequences you regret later."

In addition to controlling GMAC, Cerberus also owned Chrysler, which applied for and got a $4 billion loan from the government as part of the bailout President Bush authorized in December 2008. Then in January 2009, the Treasury decided to lend Chrysler's Chrysler Financial division $1.5 billion. Cerberus had it easier this time getting the Chrysler Financial loan because after the GMAC bailout, it could argue that GMAC now had an unfair competitive advantage over Chrysler Financial unless it, too, got bailout funds.

GMAC, despite the money it got from the government, was still going broke. It burned through $10.2 billion in the first three months of 2009 and at that pace needed more assistance or would run out of money in the fall. To save costs, it basically stopped financing new auto leases.

Perhaps the Treasury should have considered how risky it was to be buying shares in a company that did not meet bank capital reserve requirements before it invested $6 billion of taxpayer money.

Regardless, when Chrysler went bankrupt in April 2009 the government allowed GMAC to absorb Chrysler Financial, giving money-losing GMAC half of the auto-financing market. Then, in May 2009, Treasury invested another $7.5 billion in GMAC.

The government point man? Obama and czar Steven Rattner, who had been a private-equity king and Cerberus investor until he sold his shares shortly after joining the Treasury.

As the economy tumbled into recession, the Treasury initially focused on propping up industries in which there was risk of systemic collapse, like autos and banking. But Randal Quarles, the Carlyle managing director who used to be undersecretary of the Treasury under Henry Paulson, said he expected the Treasury to broaden its scope. Ultimately, as it addressed the larger issue of reducing America's debt, it would have to look at some of the 2,994 American companies PE firms bought and saddled with roughly $800 billion of loans from 2000 to 2007.

He suggested that the government should transfer toxic leveraged loans to *its* balance sheet or provide new loans so the toxic ones don't become worthless. In 2008, the ratio of total U.S. debt to GDP neared 350 percent, higher than it ever had been, even during the Great Depression. This included financial, government, nonfinancial business, and household debt. Quarles believed there was room for the government to take on some of this debt and to provide loans to prevent defaults, because the money it owed holders of debt instruments, such as Treasury notes and bonds, was 35 percent of GDP, which is not close to historic high levels. In other words, the government might provide loans directly to PE-owned companies or buy some of their toxic loans, financing the process by selling more government debt.

The government could not possibly take on the total $47 trillion total U.S. debt burden. He suspects the government would have to use a triage approach based on how significant the companies or industries are to the economy. "A lot of the highly leveraged companies owned by private-equity firms are clearly consequential. PE is now a significant player in the ownership of industrial America and the real economy," Quarles said. "I would expect that whatever triage system were developed, a number of their companies would qualify for that triage."

The government could buy shares in a broad restructuring, as it did with GMAC. This would allow it to take some control of the business but not outright ownership.

If the bailouts involve lending money, as the government did with Cerberus-owned Chrysler, Quarles believed the government should not get ownership positions in return. He conceded, though, that if it does not the public might believe the PE firms that helped create the mess were being rescued from losing their investments in bankruptcy proceedings.

United States Senator Bob Corker (R-TN) in December 2008 said he was concerned that by lending money to Chrysler, the government would enable Cerberus, which was not investing any more of its money in Chrysler, to profit from a taxpayer bailout. Cerberus still had plenty of upside in Chrysler. However, Chrysler went bankrupt less than six months later. The $5.5 billion the U.S. Treasury invested in Chrysler and Chrysler Financial proved to be wasted money.

Don Meltzer, who runs Ampad, the former Bain Capital Company, believes the approach the government took with companies like GMAC and Chrysler did not go far enough. The government, he said, should take ownership of PE companies if they save them from collapsing. Over time, Meltzer said, the government could reduce its stakes by listing each company's shares on the stock markets. He believed that struggling PE-owned companies needed to change their purely bottom-line, short-term business strategies to ones that incorporate long-term growth, and he argued that they can only do that under new ownership.

The decision as to whether the government will rescue PE companies with loans, which would save the PE firms, or by taking over their businesses, which might wipe out their investments, or by something in between, will have a direct impact on PE-fund returns and the ability of PE firms to raise much future money from investors.

There are problems, though, with any of these government approaches. Many of the larger companies that PE firms own have little chance of paying their loans, but they will not need to make any significant debt payments until 2012 or later. Ted Virtue, CEO of the PE firm MidOcean Partners, said, "I think you may have a lot of companies that are walking dead who have a huge burden of debt but have no trigger for creditors to take over and have very little liquidity to reinvest in their businesses. And that's not a healthy thing for the economy." As a result, by the time the government might attempt to rescue PE businesses, some might already be beyond repair.

Early intervention, however, is difficult. If the government wanted to invest enough money in PE-owned companies to really improve their operations before they completely collapse, it likely would need some concessions from the PE firms, whether it is shares or board seats, and PE firms are unlikely to relinquish control until necessary, because that would mean taking losses.

Even though PE firms are supposed to provide a fair valuation of their investments every quarter, the reality is that most are not very forthcoming. KKR, for example, at the end of the third quarter of 2008, claimed on its public filing that privately held hospital chain HCA's value had grown since they acquired it. But at the time, HCA's debt-to-cash flow multiple was equal to the cash flow multiple that some hospital companies were trading at in the stock markets, meaning that the company was not worth much more than the money it owed in loans. This indicated there was little value for KKR fund investors in HCA since their claims came after lenders.

Whatever approach the government might take, its resources are limited. So it can't bail out most of the roughly two thousand American PE-owned companies and the 7.5 million Americans working for them.

The Boston Consulting Group, which advises PE firms, in December 2008 predicted that almost 50 percent of PE-owned companies would probably default on their debt by the end of 2011, earlier than some other sources predict. It also believed there would be significant restructuring at these companies, leading to massive cost cuts and difficult layoffs.

If half of the PE-owned businesses go bankrupt and they fire half of their workers, that would leave 1.875 million Americans out of jobs. That is equal to about 70 percent of the 2.6 million Americans who lost their jobs in 2008, causing a massive drop in consumer spending.

By 2009, PE firms had begun negotiating with lenders to write off some of their loans, especially for the companies that couldn't even make 1 percent principal payments. But many of the businesses were so deeply in debt that a slight reduction was not going to change the eventual outcome.

As stated earlier, PE-owned companies, and not the funds, might also invest some of the little free cash they generate in buying back their own debt at a discount so they can reduce the amount they owe.

Some people suggested that the PE firms could put some of the $450 billion they have raised but not invested into their struggling businesses to stabilize operations. But it's unlikely that they will be willing to throw more money at investments that hold little potential. Besides, buyout funds investing in companies owned by prior funds typically need approval from the advisory committees of both funds, because there would be a conflict of interest between the two differ-ent sets of fund investors and that would be far from a sure thing.

No matter how bad the current recession turns out to be, eventu-ally easier credit will return. So while the public is focused on the dangers of leverage now, Congress has the chance to make tax-law changes that could prevent or at least greatly reduce the number of future damaging billion-dollar buyouts.

At an industry conference in June 2008, Carlyle cofounder David Rubenstein said the new president should think carefully before impos-ing new regulations and taxes "because we have a very good industry and we should be careful about changing it." He outlined what he would let the new president know about private equity if given the chance.

According to Rubenstein, the PE industry has been a vibrant part of the U.S. economy that has made American businesses more produc-tive. Its techniques, copied by non-PE companies, he said, contributed to twenty years of economic growth and innovation.

PE companies, Rubenstein maintained, aligned the interests of owners, managers, and employees, proving that capitalism works. He said they were also the principal source of high returns for pensions.

As an important player in the PE industry, Rubenstein may really believe that PE firms have done good things for America. But there is a lot of evidence that doesn't support his belief.

First, there's the track record. PE firms mostly buy healthy busi-nesses. These companies may not be on fast growth trajectories, but they can't get the financing for the buyouts unless they appear to have the ability to pay back the loans taken to finance the buyouts. PE firms do not target businesses that are losing money.

Yet half of the twenty-five companies that PE firms bought in the 1980s that borrowed more than $1 billion in junk bonds went bank-rupt. An investigation of the ten biggest buyouts of the 1990s, which was a decade of mainly ideal economic conditions, found that six of the ten businesses fared much worse than they likely would have had they not been acquired in LBOs. Two of those six went bankrupt. Three of the ten companies likely would have had a similar fate regardless of the buyout, and one PE firm actually improved its company (see the appendix).

This decade, predictions are that half of all PE-owned companies will collapse. The conclusion: PE firms have largely hurt their businesses in both good and difficult economic times.

Then there is the collateral damage. PE companies often reduce customer service and raise prices in order to pay debt. This hurts consumers, like hospital patients, and communities who rely on those businesses.

The actions by the PE firms often do raise operating cash flow, but not earnings when you factor in the interest the companies pay on debt. And eventually cash flow falls, because there is little focus on long-term growth. Meanwhile, principal payments loom. General Electric CEO Jeffrey Immelt, whose company finances buyouts, said that there was no magic to the way PE firms boost cash flow. "The vast majority of them only add value through financial rather than operational improvements." He said that almost any of his top managers could also nearly double cash flow if they were allowed to drop the reins on everything else.

All the cuts and the debt limit growth. Only two businesses acquired through leveraged buyouts that were not on the *Fortune* list of the 500 biggest companies when acquired were among the 250 biggest in 2008. The two were Aramark, which CEO Joseph Neubauer bought in a 1984 buyout in which management acquired 40 percent of the business, and Safeway Supermarkets, which KKR downsized during its ownership but which as a public company in the late 1990s grew by acquiring regional chains. Venture capitalists, meanwhile, can point to many businesses that made the chart, such as Google and the Staples retail chain.

By focusing on cutting costs, PE firms also starve their businesses of human capital. The comprehensive study led by University of Chicago professor Steven Davis examined buyouts of U.S. companies from 1980 through 2000, comparing them with similar companies in terms of industry, age, and size. Davis's group found that PE companies reduce jobs over their first two years of ownership by 3.6 percent more than their competitors, and according to the study, the worst job cuts happen in the third year after a buyout.

If PE companies used those savings to reinvest, this might make some economic sense. But they don't reinvest those savings, so the job cuts just weaken the businesses.

PE firms are not even earning superior returns for their investors, which are largely public pensions. Several academic studies show that PE firms generate net returns that are on par or worse than the Standard & Poor's 500 Stock Market Index. And unlike the stock market, PE firms lock investors in to twelve-year commitments with no ability to redeem their positions. Poor returns cause pensions to become more underfunded.

It is clear that PE firms hurt their businesses competitively, limit their growth, cut jobs without reinvesting the savings, and generate mediocre returns.

So despite what people in the private-equity industry claim, the only winners in private equity are the partners, who continually make money from guaranteed fees that the firms charge. Former U.S. Treasury secretary Nicholas Brady, who served under presidents Ronald Reagan and George H. W. Bush said in January 2009 that not much had changed since the buyout barbarians first appeared at the gate under his watch in the 1980s. PE firms still get large fees up front and are largely divorced from their results if their transactions fail.

The whole industry was started in order to take advantage of tax loopholes. It was not about, and never has been about, building strong, healthy companies.

Now might be the time to consider closing the loopholes.

When the first buyout boom ended badly in the late 1980s, Congress considered taking bold action. Nine congressional committees planned hearings on LBOs. Treasury Secretary Brady in January 1989 seemed to share some of Congress's concerns.

"While shareholders may . . ." walk away with "large premiums from an LBO, the corporation's employees, bond holders and the community in which the corporation is located may be adversely affected. Employees may lose their jobs if a corporation is forced to retrench or if divisions are sold in order to retire debt. Such job losses have significant collateral effects in the communities in which the employees work. [If LBOs] went to an extreme and we did this to the whole United States, I think it would be a bad thing," Brady concluded, in testimony before the U.S. Senate Committee on Finance.

Yet Dan Rostenkowski (D-IL), the chairman of the House Ways

and Means Committee, became frustrated with Brady when Treasury rejected twenty-five of the panel's twenty-seven ideas for curtailing LBOs and did not put forward any concrete measures to limit the practice: "The best you can do is tell us you are monitoring, and you are concerned?"

In the end, no major changes were made. Harvard professor Robert Reich, the future Clinton labor secretary, said at the time, "Congress and the administration were simply afraid to act, and the inhibitory mechanism was primarily Wall Street's connections with Washington." Read that: Buyout kings had the money to influence key politicians, like Brady's boss, President George H. W. Bush.

Today, twenty years later, legislation may not be much easier to pass—even with a reform-minded President Obama.

The U.S. House of Representatives Financial Services Committee held a May 2007 hearing, Private Equity's Effects on Workers and Firms, months before the credit crisis began. Massachusetts Democrat Barney Frank headed the committee. As the hearing opened, Congressman Frank said, "I assume the market is rational and that the private equity method increases value. I don't think people make deals in large numbers for no good reason." Soon after, the PE industry trotted out Jon Luther, CEO of Dunkin' Brands, the large Massachusetts company that owns Dunkin' Donuts and Baskin-Robbins, to explain how buyouts helped businesses. Frank was a big Dunkin' fan, a source said, and the softball questions to Luther undermined the seriousness of the hearings.

In the Senate, New York's Charles Schumer is the only Democrat who sits on the Banking and Finance committees, and he has often been dubbed the senator from Wall Street because of his connections there. Schumer heads the Democratic Senatorial Campaign Committee and was very successful at raising money from partners at PE firms.

In addition, four of the past eight Treasury secretaries joined the PE industry—James Baker (Carlyle), Nicholas Brady (started his own firm, Darby, to make international investments), Paul O'Neill (Blackstone), and John Snow (Cerberus)—and they have significant influence in Washington. President Bill Clinton, and both president Bushes have also advised PE firms or worked for their companies.

Besides them, current politicos and regulators, knowing that history and wanting to make fortunes after they leave office, may be reluctant to rein in the PE kings, as it would hurt their chances of future employment.

PE firms have some very high-powered lobbyists who are also pressing their case. KKR retained former Democratic House majority leader Richard Gephardt as a lobbyist and hired former Republican National Committee chairman Kenneth Mehlman as head of global public affairs.

The PE industry also knows people within the White House. At one time, Chief of Staff Rahm Emanuel interviewed for work at PE firm Madison Dearborn Partners, and MDP has donated more money to him over his career than any other contributor. To run the Small Business Administration, President Obama has tapped Karen Gordon Mills, a former managing director at PE firm Solera Capital, and in July 2009 nominated Jeffrey Goldstein, managing director at PE firm Hellman & Friedman, to be undersecretary for domestic finance at the Treasury. The president was set to name former Senate majority leader Tom Daschle as his health-care chief until it was discovered that he had not reported compensation he received as a consultant for PE firm InterMedia Advisors.

Still, after enough PE-owned companies go bankrupt, the public will be looking for answers. So it might be a good idea to consider some solutions proposed in the late 1980s.

In 1987 and 1989, members of Congress suggested closing the biggest LBO loophole, corporate tax deductions for interest payments. The provision was originally intended to encourage companies to borrow money for necessary expenses, not to take on debt to finance LBOs. This tax break actually gives PE firms an advantage when bidding against strategic buyers who make acquisitions with excess cash or stock. One 1980s proposal was to eliminate deductions for interest expense on debt used to acquire another company or to buy one's own business. The proposals never got the momentum needed for approval in Congress. However, there is precedent elsewhere.

After it became clear that buyouts were hurting its economy, Denmark on June 1, 2007, enacted a bill that reduced corporate deductible interest expenses annually to 20 million kroner ($4 million) provided other provisions were met.

Another idea would be establishing a law that encourages buyers of companies to hold on to them for at least five years. The proposal would be to give them an incentive to build long-term value. Government could impose a tax rate of, say, 45 percent, compared to the normal 35 percent, on any business that is acquired and resold within five years, and perhaps the higher rate might continue for a few years after the resale. This would cause buyers of those businesses to pay less. Because PE firms are basically the only ones quickly reselling businesses, no one else would be affected.

If Congress wanted, it, too, could limit the amount of money a company could borrow. Rand Araskog, ITT chairman, said in 1989 that a cap of a 50/50 debt-to-equity ratio would kill off LBOs.

There could also be federal restrictions on debt levels for companies in industries that are considered essential to the national interest, like health care, energy, and transportation. PE firms are very active in those sectors.

The state pensions, who are the biggest investors in buyout funds, also have leverage to change the industry. In 1989 New York governor Mario Cuomo called for the state to stop making new commitments to LBO funds until a state task force examined whether the industry put major corporations too deeply in debt and ignored the interest of their employees. Headed by Weil Gotschal lawyer Ira Millstein, the task force concluded that the state should stop investing in hostile buyouts or LBO funds in which it had no say over how its money was invested after committing to the fund so it was not unwittingly helping to fund buyouts that had an adverse effect on the state. But the state legislature never implemented the recommendations. New York has continued to invest in PE funds that maintain control over investment decisions, and at the end of 2008 had $10.3 billion, 6.7 percent of its $154 billion asset value, in alternative assets (much of which was in PE funds), and another $12.6 billion committed and not yet invested.

The Service Employees International Union, the largest health-care union, took matters into its own hands in Washington state. In July 2008, it petitioned the state legislature to introduce a ballot initiative that would require the state pension fund to consider the way a PE firm treats the employees at its companies before investing in its funds. Voters in other states could introduce initiatives to end private-equity investing altogether.

Of course, buyouts do not happen unless banks provide financing. From 2004 to 2007, commercial banks largely stopped considering whether PE companies could repay their loans, as long as the banks could resell loans and collect fees. Randal Quarles, the former undersecretary of the Treasury, said banks should be required to hold more of the risk, which would raise their reserve requirements: "When you divorce an actor from the consequences of his actions, that is a recipe for pathology in any form of human endeavor, and credit origination is no different."

Bill Isaac, the former FDIC chief, believes the government needs to get back in the business of regulating investment banks, which have been key to financing LBOs. In 2004 at the request of leading investment-bank executives, including Henry Paulson, who was then CEO of Goldman Sachs, the SEC allowed them to determine how much they needed to hold in reserves against loans. Isaac said many investment banks from 2004 to 2007 quadrupled their loan-to-reserve ratios as they constructed their own capital models. He believes the SEC needs to reinstate reserve requirements.

As for partners at PE firms, there is one suggested SEC regulation that would stop them in their tracks. Bank holding companies are required by the Federal Reserve to abide by the source-of-strength doctrine. This rule requires them to stand ready to invest available money in their banks during times of financial distress. The SEC could apply a similar rule to buyers in LBOs. If PE firms were required to be a source of strength when their companies falter, they would likely be much more careful in their acquisitions and management.

PE firms are currently unregulated, free of any government oversight. They are essentially invulnerable. President Obama in 2009 proposed a financial regulatory overhaul that included significant changes

to the PE industry, but none that would likely stop buyouts. He recommended requiring PE firms to register with the SEC. They would
then be subject to SEC examination and reporting requirements.

Another fairly simple thing that President Obama proposed in his
2009 budget was to raise taxes on the commissions PE firms make on
their buyout funds, called carried interest. Partners now pay the 15 percent capital-gains tax even though they have little or no money at risk
in their funds, instead of the 39.6 percent rate they would be paying if
commissions were considered ordinary income. A partner at one of the
largest PE firms told us, "I know 15 percent does not make sense; I have
told my colleagues to just accept it and move on." Unfortunately, while
it would help the government to collect more money, raising taxes on
profits and not making the actual investments less lucrative will not end
buyouts.

What is the downside of enacting tougher new laws and closing
loopholes? Not a lot.

Those small number of PE firms that really improve companies
could continue with little interference because they can earn money
without debt financing. Such changes would hurt only the majority
of PE firms that make fortunes by starving businesses while saddling
them with big debt burdens.

Having fewer PE firms in the game would mean that the owners of private companies looking to cash out, like Ronald Berg, who
owned Alpha Shirt, might have to look more into arranging employee
stock-ownership plans, in which the company borrows money to pay
the selling owner and ownership is transferred to the employees. Those
businesses might still have a lot of debt, but the employees would take
much better care of them than PE firms. And publicly traded companies that want to go private could just buy their own stock.

This is not an easy problem to solve. Even some people who see the
dangers of LBOs are for maintaining the status quo.

Former Treasury secretary Brady, speaking in January 2009, said
he would not propose tax-law changes to curb the industry. "PE firms
are not able to raise new money now to do LBOs. Maybe twenty-five
years from now when people have forgotten what happened, it will
happen again. In the meantime, I don't think there is anything to do

about it because no one will be investing this kind of money for buy-outs. The record of the LBO firms has not been that good."

Union leaders are the loudest voices calling for change, but they want the right to organize at PE-owned companies and seem to have little interest in ending buyouts altogether.

Not much is likely to happen until someone takes a leadership role to rally opposition to leveraged buyouts per se, which have had a very real, damaging impact on our economy for more than twenty-five years. One could reasonably argue that PE firms were significant con-tributors to the financial crisis that began in 2008, and they are defi-nitely the architects of the one that is coming by around 2012.

Joseph Rice, the PE pioneer who is chairman of Clayton, Dubilier & Rice, explained in 2007 what he would tell a critic who believed the government erred in giving PE firms a chance to regulate themselves after the 1980s: "We're going to see just how smart we have been, and if we come through this period of economic decline and everybody sails through it and the businesses are good and healthy and prosper, there will be the answer. If the businesses come up short, [if] they can't deal with the debt and we have a whole series of business fail-ures, then we didn't learn very much."

PE-owned companies are already collapsing, and tax-law changes are needed now to stop PE firms from investing so recklessly again. History has proven that regulation works.

During the 1980s buyout boom, Congress made tax-law changes so companies had to pay taxes on the gains they made from selling divi-sions of their businesses. As a result, few PE firms now buy businesses and sell off their assets, unless it is real estate or division sales that would result in losses. This has made the buy-and-bust strategy of the 1980s a thing of the past.

More recently, Congress enacted the Sarbanes-Oxley Act of 2002, forcing senior executives of public companies to certify that their busi-nesses are reporting accurate financial results. Despite its imperfec-tions, there have been no major public-company scandals like Enron since its adoption. Meanwhile, accounting frauds are becoming a reg-ular occurrence with unregulated hedge funds.

The price for inaction on buyouts has been huge.

- Because we didn't stop LBOs after the 1989 Congressional hearings, Oregon's pension authority was able to put 22 percent of its $42 billion of assets in buyout funds and now is at great risk of becoming severely underfunded. Many other pension funds are also exposed.
- The federal government lost roughly $70 billion in revenue from the companies acquired in buyouts in the 2000s that deducted bank interest from their taxes, and an additional $22.5 billion from 1990s deals.
- Between 2000 and 2008, perhaps half a million Americans lost their jobs for no reason other than that their employers needed to cut costs and pay back the money borrowed to finance leveraged buyouts.

Most important, there is the potential for the Next Great Credit Crisis, which could leave about 2 million of the 7.5 million Americans who work at PE-owned companies unemployed, and more than one thousand businesses bankrupt.

What if we do nothing now, since most of the actions that may cause the Next Great Credit Crisis have already happened?

I interviewed Carlyle's David Rubenstein, the self-appointed spokesperson for the PE industry, twice in 2007–8, once in his New York office, and asked him about the future of private equity. These were background talks, and in the end, he did not feel comfortable letting what he said be used on the record. However, he laid out his thoughts when speaking to his peers in December 2007 at the SuperReturn Middle East Conference at Jumeirah Emirates Towers, Dubai.

Private equity, he said, was going through a purgatory age, but it would be over by 2010. Then he foresaw a platinum age during which PE would be better capitalized, more resourceful, and politically sensitive. A reshaped, remodeled, chastened, and larger private-equity industry, he believed, would emerge. Why not? PE firms still had $450 billion to spend.

Rubenstein said that PE would come to be viewed as a mainstream activity and essential for the growth, enhanced productivity, and regeneration of the economies in which it operated. Basically, he was predicting that the Buyout of America would continue and spread through the rest of the world.

What a frightening thought!

For updates on the PE industry, including a list of PE-owned companies, and to comment on the book, please visit www.buyout ofamerica.com.

Acknowledgments

It seems to me I cannot make it in life on my own. I need others. And this book would not have been possible without help from the following:

First, my wife, Soma, who stood by me emotionally during the two years I worked full time on the book, giving me the freedom to find my stride. Thank you for believing in me and allowing me to pursue my goals.

Although he probably does not know it, my three-year-old son, Rahm, often kept my spirits up when it would have been easy to pack it in. He also helped me to believe in myself. I felt so much pride when he said, "Papa is leaving home to write book."

My mother initially gave me the idea to be a journalist and deserves credit as well as my father, who provided daily moral support, and Uncle Hira, who gave timely advice.

Outside the family, I'll start with Robert Dunn, who began with me on this book project more than a decade ago. After getting it jump-started, I turned to Charles Salzberg, who teaches a nonfiction writing class and became a mentor to me.

I soon joined writing groups led by Carol Rial and Tori Rowan. In one of those groups, roughly eight years ago, Bill Tipper came up with the title *The Buyout of America*.

My friend Sarah Wood introduced me to book editor Leah Spiro, who spent quality time with me preparing the book proposal. Her assistance was important.

I then made a cold call to Portfolio's publisher, Adrian Zackheim, to pitch the book. Zackheim returned the call. I appreciate the fact that he gave me a hearing. After Portfolio showed interest, I brought in agent Susan Rabiner, who has been an important ally since. Writing the book has been a challenge, and Susan helped me through some rough spots and provided great counsel. She also co-wrote several chapters and became a real advocate.

Soon after getting the contract, I worked with two freelance editors, Abigail Esman and Heather Chaplin, who both made important contributions.

Thanks also go to my Portfolio editor, Jeffrey Krames, who stuck with the project. Krames, when the book needed new direction, connected me with freelance editor Nancy Cardwell. She helped shape the final product and was a great collaborator.

The book would not have been possible without Nancy.

Once I submitted the book, I worked with Portfolio editor Jillian Gray and she, too, left her mark.

Appendix: The 1990s LBO Track Record

It's lunchtime at Citigroup's corporate headquarters in Midtown Manhattan. Four top private-equity barons are walking into the executive dining room where, away from the rest of the Citigroup employees, they wine and dine clients and, on occasion, explain the principles of what they do to skeptical reporters. On a cart behind the round dining table is salad, clam chowder, fruit, and an assortment of meats. A waiter in a suit is in constant attendance.

The leader of the group is Bill Comfort, who helped create the PE industry and in 1981 bought Aviall, a jet-engine-maintenance company, in the first Drexel Burnham Lambert buyout financed by junk bonds. Comfort is in his seventies and has the air of a man used to being at the top of the heap. He founded Citigroup's PE division, Citicorp Venture Capital (CVC) in 1979, and in 2006 he started his own PE firm, Court Square Capital Partners. (Citigroup still lets him use its executive dining room, although he is no longer employed by them.) Today Comfort, slim in a neat red sweater, is discussing the merits of the business with a couple of colleagues.

"On an overall basis, we just manage companies better," said David Thomas solemnly. He's a cofounder of Court Square and has been in the PE industry for about as long as Comfort. "We're very focused on profits, very focused on cash flow. And return on equity. So we simplify the objectives."

Comfort jumps in regarding the impossible-to-ignore question of private equity's practice of having the companies they buy borrow most of the money to fund the buyouts. He's got no problem with the topic; he believes that owing a lot of money helps businesses become more efficient. "You dump this debt on top of a company, and now you bring in a management team that does not understand or like debt," he said. "They will do everything possible to reduce that debt. You have changed their entire mindset."

Sometimes there's no better way to get at the truth than actually analyzing the facts. Comfort and his cohorts can talk all they want, but to really understand the potential—for good or ill—of leveraged buyouts, it's perhaps not entirely wise to rely on people who've amassed untold fortunes from them.

So I conducted a study of the largest ten buyouts of the 1990s, based on the list compiled by U.S. Bancorp Piper Jaffray and Securities Data Corporation. These LBOs were similar to the biggest deals that have taken place so far in the twenty-first century, both in terms of financial structure and the kinds of businesses being acquired. They offer perhaps the best way we have of understanding how buyouts affect companies in the long term.

The study allows for the benefit of time passed, which means there is no cherry-picking going on. The PE firms managed these businesses during relatively good economic times, so we can see how they fared under almost ideal circumstances. Examining these deals can help us determine if such seemingly sensible objectives—like "managing companies better"—really do go hand in hand with incentivizing managers by burdening them with mountains of debt.

Our analysis reveals a picture vastly different from the one that Comfort paints. Out of the ten deals, six companies were worse off than they likely would have been had they never been acquired in LBOs, three were largely unaffected, and only one fared better. What most of the buyouts have in common is that they made tens of millions for the private-equity firms that put them together.

TOP 10 LBOs of the 1990s

Company	PE-Induced Changes	Company Fared Better, Same, or Worse Than if Buyout Had Not Happened
General Instrument	Beat competitors in introducing new technology	*Better*
Experian	Quick flip	Same
ON Semiconductor	Grew half the business at the expense of the other	Same
Centennial Communications	Kept business strong enough to benefit from the cellular boom, but the debt stopped it from taking full advantage of what turned out to be great market conditions	Same
Riverwood International	Demand for paper products is falling and debt taken on to finance the buyout may sink the business	**Worse**
Borden	Changed business mix from food to housewares, and housewares side of business went bankrupt	**Worse**
Lin TV	Couldn't complete transition to mid-market strategy and left stranded with debt	**Worse**
Saks	Lost major ground to chief competitor	**Worse**
Valor Telecom	Customer service fell, along with company's valuation	**Worse**
Vertis	Didn't invest in business, which went bankrupt	**Worse**

Underinvesting

While all of the deals examined here have threads in common, they can also be broken into categories, based on how PE firms ran these companies differently than if they had not been bought in LBOs. For

example, as shown in the first three deals listed here, PE firms sometimes cut spending on upkeep and acquisitions more than the acquired
companies would have if they had followed their normal course.

1. Valor Telecom

Buyers: Vestar Capital Partners; Welsh, Carson, Anderson & Stowe;
Citicorp Venture Capital. *Cash Invested:* Roughly $300 million. *Company Borrowed:* $1.4 billion. *Year:* 1999. *Exit:* Windstream in 2006
bought Valor for $1.4 billion.

What came to be Valor Telecom was a group of GTE phone lines
in poor, rural areas in Arkansas, New Mexico, Oklahoma, and Texas.
Together, they provided service to about 520,000 homes and businesses.

Soon after the PE firms bought the business, revenue declined when
MCI WorldCom went bankrupt. Valor had been receiving 20 percent
of its overall revenue from long-distance providers, including MCI,
which it charged for access to its network so the long-distance companies' customers could complete interstate and intrastate long-distance
calls. Valor struggled.

With declining revenue, Valor scaled back its initial plans to expand
geographically, which was one way the PE firms intended to improve
the former GTE division. A source close to Valor said the company
considered, for example, buying US West's New Mexico phone lines for
several hundred million but dropped the idea. Valor did buy Kerville
Communications in 2002 for $128 million. GTE, which sold the lines,
was not building its rural line phone business but it was selling its lines,
and another buyer may have done more to expand the footprint.

Meanwhile Valor (see chapter 3) was letting its existing business
deteriorate. When the state of Texas approved the buyout, it did so on
the condition that Valor had to at least maintain the level of customer
service. In 2003 the Texas Public Utilities Commission concluded that
Valor was offering worse service than GTE and should stop using its bad
financial condition as an excuse. Valor had little choice but to comply.

Telephone operator Windstream bought Valor in 2006 for $1.4 billion, $300 million less than the price the PE firms had paid for the
business six years earlier.

A survey of peers in the same time period makes it hard to pin the company's troubles on the rural telecom market. In the years during its ownership by the PE consortium, Valor lost 18 percent of its value. Its competitor, Citizens Communications, on the other hand, grew 5 percent (from a valuation of $7.4 billion in fall 2000 to $7.78 billion in mid-2006.). Valor's customer base also remained stagnant. **What became Valor likely would have done better under another rural telecom company than it did under PE ownership.**

Comfort, pioneer of the LBO, is happy to talk about Valor. "It wasn't all that bad for the company," he recalled. But perhaps his memory is tainted by the fact the PE firms earned 1.6 times their money; Vestar and Welsh Carson each put in roughly $130 million and came out with more than $200 million. **Partly this was because some of the investment was in preferred shares that carried a guaranteed rate of return.**

2. Vertis

Buyer: Thomas H. Lee Company, Evercore Capital Partners. *Cash Invested:* $450 million. *Company Borrowed:* $1.5 billion. *Year:* 1999. *Exit:* Vertis filed for bankruptcy in June 2008.

The chairman of publicly traded printing company Big Flower, Ted Ammon, in 1998 sought to increase the value of his shares by breaking up the business—which had newspaper-insert, direct-marketing, and graphics-software divisions—into several publicly traded companies, by merging some of those divisions with competitors, or by selling all of Big Flower to one buyer.

PE firm Thomas H. Lee Company saw a major player in several sectors and led a $1.9 billion buyout of the entire business, renaming it Vertis. Lee already had a graphics business it planned to combine with the competing Vertis division, and the rest of the plan was expansion through acquisitions in the niches where Big Flower competed.

Probably any party that had bought part or all of Big Flower would have had a similar strategy.

Thomas H. Lee co-president Scott Sperling didn't anticipate, however, as the late 1990s became the twenty-first century, the rise of desktop publishing and the cutbacks on print advertising that sharply reduced sales. According to Sperling, the plan quickly changed to one of simply sustaining profitability and to "play out the rest of it until such time that the printing industry got better." Vertis slashed the money it spent on capital expenditures like new presses, from $115 million in 1999 to $40 million in 2002.

As Dr. Joe Webb, founding partner of PrintForecast.com, points out, there were real opportunities for Vertis—had its owner been strategically minded. Without its debt, it would have been poised at just the right time to grow internationally, where the industry was still flourishing, or through acquisitions.

When the buyout happened in 1999, Vertis was the fifth-largest printer in North America. By 2006, it was ninth, according to *Printing Impressions* magazine. Revenues dwindled during those years from $1.8 billion to $1.5 billion. The actual 17 percent decline in revenue could be attributed to merging the graphics-software business, which accounted for 20 percent of Vertis's sales, with another Thomas H. Lee company and then selling the combined business. But in the same span, its peers did better, giving some indication of how a trade buyer would have done with the business.

Printer R. R. Donnelley saw sales rise from $5 billion to $8.43 billion, because its management used the downturn in the industry to buy printers that offered other services, which gave it the ability to become a one-stop shop for clients. Valassis, a smaller competitor in the free-standing insert space, grew its sales from $795 million to $1.13 billion during the same time.

Vertis, though, collapsed, filing for bankruptcy in July 2008. The company then merged with peer American Color Graphics. **Clearly, the business, or parts of it, would have received more investment and been better off had the LBO never happened.**

3. Saks Inc.

Buyer: Investcorp. *Cash Invested:* $600 million. *Company Borrowed:* $900 million. *Year:* 1990. *Exit:* Proffitt's bought Saks in 1998 for $1.5 billion.

In 1990, Investcorp's founder and CEO, Namir Kirdar, got a hankering for a trophy property, a landmark investment that would seal his reputation as PE dealmaker extraordinaire. When British conglomerate B.A.T. Industries put the Saks retail chain up for sale, Kirdar's firm was one of several players who competed fiercely to buy the business. The retailer Dillard's and Japan's Tobu Department Stores Co. also expressed interest.

Buying it in a $1.5 billion LBO, Investcorp paid a 13.5-times-EBIT (Earnings Before Interest and Taxes) multiple for Saks. This is not unlike the inflated prices PE groups paid in 2006–7. (By comparison, private-equity firms TPG and Warburg Pincus bought Neiman Marcus in October 2005 for $5 billion, which represents less than a 12-times-EBIT multiple.)

Investcorp had trouble with Saks from the very beginning. The recession of the early 1990s hit the retailer hard, and many of its locations were in the Northeast, which was particularly affected. Saks, which had big debt payments to make, did not improve its tired stores or update its image, and better-funded competitor Neiman Marcus beat it badly when they competed in the same markets.

It's likely that if Dillard's or Tobu had bought Saks, it would have not been as deeply in debt and would have been better able to at least maintain its market share.

The recession ravaged Saks, but by 1996 Investcorp felt the company was strong enough to list on the New York Stock Exchange. Shares rose in early 1997 to $33. Considering that Investcorp had paid what amounted to $20 a share, it looked good on paper. But really, the buyout had generated less than a 10 percent compounded annual rate of return. For your average citizen, this may be perfectly decent, but PE firms tell their investors they will deliver better than 20 percent returns to justify their annual 2 percent management fees.

Seven years after the initial 1990 deal and one year after taking the company public, Kirdar held a meeting with the firm's lead partners to decide whether to get out, said a source with knowledge of the situation. PE firms like to sell their investments within five years, and it was time for Investcorp to exit.

Though the majority of partners voted that they should sell and take their modest profit, Kirdar overruled them, and Saks instead continued an aggressive, albeit woefully unfocused, expansion plan. Investcorp moved Saks into cities unlikely to support upscale retailers. It tried many different things at once, like launching stores within stores, such as an Armani-branded corner. According to the source, opening the Armani shops was not an inherently bad idea, but it should have been test-marketed first, and if successful, implemented nationally. Kirdar did not wait.

The expansion failed miserably.

The next year, 1998, Investcorp sold Saks to Southern retail chain Proffitt's in a deal valued at $1.5 billion, the same price it had fetched in the 1990 leveraged buyout. Proffitt's, which renamed itself Saks, in fall 2005 had an enterprise value of roughly $2.3 billion; far below the $5 billion PE firms paid in fall 2005 for Neiman Marcus. Yet in 1991, Neiman Marcus was slightly smaller than Saks and not that profitable. **Conclusion: A retailer like Dillard's or Tobu would have taken better care of Saks.**

Changing Direction

Another big theme that emerges is how PE firms sometimes quickly move companies into new lines of business (and/or exit certain divisions) in an attempt to boost profits beyond what they would have been without the buyout.

1. Borden

Buyer: Kohlberg Kravis Roberts & Co. *Cash Invested:* $1.9 billion stock swap for RJR Nabisco shares. *Year:* 1995. *Exit:* Apollo Management in 2004 bought what was left of Borden, its chemicals business, for $1.2 billion; Borden's appliance division, World Kitchen, in 2002 filed for bankruptcy protection.

After their much-publicized 1989 takeover of RJR Nabisco, the leveraged-buyout kings at Kohlberg Kravis Roberts (KKR) found themselves with a problem. They had taken the company back public in 1991 and by 1995 still held a 40 percent stake that they knew would be hard to sell over time without causing the share price to plummet. The strategy became to find a company it could purchase through a stock swap. KKR settled on Borden Inc., which it bought for $1.9 billion worth of RJR Nabisco stock, a modest premium to Borden's shares.

Borden was a heavily in-debt conglomerate made up of five divisions—Wise potato chips, Borden/Meadow Gold Dairies, Borden Chemicals, and packaging and plastic-film subsidiaries. PE firms are often attracted to just this sort of disorganized hodgepodge of businesses connected under one roof. It gives them the opportunity to sell off underperforming assets and use the proceeds to pay down debt and build up single divisions, which can then be brought to the public markets as new entities. If it remained a publicly traded company, Borden would have likely not moved as quickly to change its business.

KKR refocused Borden, quickly sold off all but the chemicals division, and then started looking around for something to buy with part of the sale proceeds. In 1998, it bought Corning Consumer Products (known for Corningware dishes) in a $603 million leveraged buyout. In the following year, it acquired General Housewares for $145 million and Ecko Group for $310 million, creating a giant housewares business rechristened World Kitchen, which included the brands Corelle and OXO.

Peter Campanella, president of Corning Consumer Products, said at the time he was glad to be acquired by Kohlberg Kravis Roberts, or any private-equity firm, for that matter. He figured it was better than merging with competitor Newell, which had also been sniffing around, since he would be able to continue running the business with little interference.

Be careful what you wish for.

"There were more people looking over my shoulder than I had in thirty years working for Corning," Campanella said, which included providing weekly forecasts, although the nature of the business, which sold products to Asia and big retailers, did not lend itself to that kind of short-term planning. The pressure most PE firms put on their management teams, especially right after they buy a business, can be greater than anything they will experience working for a publicly traded company. Sometimes it can backfire.

In April 2000, only two years after the takeover he'd supported, Campanella unexpectedly quit, partially because he did not like being micromanaged. Then KKR hired Nathaniel Stoddard, who relocated the headquarters from Corning, New York, to Virginia. (There was not a single factory, office, or employee in Virginia.) World Kitchen was a new company that required computer systems linking the acquired businesses, and Stoddard struggled to get it synchronized and had a hard time tracking inventory. Within a year, KKR replaced him with Steven Lamb, who oversaw World Kitchen's May 2002 bankruptcy filing. Campanella, for his part, said World Kitchen was profitable when he left. KKR's strategy had failed. Mergers are always difficult, but in this case the speed demanded in pumping profits and combining companies pushed World Kitchen too far.

Meanwhile, Borden Chemicals, the only other business inside Borden, supplied adhesives for plywood. Since the stock swap, its revenue had risen by 50 percent, roughly double the rate of inflation. In 2004, KKR sold the chemicals division to fellow PE-firm Apollo Management for about $1.2 billion—all that was left of a company it had valued at $1.9 billion.

Borden was not in any high-growth industries before the sale to KKR, but I am judging that the business would have been better off on its own.

2. LIN TV

Buyer: Hicks, Muse, Tate & Furst. *Cash Invested:* $600 million. *Company Borrowed:* $1.4 billion. *Year:* 1998. *Exit:* Company is in danger of defaulting on its loans.

Like KKR, PE firm Hicks Muse changed the direction of LIN TV and did it quickly. The firm won a contest to buy the business in a bidding war over Raycom Media, which owned twenty-five television stations. So if Hicks Muse had not bought LIN, it would have become part of privately held Raycom.

Tom Hicks of Hicks Muse had grand plans for his big foray into television. He wanted to grow the company from eleven to one hundred stations in five years. Having done well with his radio empire, comprising Capstar Broadcasting and Chancellor Media, Hicks expected to follow the same proven strategy, which was to use LIN to acquire more stations, consolidate, and reduce costs, and all as quickly as possible.

Problems emerged almost immediately, when his planned merger between LIN, Capstar, and Chancellor failed to fly on Wall Street, where analysts feared the television company would drag down the high-flying (at the time) radio stocks.

Undeterred, Hicks shifted the company's focus away from the bigger cities, where it already competed—and stations are expensive—and toward smaller markets where Hicks could purchase several channels in the same market, cut back on spending, merge staffs, and improve earnings. He sold most of LIN's stake in what had been its flagship station—Dallas-based KXAS—and bought in places like Columbus, Ohio; Albuquerque, New Mexico; and Mobile, Alabama.

The timing for LIN turned out to be wrong all the way around. National advertisers since 2003 cut back more in smaller markets than the larger ones LIN TV had focused on. Besides, it became hard to make multiple acquisitions in the same market because the regulatory constraints mandating that there be eight separate TV owners in a market didn't come off as anticipated. Other broadcasters, too, started developing similar acquisition strategies, because with new automation, it was relatively cheap to run several stations from the same broadcast center, providing competition when bidding for available stations, and raising the prices for those assets.

By 2009, LIN had only grown to twenty-seven stations, nowhere near the initial goal of one hundred.

Hicks Muse listed LIN on the New York Stock Exchange and after ten years of owning the business still controlled a 45 percent stake. LIN in 2007 sought a buyer and could not get the price it wanted. That was unfortunate, considering that LIN owed $760 million in loans. Standard & Poor's in March 2009 raised the possibility the company might break conditions in its loan agreements in late 2009 and file for bankruptcy.

LIN recently was spending much of its time trying to get cable systems to pay for airing their local television stations, so it could generate some much-needed money. Meanwhile, Raycom, also focusing on smaller markets, in 2008 spent about $10 million building a new Myrtle Beach, South Carolina, NBC affiliate from scratch and, even with advertising down across the industry, was still selectively buying stations. **The LIN stations probably would have had more**

access to funding and been better off in general if Raycom owned them.

3. ON Semiconductor

Buyer: TPG (formerly the Texas Pacific Group). *Cash Invested:* $338 million. *Company Borrowed:* $1.23 billion. *Year:* 1999. *Exit:* Company is now publicly traded, and as of January 2009 had a $2.6 billion enterprise value (shares plus debt minus cash).

In the late 1990s, Motorola was not investing much in ON. The division made sixteen thousand different varieties of low-tech chips, many selling for as low as a dollar a pop and handling such prosaic jobs as powering home appliances or timing the ignition spark in cars. Motorola planned to spin out the division to shareholders or sell it. PE firms and at least one semiconductor maker likely took interest in buying the business.

TPG saw a potential stand-alone company in a booming industry. With a bit of tinkering, ON could grow, maximize profits, *and* handle a mountain of debt, it figured.

ON was broken into three parts: 45 percent of revenue came from component (also called discrete) chips, which are simple transistors, maybe 35 percent from chips that power devices, and the other 20 percent from analog chips that are integrated circuits. Plans were to change the ratio of analog to component chips produced—analog had profit margins of about 40 percent as opposed to 20 percent for component. In August 1999, TPG bought ON from Motorola, and had ON borrow more than $1.2 billion, 75 percent of the purchase price.

The first year was great. TPG raised ON's research and development budget—the lifeline of a successful semiconductor business—from 5 percent of revenue to 6.5 percent. It also took ON public on the NASDAQ in 2000—though instead of pumping the money from share proceeds back into the business, the owners took $228 million of $515 million, 44 percent, for themselves and used the rest to pay some of the company's debt.

When 2001 came and with it the dot-com bust, the foolishness of that move became abundantly clear. Suddenly customers, like telecom equipment maker Nortel, which bought Internet routers, were cutting their orders, and annual revenue dropped from $2.1 billion in 2000 to $1.2 billion the next year. This would be an unpleasant state of affairs for any company, but for ON, which had $1.4 billion in debt to service, it was life or death. To its credit, TPG pumped $100 million into the company by buying stock, giving lenders enough confidence not to force ON into bankruptcy. (TPG later converted the investment into 49 million shares when the stock was trading near $6, giving them roughly four times their money back in five years.)

The $100 million was a life raft, though, not a solution, as the company was still seriously weakened by the industry downturn and shackled to its debt payments. TPG was left choosing which of ON's businesses to fund, component or analog, because it could not afford to develop new products for both sides. ON basically stopped investing much in component or power-chip R & D, and with a sudden glut of chips on the market, it had no choice but to drop prices right along with everyone else. Still, it needed the revenue it generated from component and power chips to fund analog R & D, so it did not sell the component side of the business.

Competitors were investing more in R & D so that when the downturn ended, they'd be ready with new products to bring to market. Once prices get slashed, they rarely go back up, which is why it's so vital to have new chips to introduce that can be sold at higher prices. By not investing in research for component chips, ON was effectively killing its own chance of playing catch-up when the semiconductor industry recovered—a particularly painful dilemma when one recalls that just around the bend was a slew of new electronic gadgets, like iPods, that needed component chips.

However, analog chips—the other side of the business—continued to grow. In 2005, analog revenue was $560 million. Analog then also accounted for almost half of ON's overall sales.

In other words, TPG succeeded in changing the ratio of analog chips. But overall sales actually dropped from $1.79 billion to $1.5 billion between 1999, the year the buyout happened, and year-end 2006, months before the PE firm sold the last of its shares. Competitors such as International Rectifier and Vishay Intertechnology spent 2001 and

2002 planting the seeds for the re-emergence of the semiconductor businesses. Unencumbered by crushing debt, they were able to significantly raise their revenues. International Rectifier became solely an analog maker and grew from a $545 million company in 1999 to a $1.32 billion one in 2006.

Looking at enterprise value (shares plus debt minus cash), International Rectifier during the same time period rose from $922 million to $2.7 billion, almost a 300 percent increase. ON's rose from $1.6 billion at the time of the LBO to $4 billion in 2006, a smaller increase of 250 percent.

Vishay, which focused on component chips in that span, saw its enterprise value rise from $1.8 billion to $2.6 billion, a smaller increase than ON.

I believe ON might have fared better or worse without the buyout. The change in product mix, which helped, might not have happened otherwise, but also, another owner—or ON if it had been a free-standing company—might have done a better job with the component side or at least sold it before it lost market share.

While I give ON a mixed grade, conditions are changing. Since TPG exited in 2006, ON expanded, making several acquisitions that have helped build the business. Meanwhile, the company at the beginning of 2009 still carried $1.2 billion in debt and announced that it would reduce planned capital expenditures to $50 million to $60 million from normalized yearly levels of approximately $130 million to $140 million. During challenging economic times, it again has to contend with the burdensome loans that date back to the TPG buyout.

4. General Instrument

Buyer: Forstmann Little & Co. *Cash Invested:* $182 million. *Company Borrowed:* $1.35 billion. *Year:* 1990. *Exit:* GI listed its shares in 1992, and Motorola bought GI in 2000 for $17 billion.

Forstmann Little & Co. has the distinction of being the only PE firm that led a Top 10 buyout of the 1990s in which it likely left the business in a better condition than it would have been otherwise.

In 1990, Forstmann Little orchestrated a $1.5 billion buyout of

General Instrument. If it had not been sold, the CEO likely would have bought shares of the public company and taken it private himself.

At the time of the buyout, GI was a conglomerate making products as disparate as racetrack tote boards, and defense electronics. The PE firm shed the less profitable divisions, cut costs, and focused on just four business lines, cable TV set-top boxes, satellite TV equipment, cable wires, and semiconductors. Forstmann Little concentrated on what became growth areas. GI, through the satellite division, developed the first digital cable box, which allowed cable companies to fit more channels in cable boxes and sell pay-per-view movies.

This investment got off to a rocky start as Forstmann Little hired former defense secretary Donald Rumsfeld as its first General Instrument CEO and then after a few years, quietly forced him out when the company was struggling. In the end, though, GI played a major role in the late-1990s cable TV boom, and the PE firm deserves credit for taking it there (see chapter 8).

Trapping Companies

Sometimes the main reason PE firms leave businesses in worse shape than they would have been otherwise is because they weigh them down with so much debt that they cannot free themselves in time to stay competitive against their peers.

1. Centennial Communications

Buyers: Welsh, Carson, Anderson & Stowe; Blackstone Group. *Cash Invested:* $414 million. *Company Borrowed:* Almost $1.5 billion. *Year:* 1999. *Exit*: AT&T agreed to buy Centennial in November 2008 for $2.8 billion.

PE firms Welsh, Carson, Anderson & Stowe and the Blackstone Group bought publicly traded Centennial Communications in a $1.9 billion LBO just as a huge boom in national cellular usage started. They left a nominal number of shares trading on the NYSE so Centennial remained a publicly traded company. In this story, there is a painful theme of opportunity lost.

Century Communications had owned more than 30 percent of Centennial and was considering ways to generate cash, including selling its Centennial stake. Centennial took matters into its own hands and found a buyer. If it had not, Centennial founder, Rudy Graf, said he would have likely tried to merge the company with a competitor like Western Wireless.

Centennial's debt doubled after the buyout, and the company became much more focused on increasing its cash flow in order to make loan payments.

The PE firms expected the regional cellular phone company to eventually lose the bulk of its profits that came from roaming charges it billed to carriers who did not provide coverage in its footprint area of Indiana, Michigan, and Louisiana, because the FCC sold new licenses in some of Centennial's markets to national players like AT&T. Once they built their own systems, the carriers would no longer need to pay Centennial to allow their customers to make and receive calls in Centennial's markets.

Initially the plan was to collect the cash from roaming profits to reduce debt as long as possible and then, when the roaming revenue fell, to hold on until cellular usage in its areas grew so much that it would compensate for the lost revenue. But the drop in roaming revenue happened in about eighteen months and was so steep it almost forced Centennial into bankruptcy.

No question, it was a challenging time for all regional carriers. The thing to remember, though, is that there was also great opportunity. From 1999 to 2007, national cellular phone use nearly tripled.

Right before the buyout, in a move predicting the growth in cellular use to come, Centennial had built a network in Puerto Rico, whose cash flow rose in 1999 from $10 million to $50 million. Because things seemed to be going so well, the PE owners began to extend Centennial's Caribbean presence, buying phone licenses in the Dominican Republic and Jamaica, as well as a Puerto Rican cable television operator. When roaming revenue fell, Centennial stopped its Caribbean development.

In 2003 its PE owners considered putting more cash in the business but then pulled out of financing talks. Centennial at the same time borrowed $500 million at 10.125 percent annual interest, which it could not prepay until June 2008 without incurring expensive penalties.

A few years later, cellular usage rose to the point that, as projected, it compensated for the roaming loss. Still, the PE owners chose not to resume their Caribbean expansion because they were ready to sell Centennial. Failing to find a buyer in 2005 willing to meet their price (which included paying lenders the penalty for early payment), the company in early 2006 borrowed $557 million to issue its owners a dividend, strapping the company again.

The company was slow to roll out new digital cellular technology as it lacked the funds to convert all its analog customers at once.

Centennial, overall, still succeeded in growing its customer base and stayed strong in its best market, Fort Wayne, Indiana. From 1999 to 2008, the number of Centennial customers rose from 454,000 to 1.1 million, which was not equal to the growth in the industry overall but enough to keep it in the ball game. (Cellular phone use was nearly tripling during this time.) AT&T agreed to buy the business in 2008, just as the prepayment penalty expired, for $2.8 billion. That seems fine until one looks at the competition.

Dobson Communications was smaller than Centennial in 2000, with 354,000 users, and teamed with AT&T Wireless in 2000 to buy another player, American Cellular. In 2007, AT&T Wireless acquired Dobson for $5.1 billion, 45 percent more than what it paid for Centennial one year later.

Or take Rural Cellular. It was less than half the size of Centennial in 1999, with 187,000 subscribers. By 2000, however, it had doubled its customer base with smart acquisitions (Triton Cellular, in particular) and by the end of 2006 had 706,000 subscribers. Verizon Wireless in 2007 bought Rural Cellular for $2.67 billion, close to what AT&T paid for Centennial.

I am ruling that the company did not clearly do better or worse than if the buyout had not happened. The PE firms did keep Centennial relevant enough in its core markets to benefit from the cellular boom, but the debt they put on the company stopped it from taking full advantage (for example, by growing its Caribbean or U.S. operations) of what turned out to be great market conditions.

The PE firms, over the course of their ten-year investment, did very well. Welsh, Carson, Anderson & Stowe made about a 165 percent gain on its $550 million investment, when one includes the loans it made to Centennial Communications along with its share of the down payment to buy the company. Blackstone posted about a 160 percent gain on the $138 million it invested.

2. *Riverwood International*

Buyer: Clayton, Dubilier & Rice; EXOR Group S.A.; Brown Brothers Harriman & Co.; Singapore-based HWH Investment Pte. Ltd.; Chase Capital Partners; First Plaza Group Trust through General Motors Investment Management Co.; Madison Dearborn Capital Partners. *Cash Invested:* $750 million. *Company Borrowed:* $2.05 billion. *Year:* 1996. *Exit:* Merged in 2003 with publicly traded Graphic Packaging International, taking the Graphic name. Riverwood after the merger held 67 percent of combined entity. Graphic in 2007 then merged with TPG's Altivity Packaging in a $1.75 billion deal, keeping the name Graphic Packaging.

In March 1996, PE firm Clayton, Dubilier & Rice (CD&R) led a $2.8 billion buyout of packaging company Riverwood International, which largely made six-pack cartons for beer and soda. Its team outbid Georgia Pacific in the auction to buy the company from bankrupt Manville Corp., so if the buyout hadn't happened GP would have absorbed Riverwood.

The only other major competitor in the beer and soda six-pack carton space was MeadWestvaco. The two split the market between them.

While beverage cartons (coated kraft paperboard) represented two thirds of sales, brown boxes (containerboard) was the rest. The plan was to move the business further into coated kraft paperboard, which was thought to be less prone to swings in paper prices than brown boxes. Transforming Riverwood would mean expanding sales beyond the soda and beer market to items like boxes that house Mattel toys.

CD&R believed coated kraft board was immune to timber price swings because there were few manufacturers of the specialized product, and steady revenue from customers like Coca-Cola for its six-pack containers would make it easy for Riverwood to pay the more than $2 billion it had borrowed to fund the buyout. A year after the deal, paper prices fell, and beer and beverage makers unexpectedly forced Riverwood to lower prices.

Other problems emerged. Soda companies soon started selling two-liter bottles and fewer six-packs. As it turned out, the coated kraft paperboard market was not so great. In 2003, CD&R merged Riverwood with similar-size publicly traded Graphic Packaging International, hoping that taking Riverwood public through the merger might give it the ability to sell its shares.

But the market saw it as a merger of two struggling companies, and the share price languished. Graphic in 2007 then merged with TPG's Altivity Packaging in a $1.75 billion deal, keeping the name Graphic Packaging. CD&R holds Graphic shares twelve years later, and the Riverwood side is worth much less than at the time of the 1996 buyout.

Riverwood has not lost or gained much market share in beverage packaging against MeadWestvaco. One would assume that Georgia Pacific would have fared the same with Riverwood's beverage boxes, and that because GP was already big in containerboard, it would have done a much better job with that smaller side of the business.

Meanwhile, Riverwood's parent, Graphic Packaging, is in trouble. Demand for paper products during the recession is falling, and the combined Graphic Packaging in January 2009 had $3.25 billion in debt and only generated $140 million in operating cash flow. The company was struggling to survive the recession.

In 2005, privately held Koch bought Georgia Pacific for $21 billion, and Koch is likely better positioned to invest in the former Riverwood operations through the recession than Graphic Packaging. **Riverwood probably would have been better off had Georgia Pacific acquired the business.**

Experian Credit

Buyer: Bain Capital, Thomas H. Lee Partners. *Cash Invested:* $200 million. *Company Borrowed:* $900 million. *Year:* 1996. *Exit:* Great Universal Stores bought Experian Credit in 1996 for $1.7 billion.

Occasionally PE firms buy and sell a company in such a short period of time that they have little impact on it. When Thomas H. Lee Partners got together with Mitt Romney's Bain Capital in 1996 to buy TRW's Experian credit-reporting system, nobody could have foretold what would happen. The plan was to quickly grow the business through acquisitions, cut costs, and sell.

While still closing the Experian deal, the PE firms were looking to buy Great Universal Stores' British-based credit-reporting business to combine with it. Great Universal Stores had just gone through a management change, and the new owner, when approached, told the PE suitors, "Instead of us selling to you, how about if we buy you?" Thomas H. Lee Co-President Scott Sperling said from the couch in his Boston office.

According to Sperling, he and his partners came up with what they thought was a ludicrously high price for Experian—$1.7 billion, when they'd signed a deal to buy Experian for $1.1 billion. Still, Great Universal Stores said yes, and Thomas H. Lee Partners and Bain Capital, which had put down a combined $200 million in the buyout, in a matter of weeks, resold the business and walked away with $800 million.

Notes

Prologue

3   **angering clients:** Josh Kosman, "DecisionOne Files Chapter 11," *TheDeal.Com*, February 14, 2000 and author interview 2000.

4   **thousand listed companies:** "The Global Economic Impact of Private Equity Report 2008," World Economic Forum, January 2008, 15.

4   **roughly ten million people:** University of Chicago Professor Steven Davis, who conducted a study on PE and U.S. employment, told us in 2008, "It's reasonable to think that since 2000 and the first half of 2007 something close to one-tenth of the private sector workforce has worked for PE-owned companies." The total private sector employment number comes from the Bureau of Labor Statistics.

5   **3,800 from 5,300:** Based on a Time Warner press release of November 24, 2003, announcing the sale of Warner Music, which listed an approximate number of Warner Music's employees, and Warner Music's Annual Report for the Period Ending September 30, 2007, which listed the number of part- and full-time employees.

5   **$1.2 billion in dividends:** Ed Christman, "WMG Issues Third Investor Return," *Billboard.com*, January 8, 2005.

6   **saving through cost cuts:** PE firms took out $1.2 billion in dividends, and Warner Music made $270 million in cost cuts in its first year (the year it made the most significant changes to the business). If one multiplies the $270 million in savings by the four years the PE firms had run the business, it equals $1.08 billion, an amount less than the $1.2 billion in dividends the PE firms declared from Warner Music.

Introduction

7   **million workers:** Robert E. Scott, "The High Price of 'Free Trade,'" Economic Policy Institute Briefing Paper, November 17, 2003.

8   **outstanding subprime mortgages:** "Will Subprime Mess Ripple Through Economy," Associated Press, March 13, 2007.

8   **by the end of 2011:** "Get Ready for the Private Equity Shakeout," Boston Consulting Group, December 2008, 4.

8   **and difficult layoffs:** ibid., 6.

8   **transactions with private-equity firms:** Global Credit Comment: Private Equity Swirling in the Eye of the Storm," Standard & Poor's, November 2008, 1.

9   **3.4 times over:** Bain & Co. senior partner Hugh MacArthur presentation at *Private Equity Analyst* conference held at New York's Grand Hyatt Hotel, September 16, 2008.

9   **of a golden age:** Peter Moreira, "Kravis: A Failure to Communicate," *TheDeal.com*, May 29, 2007.

10 **45 percent since 2000:** "Average Purchase Price and Equity Contribution by Sponsors of All Leveraged Buyout Loans 1997–1Q2008," Standard & Poor's.

10 **33 percent in 2007:** "Average Sources of Proceeds for All Leveraged Buyouts 1999–1Q2008," Standard & Poor's.

10 **to fund the buyout:** Owner of TXU debt told us, "We knew it would never produce the money from cash to make principal."

11 **by a considerable amount:** Claire Poole, "TXU Foes' Unlikely Friend in Austin," *TheDeal.com*, March 6, 2007.

11 **would repay its loans:** Remarks of James A. Baker, PR Newswire, April 11, 2007.

11 **"Vote no on the buyout":** Elizabeth Souder and Vasanth Sridharan, "Shareholders Approve TXU Sale," *Dallas Morning News*, September 9, 2007.

12 **was coming due in 2014:** Rebecca Smith and Peter Lattman, "Buyout of Utility Generates Texas-Sized Losses," *WSJ.com*, March 4, 2009.

12 **U.S. employers:** SEIU press release, "Private Equity Buyout Industry Gets Its Facts Wrong," July 11, 2008.

13 **went bankrupt:** "Masonite Sales Sliding on Loss of Major Client," *TorontoStar.com*, August 10, 2007.

13 **two years of ownership:** "The Global Economic Impact of Private Equity Report 2008," World Economic Forum, January 2008 (thorough

study done of net job loss for PE-owned companies versus peers from 1980 through 2003), 52.

13   **research and development:** Energy Future Holdings 10-Q for period ending September 30, 2008, comparing predecessor and successor capital expenditures.

13   **paying its principal:** interview with the owner of the TXU debt.

13   **through September 2006:** "Private Equity: Tracking the Largest Sponsors," Moody's Investors Service, February 2008.

14   **in unspent capital:** "Get Ready for the Private Equity Shakeout," Boston Consulting Group, December 2008, 8.

Chapter 1. How Private Equity Started

19   **of the tax code:** John Canning, chairman of the PE firm Madison Dearborn Partners and a former banker at First Chicago who helped arrange financing for Kohlberg's early deals, told us, "All of the tax gimmicks really were the reason leveraged buyouts first [happened]. . . . This was something the KKR guys discovered. It was really driven by tax benefits."

20   **a twenty-two times return:** Confirmed through Jerome Kohlberg assistant Barbara Martz and first reported by Sarah Bartlett in *The Money Machine: How KKR Manufactured Power & Profits*, Warner Books, 1991.

21   **financing leveraged buyouts:** Connie Bruck, *The Predators' Ball*, Penguin Books, 1989, 100.

22   **lifeline to the S&Ls:** interview with a cohead of a large private-equity firm.

22   **reluctance to sell:** Bartlett, *The Money Machine*, 158.

22   **discussions with Beatrice:** George Anders, *Merchants of Debt: KKR and the Mortgaging of American Business*, Beard Books, 2002, 68.

22   **of $8.7 billion:** David Carey, "Mediocrity at the Gates," *TheDeal.com*, June 1, 2001.

22   **divesting those pieces:** Anders, *Merchants of Debt*, 71.

22   **for the entire company:** Adding up sales of spun-out E-II Holdings, $2.7 billion; Playtex, $1.25 billion; Coca-Cola Bottling, $1 billion; Tropicana, $1.2 billion; Avis, $1.6 billion, which equals $7.75 billion.

22   **sum of the whole:** Carey, "Mediocrity at the Gates."

23   **Gordon Gekko:** Bartlett, *The Money Machine,* 3.

23   **on the gains:** Bruce Wasserstein, *Big Deal: Mergers and Acquisitions in the Digital Age,* Warner Books, 2001, 108.

24   **worth $1.1 billion:** "The 400 Richest Americans," *Chicago Sun-Times,* August 10, 1989, 4.

24   **then nearly bankrupt:** Max Holland, "How to Kill a Company; Anatomy of a Leveraged Buyout," *Washington Post,* April 23, 1989, C1.

24   **to build a factory:** Laura Saunders, "How the Government Subsidizes Leveraged Takeovers," *Forbes,* November 28, 1988, 192.

25   **billion in 1989:** The 1981 number comes from "Leveraged Buyouts and Corporate Debt," testimony before the U.S. Senate, Committee on Finance, January 26, 1989; the 1989 number from *Buyouts Newsletter;* January 13, 1997, 18.

25   **times earnings:** "Ohio Mattress to Be Acquired," Dow Jones News Service, March 6, 1989.

25   **times annual earnings:** Calculation for payment equal to twenty-eight times earnings is based on taking its $70 million in 1988 earnings before interest and subtracting its $828 million in 1989 long-term debt at 5 percent interest (a very conservative figure), which is $41 million. That equals $29 million. Then I divided 828 by 29, and that equals twenty-eight years.

25   **tax on dividends:** "Leveraged Buyouts and Corporate Debt," testimony before the U.S. Senate, Committee on Finance, January 24, 1989.

26   **Brady concluded:** ibid.

27   **postcollege job:** Bartlett, *The Money Machine,* 268.

27   **$550,000:** ibid.

27   **GOP Team 100:** ibid., 258.

27   **donated $100,000:** ibid., 268.

27   **"with respect to supervision":** "Leveraged Buyouts and Corporate Debt," testimony before the U.S. Senate, Committee on Finance, January 26, 1989.

27   **included insider trading:** Stephen Labaton, "Junk Bond Leader Is Indicted in U.S. in Criminal Action," *New York Times.com,* March 30, 1989.

27   **served twenty-two months:** Matt Spetalnick, "Milken Relased from Prison to Halfway House," Reuters, January 4, 1993.

27   **in fines:** Connie Bruck, *The Predators' Ball*, Penguin Books, 1989, 369.

28   **in junk-bond losses:** Kenneth Thomas, lecturer in finance at the Wharton School and an expert on the 1980s S&L bailout, told us the only way to estimate the proportion of the total loss caused by junk bonds is to identify which thrifts failed primarily due to them and what was their cost. Those big S&Ls include Centrust, Columbia Savings, Far West Federal, and Lincoln. He concluded the cost to the taxpayers as per the FDIC estimates were in the $5 billion range or about $15 billion counting interest.

29   **had not gone bankrupt:** interview with someone directly involved in raising the Blackstone fund.

32   **to police itself:** Dr. Cordell Esplin, a longtime St. Luke's physician and executive committee member, said, "[The practice] claims peer review by saying it is reviewed by partners in its labs"; second St. Luke's executive committee member who while a member tried to get the practice under peer review; and a well-placed former senior St. Luke's physician both said the practice did not operate under hospital peer review.

33   **at its hospital:** United States of America, Ex Rel. Jerre Frazier, Plaintiffs; Case No. CV-05-0766 in the United States District Court for the District of Arizona.

34   **bankruptcy in 2008:** interview with Mark Michelson, editor in chief of *Printing Impressions* magazine.

34   **during the decade:** Michael Kliegman, a partner at PriceWaterhouseCoopers, explained to us how to calculate how much PE-firm-owned companies save on taxes through interest deductions. If a PE firm puts $500 million down to buy a company for an eight times EBITDA multiple, $2 billion, the company might borrow $1.5 billion at a combined 8 percent interest rate, which equals $120 million. It can then deduct the $120 million from taxes. The company would likely have a 40 percent tax rate when combining state and federal taxes: 120 x .40 = 48. The company saves $48 million annually from taxes. That would represent 19 percent of the company's EBITDA. That also equals 2.4 percent of the $2 billion purchase price. Taking the roughly $207 billion in 1990s LBOs of U.S. companies and multiplying it by 2.4 percent (what $48 million of $2 billion represents) gets you $5 billion. Multiplying $5 billion by the average

number of years PE firms owned companies from 1994 to 1999 (based on the World Economic Forum study), 4.5, gets us $22.5 billion.

34 **stock-market index:** Steve Kaplan and Antoinette Schoar, "Private Equity Performance: Returns, Persistence and Capital Flows," MIT Sloan School of Management Working Paper 4446–03, November 2003, 2.

Chapter 2. The Next Credit Crisis

36 **2001 and 2007:** "The Global Economic Impact of Private Equity Report 2008," World Economic Forum, January 2008, iii.

38 **rate their CLOs:** "Summary Report of Issues Identified in the Commission Staff's Examination of Select Credit Rating Agencies," U.S. SEC, July 2008, 23.

38 **loan portfolio:** interview with CLO portfolio manager who managed and raised CLOs for an international bank.

38 **when issuing ratings:** "Summary Report of Issues Identified in the Commission Staff's Examination of Select Credit Rating Agencies," throughout report, including 32.

38 **after that, $97 billion:** Thomas Lee presented these Bear Stearns numbers on CLO issuance February 9, 2007 at the Columbia Business School's 13th Annual Private Equity and Venture Capital Conference.

38 **$270 billion in loans:** A top executive at an investment bank that raised CLOs gave us this number on background in June 2008.

38 **mostly for private-equity–owned companies:** The CLO portfolio manager referred to in earlier endnote said in 2006 that as much as 75 percent of loans CLOs bought were those made to PE-owned companies, when one includes their recapitalizations.

39 **7.7 times those earnings:** Based on Standard & Poor's "Average Purchase Price and Equity Contribution by Sponsors of All Leveraged Buyout Loans 1997–1Q2008" chart that shows EBITDA multiple purchase prices rose 15 percent from 2004 to 2005; and mergermarket data on EBITDA multiple paid for Toys "R" Us based on year ending January 30, 2006 figures.

39 **8.4 in 2005:** ibid.

40 **from their peers:** I arrived at this number by looking at all the 2005

U.S. buyouts as compiled by the *Buyouts Newsletter* and adding up secondary buyouts while subtracting add-on (or platform) investments.

40 **through 2007:** "Private Equity: Recent Growth in Leveraged Buyouts Exposed Risks That Warrant Continued Attention," U.S. Government Accountability Office, September 2008, 69.

41 **to fund the buyout:** Robert Barnwell says this was the case in LBOs done in 2003–4.

42 **increases in cash flow:** Specialty Retail 2006 Trend Report: "High Leverage Is IN, Cash Is OUT," Moody's Investors Service, January 2007.

42 **investment discipline:** Dow Jones Private Equity Analyst Conference, Waldorf Astoria, New York, N.Y., September 27, 2006.

43 **closed operations:** Al Lewis, "Retailer Liquidation One of Those Things," *Dow Jones Newswires* column, October 16, 2008.

43 **buy the business:** "Affiliates of the sponsors collectively contributed approximately $648 million as equity to Linens Merger Sub Co. immediately prior to the merger," Linens 'n Things 10-K for period ending December 30, 2006.

43 **17,500 employees:** Linens 'n Things 10-K for period ending December 29, 2007.

43 **made the down payment:** Based on terms in Apollo Investment Fund V, L.P. memorandum that I have (Apollo's Fund V managed this investment). The firm said its principals would invest $100 million and was seeking commitments aggregating $4.5 billion (2.2 percent of the fund).

43 **when the business collapsed:** $648 million in equity times 2.2 percent = $14.3 million.

43 **for two years:** "The Companies agree to pay to the Managers a transaction fee in the aggregate amount of $15,000,000 (the *"Transaction Fee"*), plus reimbursement to Apollo of out-of-pocket expenses incurred by Apollo in connection with the services provided in connection with the Acquisition. . . . " Apollo received a $1.5 million annual general services fee and investment partner NRDC an annual $500,000 real-estate fee. Investor Silver Point did not collect a management fee. Management Services Agreement dated as of February 14, 2006, among Linens 'n Things, Linens Holding Co., Apollo Management V, L.P., NRDC Linens B LLC, and Silver Point Capital Fund Investments LLC.

43 **collected for themselves in fees:** Based on terms in Apollo Investment

Fund V, L.P. memorandum (Apollo's Fund V managed this investment). The firm said its management fee would be 1.5 percent of total commitments. Also, the memorandum says 50 percent of all closing fees, consulting fees, advisory fees, transaction fee, and break-up fees paid to the manager will be applied to reduce the management fee paid by the limited partners.

43 **over two years:** $648 million x 1.5 percent = $9.72 million; over two years that is $19.4 million. Then I reduce it by half of the $9.5 million in fees the firms kept for themselves ($4.75 million) and it equals $14.69 million.

43 **a better than 50 percent return:** The PE firms kept $9.5 million in fees (half of the $15 million transaction fee and $4 million in management fees) and $14.7 million in fund management fees (see above endnote "over two years") equals $24.19 million. Meanwhile, they risked $14.3 million and that was likely lost in the bankruptcy.

43 **2005 and 2007:** Standard & Poor's, "Average Purchase Price and Equity Contribution by Sponsors of All Leveraged Buyout Loans 1997–1Q2008."

43 **33 percent in 2007:** Standard & Poor's, "Average Sources of Proceeds for All Leveraged Buyouts 1999–1Q2008."

44 **financing buyouts:** Financial Sponsor—Bank Fee Ranking—2006, Dealogic Financial Sponsor Review Year End 2006.

44 **than its peers:** Interview with Barnwell.

45 **4.5 times their money:** A.N., "Leonard Green, TPG Aim to Relive PETCO Glory," *Buyouts Newsletter*, July 24, 2006.

45 **stayed the same:** The 2002 IPO price was $19 a share, and the pre-takeover announcement price in 2006 was $19.45 a share.

45 **be in trouble:** Dow Jones Private Equity Analyst Conference.

46 **$258 billion in 2006:** The Carlyle Group in presentation at December 2007 SuperReturn Middle East Conference at Jumeirah Emirates Towers, Dubai, December 10–12, 2007. Carlyle attributed data to Thomson.

47 **worth $659 billion:** Dealogic Financial Sponsor Review, January 6, 2009.

47 **professor Steven Davis:** University of Chicago professor Steven Davis, who conducted a study on PE and U.S. employment, told me in 2008, "It's reasonable to think that since 2000 and the first half of 2007 some-

thing close to one-tenth of the private sector workforce has worked for PE-owned companies." The total private sector employment number comes from Bureau of Labor Statistics.

47 **"dating our daughters":** Dow Jones Private Equity Analyst Conference.

48 **holding the bag in 2007:** Walden Siew and Megan Davies, "LBO Debt Logjam Threatens Further Write-downs for Banks," Reuters, January 4, 2008.

48 **more forgiving:** interview with Chris Taggert from CreditSights, "Many will tap revolvers and survive until refinancing."

48 **maturing later:** Wharton Private Equity Review: Harnessing the Winds of Change, Spring 2008, 4.

49 **instead of paying interest:** "Blackstone, Others Toggle to Help Preserve Cash," *Buyouts Newsletter*, December 1, 2008.

49 **its own buyout:** "Star Tribune Employees Put Some Blame on P.E. Debt," *New York Times DealBook*, January 16, 2009.

50 **struggling businesses:** Dow Jones Private Equity Analyst Conference, Waldorf Astoria, New York, N.Y., September 16, 2008.

50 **state pensions:** "Top 25 Alternative Investors," *Private Equity Analyst Directory of Alternative Investment Programs*, 2007 edition.

51 **the loans themselves:** "Private Equity: Recent Growth in Leveraged Buyouts Exposed Risks That Warrant Continued Attention," U.S. Government Accountability Office, September 2008, 57.

51 **at deep discounts:** interview with Jon Moulton from Alchemy who said Cerberus was already buying a lot of leveraged loan debt positions in Europe.

51 **out of work:** From the introduction: PE firms own companies that employ about 7.5 million Americans. Half of those companies, with roughly 3.75 million workers, may collapse between 2012 and 2015. Assuming that those businesses file for bankruptcy and fire only 50 percent of their workers, that leaves 1.875 million Americans out of jobs.

Chapter 3. Doctoring Customer Service

55 **the following year:** interview with Susan Nick, who was the chief nursing officer of Louis Weiss at the time of the 2002 buyout and for a few years after.

56   **these purposes:** A former high-ranking Vanguard exec said quality was not a fundamental focus.

57   **other businesses:** Vanugard, in a May 2006 internal memo to its chief nursing officers titled "Quality as a Strategy," said in the past, "Public accepted quality of hospitals at lower levels than almost any other industry."

57   **for-profit chains:** based on *Modern Healthcare's* list of the largest for-profit hospital chains published March 5, 2007, and factoring in that Community Health bought Triad after the list was published. The seven PE-owned chains are HCA, Vanguard, Ardent Health Systems, Iasis Healthcare, MedCath Corp., Essent Healthcare, and United Surgical Partners.

57   **five thousand hospitals:** interview with an investment banker at a major lender who helps lead their health-care practice.

58   **quality of care:** California Nurses Association Web site under HCA.

58   **the only reaction:** Department of Health and Human Services Centers for Medicare and Medicaid Services Statement of Deficiencies and Plan of Correction, printed October 21, 2004.

58   **essentially probation:** When I ran this by Vanguard Vice Chairman Keith Pitts he said a competing hospital in Massachusetts was put on similar notice.

59   **Richards's arm:** Ted Erikson and Diane Richards, "A Dying Diatribe," found on http://www.sdogv.com/DIATRIBE.html, also interviewed Erikson.

59   **two years earlier:** Erikson interview.

60   **as safe as other facilities:** Dr. Himmelstein bases the number on a summary of all of the reliable studies ever conducted, comparing quality of care for comparable patients at for-profit and not-for-profit hospitals that colleagues from McMaster University published in the *Canadian Medical Association Journal.*

60   **14.3 percent:** I came up with this number by studying Texas Department of State Health Services statistics. Vanguard's Counsel Soltman confirmed the figure.

60   **Texas Department of Health Services:** I came up with this number for the other San Antonio hospitals also by studying Texas Department of State Health Services statistics.

61 **none were above:** The joint commission gives Vanguard's five San Antonio hospitals one combined grade and two of its three Massachusetts hospitals one combined grade. I say that if the San Antonio group got a combined "performed at a level below most accredited organizations," then five hospitals are performing at that level.

62 **inform Medicare:** Kerry Fehr-Snyder, "State Cites Phoenix Baptist for Licensing Rules Violations; Hospital Could Face Hefty Fines," *Arizona Republic*, May 8, 2003, B3.

64 **it kept in the business:** Vyvyan Tenorio and David Carey, "Blackstone Leads Vanguard Recap," *TheDeal.com*, July 27, 2004.

64 **$24.3 million:** Joseph Mantone, "Martin Off Vendor Board," *Modern Healthcare*, August 28, 2006, 20.

64 **by 6 percent:** Vanguard Health Systems 10-K for year ending June 30, 2008. Divided the total discharges by the number of beds. In 2004, Vanguard had 126,356 discharges and 3,133 beds at its 12 hospitals (an average of 40.3 patients per bed), and in 2005, 147,798 discharges and 3,907 beds at its 15 hospitals (a 37.8 average).

64 **the second buyout:** ibid.; net interest $41.4 million for fiscal 2004 and $82.3 million for fiscal 2005.

65 **due in September:** ibid., "The senior credit facilities consist of $774.1 million in term loans maturing in September 2011."

66 **"return to investors":** Thomas Heath, "Under Pressure, Carlyle Issues Patient Promise," *Washington Post*, October 22, 2007, D01.

66 **the *Times* reported:** Charles Duhigg, "More Profit and Less Nursing at Many Homes," *New York Times*, September 23, 2007.

66 **provisional license:** Michele Canty, "Second ManorCare South Death in Less Than Five Months: State Health Officials Fined the York Township Home More Than $7,000," *York Daily Record*, July 21, 2008.

67 **Haskell [Texas]:** Jennifer Files, "GTE to Sell Rural Service in Texas, New Mexico to Hispanic Investors," *Dallas Morning News*, September 8, 1999.

67 **phone service:** Valor 10-K for year ending December 31, 2004. "We received 25.3%, 24.1% and 23.7% of our 2002, 2003 and 2004 revenues, respectively, from Universal Service Fund payments, or USF, from the State of Texas and the federal government to support the high cost of providing local telephone service in rural areas."

67 **to the PE investors:** Jonathan Higuera, "Valor on the Front Lines," *Hispanic Business* magazine, October 2001.

67 **totaling $1.7 billion:** "GTE to Sell All Local Properties in Oklahoma to dba Communications, LLC," Business Wire, October 26, 1999.

67 **$130 million in cash:** interview with an investor in one of the buyout funds that acquired Valor Telecom.

67 **twelve Hispanic investors:** interview with one of the twelve Hispanic Valor investors.

68 **$70 million:** Valor Communications Group S-1, May 28, 2004.

68 **expenditures:** interview with the director of communication practice at a large corporate consulting firm.

68 **percent in 2003:** Divided $497.334 million in 2003 operating revenue for year ending December 31, 2003 by $69.85 million in capital expenditures. Valor Communications Group S-1, May 28, 2004.

68 **service interruptions:** Texas Public Utility Commission; Case 27474-10. Filing description "Open Meeting May 9, 2003."

68 **for five days:** Texas Public Utility Commission; Case 27474-21. Filing description "Open Meeting Cover Sheet; Meeting Date July 25, 2003," 1–3.

68 **worse service:** interview with Texas Public Utility Commission spokesperson Terry Hadley. "When we said Valor fell short of monthly performance standards that meant standards had fallen short of where they were before the buyout."

68 **as an excuse:** Texas Public Utility Commission; Case 27474-21, 28.

69 **empowering Hispanics:** interview with one of the twelve Hispanic Valor investors.

69 **$585 million:** Chris Nolter, "Valor Banks on IPO to Raise Cash," *The Deal.com*, January 12, 2005.

69 **$410 million after expenses:** Form 10-K for the year ending December 31, 2004. "The proceeds from the offering, net of underwriting discounts and other expenses, were $409.6 million."

69 **times their money:** interview with an investor in one of the buyout funds that acquired Valor Telecom.

69 **did not go bankrupt:** Texas Public Utility Commission; Case 27474-21, 27.

69   **wireless providers**: Dionne Searcey, "Hawaiian Telcom Is No Para-
      dise for Carlyle Group," *Wall Street Journal*, March 28, 2008; B1.

Chapter 4. Lifting Prices

72   **rose 54 percent:** International Sleep Products Association statistics.
      1997: 35.3 million mattress and foundation units were sold to retailers
      at $3.6 billion = $102; 2006: 43.115 million mattress and foundation
      units were sold to retailers at $6.78 billion = $157.
72   **in the general economy:** U.S. Department of Labor, Bureau of Labor
      Statistics, CPI inflation calculator.
74   **3.2-times return:** Gibbons Green in 1989 put $170 million down and
      lost all its money; Zell-Chilmark put $100 million down in 1993 and
      collected $590 million; Bain led investors that in 1997 put $140 million
      down and collected $740 million. Total $410 million down and $1.3 billion
      collected.
74   **3.7-times return:** Wesray Capital in 1986 put $5 million down and
      collected $100 million; Merrill Lynch in 1991 put $40 million down
      and collected $120 million; Investcorp in 1996 put $85 million down
      and collected $193 million; and Fenway Partners in 1998 put $148 mil-
      lion down and collected $620 million. Total $278 million down and
      $1.03 billion collected.
74   **by 66 percent:** Willard Mueller and Frederick Geithman, "An Empir-
      ical Test of the Free Rider and Market Power Hypothesis," MIT Press
      in its *Journal of Economics & Statistics*, May 2, 1991, 301–8.
74   **foundations sold:** "Ohio Mattress to Be Acquired," Dow Jones News
      Service, March 6, 1989.
75   **consider a sale:** This version of events came from an interview I had
      with an Ohio Mattress board member at the time who requested ano-
      nymity, except for the part explaining what Wuliger and Trzcinski were
      fighting about, which came from an interview with an Ohio Mattress
      director.
75   **$170 million:** Robert Cole, "Deal to Buy Division of Ohio Mattress
      Fails," *New York Times*, February 15, 1990, says Leonard Green put
      down $170 million to buy Ohio Mattress. In a public filing, Ohio Mat-
      tress reported that for the year ending November 30, 1989 it had

$829 million in long-term debt. The $980 million purchase price minus $829 million leaves $151 million, roughly the same number.

75 **1.5 percent:** International Sleep Products Association statistics. Number of U.S. mattresses and foundations sold; 1988, 28,413,000 and 1989; 27,985,000, a 1.5 percent fall.

75 **and raised prices:** interview with the Ohio Mattress director referenced to in endnote "consider a sale" who stayed with the company under LBO management.

75 **after the sale:** interview with the Ohio Mattress board member referenced to in the note "consider a sale."

75 **generated this way:** interview with an executive who helped run Simmons and requested anonymity.

75 **losing money:** Barbara Solomon, "Bed Wars: A Sealy Licensee Causes Sleepless Nights," *Management Review*, December 1, 1990.

76 **and co-investors were paid:** interview with the executive referenced in endnote "generated this way" who helped run Simmons and requested anonymity.

76 **company shares:** "By November of 1991, First Boston owned approximately 94% of the Company's stock," Sealy History, MattressDirect-OnLine.com.

76 **more expensive beds:** Gary Fazio said Beggs pushed the sales team to sell more expensive mattresses under its "high-end" Stearns & Foster line and dropped lower-priced models representing 38 percent of revenue (there is a quote about that a few paragraphs ahead of this endnote).

78 **by 2.5 percent:** Simmons 10-K for fiscal year ending December 27, 1997.

78 **over two years:** Simmons 10-K for fiscal year ending December 31, 2001.

79 **buy from Sealy:** interview with Sealy CEO at the time Ron Jones.

79 **were not growing:** interview with the CEO of a competing bedding retailer.

80 **clearly improved:** Simmons 10-K for fiscal year ending December 28, 2002. Calculations based on comparing net sales and adjusted EBITDA for the years ending December 25, 1999 and December 28, 2002.

80 **no-flip design:** David Perry, "Sealy Flips to One-Sided," *Furniture Today*, February 3, 2003.

80 **case today:** interview with owner of Sealy supplier.

80 **increased 12.1 percent:** International Sleep Products Association statistics.

82 **Sealy outlay:** John E. Morris, "Sealy Hops from Bain to KKR," *The Deal.com*, March 5, 2004 (for the amount of cash PE firms put down in 1997 to buy Sealy; the rest of the data in this paragraph comes from Sealy and Simmons public filings).

82 **a dividend:** Simmons 10-K for the fiscal year ending December 25, 2004. "On December 15, 2004, our indirect parent, Simmons Company, completed a private placement for approximately $165.1 million aggregate gross proceeds from its issuance of 10% senior discount notes due 2014 (the "Discount Notes"). The proceeds from the offering were used to make a dividend distribution to its class A stockholders and to pay expenses related to the sale and distribution of the notes."

82 **pay their debt:** Sealy did not introduce its first memory foam bed until spring 2005 with a rollout throughout the summer, as reported by David Perry, "Sealy Offers POP Support for First Memory Foam Bed," *Furniture Today*, April 15, 2005.

82 **increased 7.2 percent:** International Sleep Products Association statistics.

82 **again the next year:** ibid.

83 **low-end makers:** interview with the CEO of a leading mattress manufacturer.

83 **to entice buyers:** "Sealy Shares Fall as Price Cuts Pressure Margins," Reuters, April 5, 2007.

83 **when the first buyout happened:** The present market share is based on Sealy public filing, which says it had a 20.9 percent market share in 2007. The 1989 market share comes from "Ohio Mattress to Be Acquired," Dow Jones News Service, March 6, 1989.

85 **on other deals:** "Predatory Equity Watch-List," www.saveourhomes.org.

85 **higher rates:** Gretchen Morgenson, "Questions of Rent Tactics by Private Equity," *New York Times*, May 9, 2008.

85 **nothing wrong:** ibid.

85 **city average of 5.6 percent:** Terry Pristin, "Square Feet: Fear of Defaults After a Flurry of Apartment House Sales," *New York Times*, August 27, 2008.

85 **mortgage payments:** Adam Pincus, "Financial Woes Plague Multi-Family Portfolios," *The Real Deal,* January 7, 2009.

Chapter 5. Starving Capital

87 **an additional $100 million:** Hertz 10-K for year ending December 31, 2006. "Revenue earning equipment expenditures in our car rental and equipment rental operations for the year ended December 31, 2006 decreased by 8.2% and 5.6%, respectively, compared to the year ended December 31, 2005"; "Property and equipment expenditures in our car rental, equipment rental and 'corporate and other' operations for the year ended December 31, 2006 decreased by 38.6%, 21.2% and increased by 6.9%, respectively, compared to the year ended December 31, 2005."

87 **outsourcing:** interview with a former high-ranking Hertz executive.

88 **early 2009:** The Hertz market share in 2005 is based on Hertz 2006 Annual Report (found at https://images.hertz.com/pdfs/HTZ_2006_annual_report.pdf); the 2009 market share is from Hertz EVP and CFO Elyse Douglas, speaking February 3, 2009 at JPMorgan Global High Yield and Leveraged Finance Conference.

89 **fund the LBO:** Mervyn's Holding, LLC Debtors, Mervyn's LLC, Plaintiff; Case No. 08-11586 (KG) in the U.S. Bankruptcy Court for the District of Delaware, 18.

89 **more than $22 million:** ibid., 40–41.

89 **to $172 million:** ibid., 16.

89 **below-market rents:** interview with George Whalin, who runs Retail Management Consultants.

89 **33 percent of its stores:** Calculated by taking the number of stores reported September 8, 2005 in "Mervyns Plans to Shutter 62 Stores, Cut 4,800 Jobs," *Los Angeles Times,* where Castagna said they are cutting 62 stores and will be left with 193, meaning that there were 255 stores. When she left, David Mornin, "Castagna Exiting Mervyns," *Women's Wear Daily,* January 22, 2007, 2, said Mervyn's operated 172 stores. 255 − 172 = 83 stores (33 percent closed).

89 **remaining stores:** Emily Thornton, "How Private Equity Strangled Mervyn's," *BusinessWeek,* November 26, 2008.

89 ***Women's Wear Daily:*** Mornin, "Castagna Exiting Mervyns."

90   **in the buyout:** Mervyn's Holding, LLC Debtors, Mervyn's LLC, Plaintiff; Case No. 08-11586 (KG) in the U.S. Bankruptcy Court for the District of Delaware, Dated: September 2, 2008, p. 19.

90   **paying in rent:** Mervyn's Holding, LLC Debtors, Mervyn's LLC, Plaintiff; Case No. 08-11586 (KG) in The United States Bankruptcy Court for the District of Delaware, Dated: September 2, 2008, 10, 16.

90   **heartbreaking:** Peter Lattman, "Making a Bundle on Mervyn's," *WSJ.com*, November 24, 2008.

90   **following the buyout:** Mervyn's Holding, LLC Debtors, Mervyn's LLC, Plaintiff; Case No. 08-11586 (KG) in the U.S. Bankruptcy Court for the District of Delaware, Dated: September 2, 2008, 33.

90   **middle of a recession:** Prabha Natarajan, "Losses on Mervyns-Backed Bonds Could Get Grimmer," *WSJ.com*, January 22, 2009.

91   **depreciation and amortizations:** interview with Scott Sperling, who led the investment for the PE firm Thomas H. Lee Partners.

92   **(OIBDA):** Warner Music provided the number that came from an Ernst & Young audit.

92   **companywide:** Warner Music S-1 Filing, April 18, 2005, "The number of employees identified to be involuntarily terminated approximated 1,600."

92   **of the staff:** The number of employees at the time of the buyout, approximately 5,300, comes from a Time Warner news release announcing the sale of the business titled "Investor Group Led by Thomas H. Lee Partners, Edgar Bronfman, Jr., Bain Capital and Providence Equity Partners to Purchase Warner Music Group and Create One of the World's Largest Independent Music Companies," November 24, 2003.

92   **senior-level Elektra executives:** interview with a former senior Elektra executive.

92   **laid to rest:** interviews with two former senior Elektra executives, including the one mentioned in endnote above, and a record industry competitor.

93   **exist anymore:** Jenny Eliscu, "Warner to Ax Eighty Artists," *Rolling Stone*, June 3, 2004.

93   **to the PE firms:** Ed Christman, "WMG Issues Third Investor Return," *Billboard.com*, January 8, 2005.

93   **as a dividend:** Warner Music S-1 Filing, April 18, 2005.

93   **down payment:** "Moody's Rates Warner Music's New Holding Co. Notes Caa2; Existing Ratings Affirmed; Outlook Changed to Negative," Moody's Investors Service, December 16, 2004.

93   **the next year:** Nielsen Soundscan numbers for total album sales 2005 and 2006.

94   **to propel sales:** Warner Music Group Citigroup Analyst Report, December 9, 2005.

95   **rival Universal Music:** Ray Waddell, "Life in the Express Lane," *Billboard.com*, October 30, 2007.

95   **radio advertising:** Brian Garrity, "Eagles Soar," *New York Post*, February 17, 2008.

95   **while Universal jumped 3.4:** comparing Nielsen's Year-End 2003 and 2008 total albums (current and catalog titles) figures.

97   **for the project:** Jeffrey McCracken and Jamie Butters, "Ford Refuses New Business for C&A," *Detroit Free Press*, May 17, 2005.

97   **outright deceit:** Jeffrey McCracken and Jamie Butters, "Tracing C&A's Spiral Toward Bankruptcy; Auto Supplier Burned by Cuts, Dud Deals," *Detroit Free Press*, May 18, 2005.

97   **personnel in attendance:** MacKay Shields, Plaintiff; Heartland Industrial Partners, Defendant, Case 05-520229 CZ, State of Michigan in the Circuit Court for the County of Wayne, 82.

98   **the suit said:** ibid., 30–31.

99   **after the LBOs:** "The Global Economic Impact of Private Equity Report 2008," World Economic Forum, January 2008, 57.

99   **than in prior times:** ibid., 60.

100   **real-estate businesses:** ibid., 61.

100   **from other PE firms:** ibid., 62–63.

100   **"be more positive":** Andrew Ross Sorkin, "Study Says Private Equity Isn't Big Job Killer," *New York Times*, January 25, 2008.

100   **ten million people:** See prologue endnote "roughly 10 million people."

100   **five million Americans:** "The Global Economic Impact of Private Equity Report 2008," 55.

100   **two years of ownership:** 10 million jobs times 3.6 percent net job loss (including jobs destroyed and created) = 360,000.

100   **its workforce:** The third year after the buyout is December 2007–December 2008. Job losses are listed in Hertz 10-Q November 7, 2008

(adding up the 2008 job losses of 950, 180, 220, and 1,400 jobs detailed in filing = 2,750 losses). Then I took a company press release from January 16, 2009, when Hertz said it was laying off 4,000 people, and that represented 10 percent of the workforce, and calculated that 2,750 represented about 7 percent.

101 **higher-value directions:** "The Global Economic Impact of Private Equity Report 2008," 45.

103 **was not profitable:** Christopher Barton, "North Carolina-Based Mattress Maker to Close Memphis, Tenn., Factory," *Knight Ridder Tribune Business News*, March 2, 2001.

103 **Texas, plant:** The Sealy executive referenced in Chapter 4 endnotes.

104 **to Harrisburg:** 121 workers at warehouse according to Natalie Kosteini, "S. Walter Packaging Wraps Up Lease of Phila. Distribution Center," *Philadelphia Business Journal*, March 7, 2008.

Chapter 6. Plunder and Profit

105 **would choose him:** Susan Page, "Obama Now Virtually Tied with Clinton, Poll Shows; May Be Sign of 'Whose' Messages Are Sticking," *USAToday.com*, June 5, 2007.

105 **"reinvested in growth":** http://transcripts.cnn.com/TRANSCRIPTS/0706/05/se.01.html.

106 **in the first year:** "Private Equity: Tracking the Largest Sponsors," Moody's Investors Service, February 2008.

106 **that later collapsed:** David Kirkpatrick, "Romney's Fortunes Tied to Business Riches," *New York Times*, June 4, 2007.

106 **1992 and 2001:** Bain, through its spokesperson, was asked in writing about Romney's ownership of Bain Capital and declined comment. I contacted Romney spokesperson Eric Fehrnstrom on his cellular phone and left a direct message about this chapter, and he did not return the call.

106 **"abdicate":** Jill Lieber, "Romney's Goal: Return Soul, Character to 2002 Games," *USA Today*, October 2, 2000.

108 **for public office:** interview with a Bain Capital managing director who worked with Mitt Romney.

108 **venture-capital investments:** interview with Geoffrey Rehnert, who helped start Bain Capital.

108 **ownership of Bain Capital:** David Snow, "The House That Mitt Built," *Private Equity International*, September 9, 2007, reports that while Bain & Co. owned a stake in the early Bain Capital funds, the creation of Bain Capital Inc. in 1992 saw Romney become the 100 percent owner of the firm's management company, which technically gave him control of decision making at the firm.

109 **small venture deals:** interview with Geoffrey Rehnert, who helped start Bain Capital.

109 **to $27 million:** Dade International 10-K for the year ending December 31, 2006.

110 **of sales to R & D:** interview with stock analyst who covers the space.

110 **$88.2 million in 1998:** Dade Behring 10-K for the year ending December 31, 1999.

111 **owed in 1999:** The exact details are based on a former affected Dade executive who spoke on background; broad outlines of change and date of change of plan in Dade public filing, which says that Dade transitioned its pension plan from a final average pay to a cash balance plan design.

111 **company stake:** Dade Behring 10-Q for the quarter ending June 30, 1999.

111 **buy the company:** Kelly Holman, "Dade Behring Sponsors Largely Unhurt," *Daily Deal*, August 3, 2002.

111 **business conditions:** "Dade Behring Corp/ S&P -2: Rating Outlook Stable", Dow Jones News Service, June 28, 1999.

112 **Miami employees:** "Mellon Bank Corp. to Buy United National Bank of Miami," *South Florida Business Journal*, November 28, 1997.

112 **for company shares:** Dade Behring 10-K for the fiscal year ending December 31, 2002; "A restructuring of the Company's debt occurred that reduced the principal amount of the Company's outstanding indebtedness by approximately $678.2 million and converted that debt into equity."

112 **more than 8 percent of revenue:** Dade Behring 10-K for the year ending December 31, 2005.

113 **time of the bankruptcy:** Siemens paid $77 a share, and the high and low sales price for Dade's common stock from October 3, 2002 through December 31, 2002 was $17.05 and $12.75, respectively, based on the Dade 10-K for the year ending December 31, 2002.

113 **exposing the Marion layoffs:** Peter Kilborn, "The 1994 Campaign: Labor; Bitter Strike in Indiana Echoes in Massachusetts," *New York Times*, October 10, 1994.

113 **other factories:** American Pad & Paper 1998 Annual Report (sec.edgar-online.com/american-pad—paper-co/10-k-annual-report/1998/03/27/Section2.aspx).

113 **twenty-times return:** former Bain Capital director with direct knowledge of the Ampad returns.

114 **Ampad to achieve its growth objectives**: "Results; Reports EPS of $0.18 Versus Pro Forma EPS of $0.17," PR Newswire, July 16, 1997; "American Pad and Paper Company Announces Preliminary Results for First Quarter," PR Newswire, April 1, 1997.

114 **in five trading sessions:** *Allan Zishka and Gerald R. Dailey vs. American Pad & Paper, Bain Capital,* U.S. District Court, Northern District of Texas, Dallas Division, Civ. No. 98CV0660-D, filed March 10, 1998, 12.

116 **$55 million in cash:** Craig Douglas, "Bain Capital Accused of Raiding KB's Piggy Bank," *Boston Business Journal*, March 24, 2006.

116 **more than $85 million:** *Big Lots Stores vs. Bain Capital Fund VII, LLC,* Court of Chancery of the State of Delaware in and for New Castle County, Filing ID 5108097, EFiled February 9, 2005, 3.

116 **on the $18 million:** ibid., 2.

117 **and Robert White:** CEO Glazer in an interview said it was a 4–0 board vote to approve the dividend, and the board included three Bain Capital representatives. Bain, in its brief to dismiss the case against Big Lots referred to in the above endnotes, Civil Action 1081-N, on page 5 names its managers who were on the KB board at the time of the dividend.

Chapter 7. Leaving Little to Chance

121 **safety net underneath them:** interview with the Academy of Achievement (http://www.achievement.org/autodoc/page/kra0int-1), February 12, 1991.

121 **$3.78 billion:** HCA 10-K for the year ending December 31, 2006. "The aggregate purchase price paid for all of the equity securities of the Company was $20.364 billion, which purchase price was funded by $3.782 billion of equity contributions from the Investors, certain

members of management and certain other coinvestors and by incurring $19.964 billion of indebtedness through bank credit facilities and the issuance of debt securities."

122 **put down the firm's $1.02 billion share:** interview with a Bain 2006 fund investor whom we'll call Bain Investor One.

122 **6.3 percent of those funds:** a large Bain fund investor, whom I will call Bain Investor Two, said Bain, the firm, invested $500 million in its 2006 $8 billion fund, 6.3 percent of the fund.

122 **even if their funds lost money:** interview with a banker who made these loans, and an interview with a second bank executive at another bank who knew they were being considered and assumes they were made.

122 **which it kept for itself:** Bain Investor Two said in an interview that Bain in the 2006 funds kept all the transaction and management fees unless they totaled beyond a certain percentage of the overall value of a particular buyout, and fees appeared to be well below that percentage in HCA; and in a blog posting, Dan Primack, "HCA Already Paying Dividends," on peHub.com said, "Not all private equity firms share either the transaction or management fees with limited partners.... Bain, for example, almost never shares any of those fees with LPs." A Bain spokesperson asked about Bain's fees declined to comment.

122 **without sharing with its fund investors:** Bain Investor Two said Bain did not share management fees.

123 **1 percent fee when they sell HCA:** a breakdown of all fees in HCA 10-K for the year ending December 31, 2006 under the Sponsor Management Agreement and Management Agreement.

123 **give fund investors the rest:** The second Bain fund investor said that Bain shared transaction fees with investors once they exceeded 1 percent of the value of the buyout, and expenses were paid. By the time Bain would collect this fee, HCA transaction fees might surpass the 1 percent threshold.

123 **risked in the HCA buyout:** $180 million in fees divided by $64 million risked = 2.8 times the money the firm is risking.

123 **2 percent management fee:** Bain Investor One said Bain will charge a 2 percent annual management fee until December 31, 2011, when the charge will be reduced by HCA distributions or write-offs, to investors;

interview with Bain Investor Two; interview with Bain investor who passed on investing in 2006 fund because of high fee structure; and Laura Kreutzer, "Bain Capital Collects $8 Billion for Fund IX," Dow Jones Newswires, April 4, 2006.

123 **another $96 million:** $956 million HCA investment if held for five years at 2 percent = $96 million.

123 **$276 million *in fees alone:*** $180 million in fees charged to HCA plus $96 million charged fund investors.

123 **retains 30 percent:** Bain Investor Two; and Kreutzer, "Bain Capital Collects $8 Billion for Fund IX."

123 **money out through dividends:** Primack, "HCA Already Paying Dividends."

123 **eleven times its money:** The profit would come from $956 million fund down payment from outside investors. If the investment doubled it would produce a $956 million profit, multiply that by Bain's 30 percent commission = $287 million. Add the $64 million profit on Bain's own fund investment (double what it put down), the $64 million it invested, and the $276 million fee haul and one collects $691 million.

124 **for the HCA buyout:** Adding $125 million fund management fee ($956 million times 2 percent times 6.5 years), $58 million transaction fee, plus $47 million HCA management fee = $230 million.

124 **financing evaporated in mid-2007:** Dealogic Financial Sponsor Review, January 6, 2009, 2.

124 **a $10.6 billion agreement:** Hexion press release, July 12, 2007.

124 **was no longer viable:** "Hexion Files Suit Alleging That Transaction with Huntsman Is No Longer Viable," Hexion press release, June 18, 2008.

124 **their firm for damages:** "Huntsman Sues Apollo and Two Partners for Fraud and Tortious Interference," Huntsman press release, June 23, 2008.

124 **breached the merger agreement:** The Deal Professor, "Lessons from Huntsman v. Hexion," *New York Times Dealbook*, October 2, 2008.

125 **but allegedly backed out:** "Hexion Files Suit Against Credit Suisse and Deutsche Bank for Failure to Fund Merger with Huntsman," Hexion press release, October 29, 2008.

125 **exposure for much of that amount:** Peter Lattman, "Apollo, Huntsman Reach Amicable Split," *WSJ.com*, December 15, 2008.

125 **hammer out a settlement:** Jack Kaskey, "Huntsman, Apollo's Black Reached Agreement in 3 Days," Bloomberg, December 15, 2008.

125 **help Hexion buy Huntsman:** Laura Kreutzer, "LPs Bristle at Apollo's Plans for Huntsman Settlement," *WSJ.com*, December 22, 2008.

125 **by insurance policies:** "Apollo Makes a Bad Call," peHub.com, December 18, 2008.

125 **loan Hexion $325 million:** "Hexion Specialty Chemicals Announces Termination of Merger Agreement with Huntsman Corp. and Settlement," Hexion press release, December 14, 2008.

125 **was charged $155 million:** "Apollo Makes a Bad Call."

126 **9 percent:** Carlyle Group in presentation at December 2007 Super-Return Middle East Conference at Jumeirah Emirates Towers, Dubai, December 10–12, 2007. Carlyle attributed data to Thomson Venture Economics.

126 **with only twenty-five in 2000:** Andrew Ross Sorkin, "The Money Binge," *New York Times*, April 4, 2007, who referred to a Wilshire Associates report.

127 **contributions to fund investments:** written response from Ann S. Fuelberg, executive director of the Employees Retirement System of Texas.

127 **than the 2003 level:** "U.S. Private Equity Firms Raise a Record $302 Billion in 2007, Up 19% Over 2006," Dow Jones Private Equity Analyst press release, January 8, 2008; and for the 2003 number, Zachery Kouwe, "LBO Deals, Fund-Raising Set for Another Boom Year in '05," Dow Jones News Service, January 10. 2005.

129 **"negative, very negative":** Martin Arnold, "Private Equity Picture Remains Bleak," *Financial Times.com*, November 20, 2008.

129 **of being a limited partnership:** interview with NYPPEX managing member Laurence Allen.

130 **"coming out of private equity":** Michael Flaherty, "Bonderman's Investor Kiss," Reuters, November 17, 2008.

130 **tied into alternative investments:** interview with CalPERS information officer Clark McKinley.

130 **slow down their investment pace:** Peter Lattman, Craig Kamin, and Pui-wing Tam, "Private Equity Is Getting the Cold Shoulder—Big U.S. Institutions Rethinking Strategy; Harvard in Sell Mode," *WSJ.com*, November 5, 2008.

130 **cut its fund management fees by 10 percent:** Peter Lattman, "TPG Will Let Clients Trim Cash Pledges by Up to 10%," *WSJ.com*, December 23, 2008.

131 **how its funds performed:** interview with Permira director of communications Chris Davison.

132 **top quartile performances:** KKR fund figures are from the Oregon Public Employees' Retirement Fund Alternative Equity Portfolio record as of September 30, 2008; and fund performance return numbers for the industry are from Cambridge Associates for the period ending December 31, 2006.

133 **more than $2.5 million:** Nortek 14A public filing October 2, 2002 says, "The basic annual salary for Mr. Bready during the employment term will be not less than $1,068,767, which is his current salary, for the year ending December 31, 2002 and not less than $2,500,000 per year during the remainder of the [new five-year] employment term."

133 **16 percent ownership stake:** ibid.: "Some of the management investors, including Mr. Bready, will sell or 'cash-out' a portion of their current equity interest in Nortek as part of the recapitalization and will retain or 'roll over' their remaining equity interest. In the aggregate, the management investors will receive approximately $18.6 million through the sale of 392,786 shares and the 'cash-out' of 22,500 stock options, including approximately $17.2 million to be paid to Mr. Bready as a result of the sale of 373,182 shares. The management investors will, in the aggregate, 'roll over' 293,860 shares."

133 **for essentially replacing them:** David Carey, "Deliver and You Get Paid," *The Deal.com*, June 1, 2007.

133 **continued employment:** Bready in 2001 earned about $8 million including bonuses (public filings) and received $17.2 million in the sale without losing his stake in the business. That is slightly more than twice his salary and bonus, and the average compensation for a fired public company CEO is three times salary and bonus.

133 **4.3 percent of the business:** Nortek 14A public filing October 2, 2002 says, "Nortek will grant Mr. Bready, upon the consummation of the recapitalization, (1) Class A options to purchase approximately 1.4% of the fully diluted equity of Nortek at the closing of the recapitalization

and (2) Class B options to purchase approximately 2.9% of the fully diluted equity of Nortek at the closing of the recapitalization."

134 **if he stuck with the business:** ibid.

134 **premium over the stock price:** "Company News; New York Equity Company Shows Interest in Nortek," *New York Times*, April 9, 2002, reports stock went up 9 percent to $40.75 on news of the offer; and mergermarket in its database said Nortek traded at $37.50 a share March 13, 2002, which would make a $40 offer a 7 percent premium to that price.

134 **47 percent average premium:** "Why Do Private Acquirers Pay So Little Compared to Public Acquirers?" study by professors Leonce Bargeron, Frederick Schlingemann, Rene Stulz, and Chad Zutter, May 2007.

134 **the Kelso offer:** "Nortek Offer May Be Evaluated," *Plastics News,* April 22, 2002.

134 **would work only with Kelso:** from Nortek public filing describing the circumstances leading to the sale, "At this meeting, Kelso stated that if the special committee was not prepared to recommend an agreement on such revised terms, Kelso intended to withdraw its proposal and that it understood Mr. Bready would also withdraw his interest in participating in a transaction to acquire the public shares of the company." Also, other PE firms that were bidding told me at the time that they would not be able to partner with Bready.

134 **how the auction was developing:** Nortek 14A in Background of the Recapitalization section, filed November 27, 2002.

135 **Kelso or anyone else:** ibid.

135 **from competing suitors:** ibid.

135 **open, competitive process:** Josh Kosman, "Nortek Early in Process of Selling Itself, Source Says," mergermarket, June 14, 2004.

135 **7.4-times-EBITDA multiple:** David Carey, "Kelso Cashes Out of Nortek," *TheDeal.com,* July 16, 2004.

135 **Kelso had paid:** took Kelso purchase price of $1.6 billion for deal that closed January 2003 and divided it by $236.4 million Nortek EBITDA figure found in Nortek annual report filed in 2004.

135 **since the Kelso buyout:** Carey, "Kelso Cashes Out of Nortek," reported that Kelso's 80 percent share of Nortek after resale was worth more than

$1 billion. Bready and management owned the remaining 20 percent, which then would be worth more than $250 million. Kelso, according to the Carey article, made a better than 2.6 times return on its money.

135 **a $30 million profit:** Bready had the option to buy 4.3 percent of the company's shares, which he likely did since they rose in value; 4.3 percent of the company would be worth more than $50 million based on the overall $1.25 billion valuation in the Carey article referred to above. Since those shares rose 2.6 times in value, Bready likely pocketed a better than a $30 million profit on the options.

136 **competitive auction:** in the buyouts of TXU, HCA, Harrah's, and Kinder Morgan, management partnered with a PE firm before starting a formal sales process (Equity Office Properties is the lone top five buyout that was competitive early on). Only in Harrah's did the board aggressively then try to attract other bidders.

136 **only benefited themselves:** Roland Grover, "Just Don't Call Him a Raider," *BusinessWeek*, March 5, 2007.

137 **and cultural institutions:** Julie Creswell, "In Private Equity, the Limits of Apollo's Power," *New York Times*, December 7, 2008.

137 **Vail Valley Foundation:** according to an Apollo Investment Fund V, L.P. memorandum that I have.

137 **"from barbarians":** Creswell, "In Private Equity."

Chapter 8. A Different Approach

139 **moneymakers ever:** Thomas Stewart, "General Instrument: How a High-Tech Bet Paid Off Big," *Fortune Magazine*, November 1, 1993.

140 **electronic betting systems:** General Instrument company history found at FundingUniverse.com.

140 **CEO of Monsanto:** interview with a former top General Instrument executive who was there during the time Hickey chose a successor.

140 **other pay television stations:** General Instrument company history found at FundingUniverse.com.

141 **their own operations:** interview with Krisbergh, who ran the cable division and said Hickey didn't get involved in his business.

141 **decline in that business:** interview with a former top General Instrument executive who was there during the time.

141 **proved to be a bust:** General Instrument company history found at
FundingUniverse.com.

142 **GI's stock price:** Vivian Marino, "Forstmann Announces Takeover,"
Los Angeles Daily News, July 3, 1990. Our calculation of around a
15 percent premium is based on the share price the day before the
deal was announced (in the cited article above) and then assuming
that Forstmann's initial offer was less than the $44.50 agreed price,
and likely around $42 a share. Forty-two dollars would be a 15 percent
premium to $36.50 a share.

142 **Bush's presidential campaign:** Stephen Taub, David Carey, Richard
Coletti, and Tom Bancroft, "The Wall Street 100," *Financial World*,
July 10, 1990.

143 **$1.4 billion in annual sales:** calculated by taking General Instrument
company history found at FundingUniverse.com that said Rumsfeld
sold businesses representing nearly $400 million in sales and adding
that to the $929 million in sales reported for its core segments in 1991.
And $1.329 billion divided by 400 = 30 percent

143 **at the New York office:** General Instrument company history found
at FundingUniverse.com.

143 **$65 million in overhead:** Stewart, "General Instrument."

144 **$3.4 billion market capitalization:** Ciena company history found at
FundingUniverse.com.

144 **worth more than GI:** Toni Mack,"Communications: The Next Wave,"
Forbes, October 6, 1997.

145 **$5.23 a share:** John Higgins, "GI Stock Sale Falls a Wee Bit Short,"
Multichannel News, June 15, 1992.

145 **to pay down debt:** Robert Rose, "Top Managers at General Instrument Show $45 Million Paper Profit on Stock," *Wall Street Journal*,
July 17, 1992.

146 **in one million American homes:** Paula Parisi, "Revolution to Run on
High-Powered Converters," *Hollywood Reporter*, December 4, 1992.

146 **to buy them:** "GI Signs Agreement with TCI," HDTV Report Phillips
Business Information, July 7, 1993.

146 **than a year earlier:** Stewart, "General Instrument."

146 **three-year investment:** ibid.

147 **8.2 percent of its sales:** figures are calculated from General

Instrument's 2004 annual report, which says R & D spending increased to $74 million in 1993 from $58 million in 1992 and that net sales were $1.393 billion, and Scientific-Atlanta's reported figures in its annual report of $60.1 million in 1993 R & D spending compared to $52.3 million in 1992 and $730.6 million in sales.

148 **looking for a replacement:** John Van, "MCI Exec to Replace Rumsfeld as General Instrument Chief," *Chicago Tribune*, August 12, 1993.

149 **$28 million in shares:** Frederick Lowe, "Rumsfeld Resigns at General Instrument," *Chicago Sun-Times*, August 12, 1993.

149 **a lot of dreaming, Krisbergh said:** Hal Krisbergh, "Guest Commentary: Digital Set-Tops Take Cable to the Next Level," *Electronic Media*, November 27, 2000.

149 **in GI's technology:** Jeffrey Trachtenberg and Mark Robichaux, "Bell Alliance to Buy over $1 Billion of Set-Top Boxes to Offer Wireless TV," *Wall Street Journal*, September 22, 1995, and an interview with a top executive of Bell Alliance who explained why they chose Thomson.

150 **dropped 35 percent:** Peter Elstrom and Peter Coy, "Dustup on the Set-Top: General Instrument's Cable Hegemony Is Over," *Business-Week*, April 22, 1996.

150 **fired Friedland:** A General Instrument executive who worked under Forstmann, one of the two well-placed sources, added that Forstmann also took away Friedland's options.

Chapter 9. The Next Great European Credit Crisis

156 **to 10 percent:** Ronald Cohen, *The Second Bounce of the Ball*, Weidenfeld & Nicolson, 2007, 36.

156 **1997 to 1999:** Laura Holson, "Can Europe Learn to Love Americans at the Gate," *New York Times*, April 25, 1999.

156 **and fire workers:** interview with Professor Mike Wright, the director of the Centre for Management Buyout Research, who said detailed analysis of 1,350 UK buyouts between 1999 and 2004 showed employment fell in companies acquired through management buy-ins (where management did not have a significant stake in the business) six years after the acquisitions by more than 18 percent. Meanwhile, employment

in management buyouts (where management had a controlling interest) grew 36 percent over the same time frame.

156 **introduced junk bonds:** Phred Dvorak and G. Thomas Sims, "Milken Protege Teaches Europe to Love Junk—Deutsche's Mr. Virtue Targets Japan, Too—'You Must Be Mad,' a Fund Manager Said," *Wall Street Journal*, August 14, 2000.

157 **from Hugh Osmond:** "Texas Pacific Group Invests in Punch Taverns, Backing Senior Management Team," *Business Wire*, May 19, 1999, where TPG announced it bought a majority stake in Punch.

157 **traded brewer Whitbread:** Christoper Sims, "Punch Eye Allied's 3600 Pubs," *The Herald* (Scotland), May 15, 1999.

157 **was expected to close:** Andrew Verity, "Punch Vows to Trump Whitbread's Allied Deal," *The Independent,* May 26, 1999.

157 **would be voted on:** David Jones, "Focus—Punch Delivers Bid for Allied's Pubs," Reuters, June 22, 1999.

157 **a superior proposal:** "Allied/Punch: Says Whitbread Offers More Benefits," Dow Jones News Service, June 23, 1999.

157 **more attractive?:** Ernest Beck and Jeffrey Hiday, "British Bar Brawl Ends with Osmond's Winning Punch—Victory Caps Pizza Entrepreneur's Lengthy Duel with U.K. Titans Allied Domecq and Whitbread," *Wall Street Journal*, July 23, 1999.

157 **by 6 percent to £2.85 billion**: "Whitbread Falls as Punch Lifts Allied Offer," Reuters, June 29, 1999.

157 **with Allied for the pubs:** "K's Allied Recommends Whitbread Pubs Offer," Reuters, July 6, 1999.

158 **of the private sector:** interview with Nathan Williams of the British Venture Capital Association.

159 **"shakes our banking system":** David Gow, "Private Equity Firms Drinking at Self-Regulation's Last-Chance Saloon, EU Warns," *The Guardian*, December 12, 2008.

159 **Financial Assistance Scheme:** "Private Equity Dumps More Than £2 Billion Unfunded Liabilities in 96 Insolvent Pension Funds on UK Taxpayers/Other Pension Funds," GMB Union press release, June 3, 2007.

160 **"dependent on the state":** ibid.

160 **to enter heaven:** Martin Waller, "Needled; City Diary," *The Times*, May 23, 2006.

160 **the impact of private equity:** Christopher Adams, "Labour MPs Raise Buy-Out Concern," *Financial Times*, February 13, 2007.

160 **($18.74 billion):** Rachel Sanderson and Dominic Lau, "KKR Offers 9.7 Bln Pounds for Alliance Boots," Reuters, March 9, 2007.

161 **Somerfield PLC in a leveraged buyout:** Lauren Mills, "Apollo Plots Somerfield Buy-Out," *Telegraph*, March 21, 2001.

161 **cut R & D spending:** Parliament Select Committee on Treasury Minutes of Evidence, June 12, 2007, Q160 (http://www.publications.parlia ment.uk/pa/cm200607/cmselect/cmtreasy/567/7061212.htm).

161 **brought down to size:** Matthew Engel, "A Modern Gibbet for the Sharp of Suit Matthew Engel," *Financial Times*, June 21, 2007.

162 **"is value creation":** Parliament Select Committee on Treasury Minutes of Evidence, June 20, 2007, Q 305–313 (http://www.publications.parlia ment.uk/pa/cm200607/cmselect/cmtreasy/567/7062009.htm).

162 **"sale of Wickes":** Parliament Select Committee on Treasury Minutes of Evidence, July 3, 2007, Q607 (http://www.publications.parliament .uk/pa/cm200607/cmselect/cmtreasy/567/7070310.htm).

163 **"or growing throughout":** Parliament Select Committee on Treasury Minutes of Evidence, July 3, 2007, Q566–567.

163 **hundreds of layoffs:** Helen Power, "Bill's Focus Is on Fixing Troubled DIY Stores," *Daily Telegraph*, December 17, 2007.

163 **PE-owned companies:** Martin Arnold, "No Naming and Shaming for Private Equity," *Financial Times*, January 11, 2009.

165 **biggest corporate taxpayer:** "Regulating Private Equity—Overview of Recent Parliamentary Hearings and Legislative Initiatives," TUAC Secretariat, November 12, 2007, 13.

165 **University of Denmark:** William Melody, "The Private Equity Take-over of Telecom Infrastructure in Denmark: Implications for Network Development and Public Policy," June 2007 (study found on regula teonline.org).

165 **forty-fifth and fiftieth:** ibid.

165 **staff planned for 2007:** "TDC Discusses Further Job Cuts in Denmark," *Danish News Digest*, May 18, 2006.

166 **collected corporate tax:** Denmark Ministry of Taxation Web site says the country collected DKK 71 billion in 2006 corporation tax; 71 billion divided by 2 billion estimated loss = 3 percent.

166   **15 billion kroner ($2.9 billion):** Thao Hua, "Danish Regs Could Have Domino Effect; Other Countries Mulling Tax Hike for Private Equity Firms," *Pensions & Investments*, July 9, 2007.

166   **to another telecom operator:** interview with a TDC analyst on background.

166   **"action the better":** Paul Hodkinson and Vivek Ahuja, "Financial News: Private Equity Gets a Break in Vote—EU Legislative Body Softens Its Proposals on Cross-Border Rules," *Wall Street Journal Europe*, September 12, 2008.

166   **Sweden, and Denmark:** Copublication of the World Bank, International Finance Corporation, Oxford University Press, "Doing Business in 2004" (http://www.doingbusiness.org/Documents/DB2004-full-report.pdf). The report says that "the optimal level of regulation is not none, but may be less than what is currently found in most countries."

168   **and move on:** "Marx or Markets: German Politicians Debate the Dangers of Capitalism," *SpiegelOnline*, May 5, 2005.

168   **supervisory board:** John Morris, "Blackstone's German Puzzle," *TheDeal.com*, May 26, 2006.

168   **may sell their shares:** Paul Betts, "Will Deutscheland AG Battle with the Giant Locusts," *FinancialTimes.Com*, November 7, 2007.

169   **"protect its companies":** "Sarkozy Vows to Defend French Companies from Foreign Funds," Dow Jones Newswires, January 8, 2008.

169   **had it gone further:** Lina Saigol and Adam Jones, "KKR Put Up Euro 40BN Offer for Vivendi," *Financial Times*, November 3, 2006.

170   **"organization adrift":** "Armani May Seek Investors," Reuters, November 6, 2007.

170   **"Italy is missing out":** Ambassador Ronald Spogli speech given at the National Italian American Foundation (NIAF) Business Roundtable at his Villa Taverna home in Rome, June 20, 2006.

170   **the $335 million buyout:** Ian Rodger, "Austria Tabak Poised to Buy Head Sports Group," *Financial Times*, March 22, 1993.

170   **just assuming its debts:** Ian Rodger, "International Company News—Austrian Banks Approve Bid for HTM," *Financial Times*, November 27, 1995.

170   **three times its money:** Carol Matlack, "Cowboys on the Continent;

Texas Pacific Keeps Roping In European Companies," *BusinessWeek*,
December 29, 2003.

170 **December 2010:** Dominic Walsh, "Punch Questions Zombie Rumors,"
The Times, December 12, 2008.

171 **European corporate loans:** Private Equity Beat column, "A Window
into Apollo," *WSJ.com*, March 31, 2009.

171 **taken over by creditors:** Helia Ebrahimi, "Distressed Debt Investors
Alchemy and Oaktree Take Control of Countrywide," *Telegraph.co.uk*,
February 17, 2009.

171 **repossessed business:** Jonathan Braude, "PAI Pullback from Monier,"
TheDeal.com, June 11, 2009.

Chapter 10. What's Next?

175 **control IndyMac:** A spokesperson for the new bank owners said she
could not disclose the financing terms for the buyout or the ownership
shares of the individual firms within the buying group.

175 **typical fund investment:** interview with Mark Patterson, chairman
of MatlinPatterson.

177 **chairman of Mitsubishi:** Phred Dvorak, "How a Japanese Bank Fell
to Foreigners—Two Deal Makers Put Ripplewood on Tokyo's Radar as
a Suitor for LTCB," *Wall Street Journal*, March 23, 2000.

177 **most serious suitor:** interview with a member of the buying group
that acquired Shinsei.

177 **against those losses:** basic agreement between buyers and government found on http://www.fsa.go.jp/frc/newse/ne014b.html.

177 **to the Flowers team:** interview with a member of the buying group
that acquired Shinsei.

177 **including bankruptcy:** ibid.

177 **loans abruptly:** ibid.

177 **on the guarantee:** ibid.

178 **one third of book value:** ibid.

178 **'Absolutely not'":** Columbia Business School, "Center on Japanese
Economy: Program on Alternative Investments," which reprinted much
of the September 22, 2004 speech (http://app.cul.columbia.edu:8080/
ac/bitstream/10022/AC:P:51/1/fulltext.pdf).

178 **others into bankruptcy:** found in "American Embassy in Tokyo's Daily Summary of Japanese Press" reprint of *Yomiuri Shimbun* article published July 13, 2000.

178 **"wrecking its business partners":** ibid.

178 **clients to survive:** interview with a member of the buying group that acquired Shinsei.

179 **$626 million profit:** "Shinsei Bank 04/05 Profit Up 1.6%; Sees Fall in 05/06," Reuters, May 24, 2005.

179 **credit card business:** "Case Study—Shinsei: Setting a Path to Recovery," *Retail Banker International*, April 18, 2007.

179 **Holding AG, soured:** Finbarr Flynn and Takako Taniguchi, "Lehman, Hypo Risks Created 'Messes' for Flowers's Japanese Bank," *Bloomberg*, February 19, 2009.

179 **best breaking even:** Allison Tudor, "Crisis on Wall Street: Shinsei CEO Says He Has Repair Plan; Loss Near," *Wall Street Journal*, December 23, 2008.

179 **U.S. investors:** Katherine Hyde, "Vultures or Doves? How Changing Japanese Laws & Shifting Perceptions Will Impact U.S.-Japan M&A," Japan Society, September 25, 2007.

179 **of the buyers:** "Beyond the Boldface Names in the IndyMac Deal," *New York Times DealBook*, January 12, 2009.

180 **"have all the upside":** Eric Lipton, "As Investors Circle Ailing Banks, Fed Sets Limits," *New York Times*, May 5, 2009.

180 **bank to file for bankruptcy:** Peter Lattman, "TPG Will Let Clients Trim Cash Pledges by Up to 10%," *Wall Street Journal*, December 23, 2008.

180 **fell deeper in value:** "Merrill Lynch Announces Substantial Sale of U.S. ABS CDOs, Exposure Reduction of $11.1 Billion," Merrill press release, July 28, 2008, in which it says, "Merrill Lynch will provide financing to the purchaser for approximately 75 percent of the purchase price. The recourse on this loan will be limited to the assets of the purchaser. The purchaser will not own any assets other than those sold pursuant to this transaction."

181 **losses beyond that point:** Interview with managing director at PE firm who bought some of these loans and laid out how they were structured.

182 **lowering their debt:** interview with someone told about the lobbying effort from a firsthand source.

182 **for five years:** in the text of the American Recovery and Reinvestment Act of 2009, page 123, Stat. 339 under Rules Relating to Debt Instruments (http://frwebgate.access.gpo.gov/cgi-bin/getdoc.cgi? dbname=111_cong_public_laws&docid=f:publ005.111).

182 **"to the debt holders":** Peter Lattman and Jeffrey McCracken, "Buyout Shops Swoop in for a Feast on the Cheap," *Wall Street Journal*, December 31, 2008.

183 **Delaware Supreme Court:** Michael Qunit, "COMPANY NEWS; Interco Wins Reprieve on 'Poison Pill' Ruling," *New York Times*, November 3, 1988.

183 **on the New York Stock Exchange:** interview with Lynn Chipperfield.

184 **brand's image:** interview with a Florsheim executive who preferred not to be quoted.

184 **25 percent annual return:** numbers were found in Apollo Investment Fund V, L.P. memorandum.

184 **bankruptcy protection:** "Company News; Florsheim Files for Bankruptcy and Sells Most Assets," *New York Times*, March 5, 2002.

185 **survive the recession:** Julie Creswell, "In Private Equity, the Limits of Apollo's Power," *New York Times*, December 7, 2008.

185 **are not far behind:** Cambridge Associates Benchmark Statistics for Private Equity as of September 30, 2008, ranking returns based on pooled mean net to LPs.

Chapter 11. Handling the Fallout

186 **bring down GM:** Leslie Wayne, "GMAC's Bondholders Near Crucial Deadline," *New York Times*, December 24, 2008, in which it says, "Both GMAC and several ratings agencies have raised the possibility that if bondholders did not go along with the exchange program, GMAC might have to file for bankruptcy."

186 **into a bank:** Damian Paletta and John Stoll, "GMAC Seeks Access to Bank Bailout Funds," *Wall Street Journal*, October 29, 2008.

186 **over fifteen months:** Bryan Keogh, "GMAC Completes Debt Swap After Falling Short of Goal," Bloomberg, December 31, 2008.

187 **for paper worth less money:** Caroline Salas and David Milden-
berg, "GMAC Rescue Plan Falters, Raising Bankruptcy Concern,"
Bloomberg, December 10, 2008.

188 **expedited basis:** Federal Reserve system order approving the forma-
tion of bank holding companies and a notice to engage in certain non-
banking activities.

188 **two blind trusts:** interview with GMAC media relations associate
manager Beth Coggins.

188 **make on its investment:** Treasury Department press release, "Treasury Announces TARP Investment in GMAC," December 29, 2008,
says, "Under the agreement GMAC must be in compliance with the
executive compensation and corporate governance requirements of
Section 111 of the Emergency Economic Stabilization Act, as well as
enhanced restrictions on executive compensation." None of those conditions puts restrictions on compensation to Cerberus.

188 **seven-member GMAC board:** GMAC Financial Services press release,
"GMAC Announces Interim Changes to Its Board," January 9, 2009.

189 **$1.5 billion:** Treasury Department press release: "Treasury Announces
TARP Investments in Chrysler Financial," January 16, 2009.

189 **new auto leases:** Josh Kosman, "Seared Cerberus," *New York Post*,
May 8, 2009.

189 **joining the Treasury:** Greg Gardner, "Auto Task Force Chief Rattner
Is No Stranger to Success, Wealth," *Detroit Free Press*, June 7, 2009.

190 **from 2000 to 2007:** data based on a Government Accountability
Office analysis of Dealogic Data and taking the total value of deals and
multiplying it by 75 percent since PE firms on average this decade put
down about 25 percent of the purchase price in buyouts.

190 **35 percent:** Edward Harrison, "Chart of the day: Total US Debt,"
www.creditwritedowns.com, August 21, 2008.

190 **$47 trillion:** Harrison, ibid., where he reports total U.S. debt for 1Q
2008 was $47.4 trillion.

190 **taxpayer bailout:** John Stoll and Stacy Meichtry, "Chrysler-Fiat Deal
Needs U.S. Loans," *Wall Street Journal*, January 21, 2009; and David
Welch and David Kiley, "As a Bailout Takes Shape, Chrysler Doubts
Grow," *BusinessWeek*, December 9, 2009.

192 **owed in loans:** Andrew Bary, "Ka-Boom!" *Barron's*, February 2, 2009.

192 **difficult layoffs:** Boston Consulting Group report "Get Ready for the Private Equity Shakeout," December 2008, 4–6. Found at http://www. bcg.com/impact_expertise/publications/files/Get_Ready_Private_ Equity_Shakeout_Dec_2008.pdf.

193 **returns for pensions:** Peter Lattman, "10 Things the Next President Needs to Know About Private Equity," *Wall Street Journal,* June 4, 2008.

194 **everything else:** Francisco Guerrera, "The Man Behind GE's Quiet Revolution," *Financial Times,* November 6, 2006.

195 **healthy companies:** interview with John Canning, who funded some of the earliest LBOs and founded the PE firm Madison Dearborn. He said, "This [LBOs] was something the KKR guys discovered. It was really driven by tax benefits."

195 **Senate Committee on Finance:** "Leveraged Buyouts and Corporate Debt," testimony before the U.S. Senate Committee on Finance, January 24, 1989.

196 **"you are concerned?":** Max Holland and Viveca Novak, "Buyouts: The LBO Lobby Makes Its Move on Washington," Common Cause, September/October 1989, and reprinted in *Washingtondecoded.com.*

196 **"connections with Washington":** ibid.

196 **partners at PE firms:** Raymond Hernandez and Stephen Labaton, "In Opposing Tax Plan, Schumer Supports Wall Street Over Party," *New York Times,* July 30, 2007.

197 **as a lobbyist:** "Union's Buyout Protests Go Global," *New York Times DealBook,* June 4, 2008.

197 **Madison Dearborn Partners:** Michael Luo, "In Banking, Emanuel Made Money and Connections," *New York Times,* December 3, 2008.

197 **any other contributor:** info on opensecret.org, which reports, "Private equity firm Madison Dearborn Partners has given Emanuel more than any other contributor over his career at $93,600."

198 **kill off LBOs:** Max Holland and Viveca Novak, "LBOs: Enough Already!;...While on Capitol Hill, Lobbyists and Loopholes Keep Congress in Line," *Washington Post,* October 22, 1989.

198 **not yet invested:** from the Dow Jones 2009 Directory of Alternative Investment Programs.

199 **reserves against loans:** Stephen Labaton, "Agency's 04 Rule Let Banks Pile Up New Debt," *New York Times,* October 2, 2008.

202 **severely underfunded:** Ted Sickinger, "Oregon Public Pension Fund
Gets Preview of Fiscal Health," *The Oregonian*, March 8, 2009.

202 **$22.5 billion from 1990s deals:** Michael Kliegman, a partner at
PriceWaterhouseCoopers, explained to us how to calculate how much
PE-firm–owned companies save on taxes through interest deductions. If
a PE firms puts $500 million down to buy a company for an eight times
EBITDA multiple, $2 billion, the company might borrow $1.5 billion at
a combined 8 percent interest rate, which equals $120 million. It can
then deduct the $120 million from taxes. The company would likely have
a 40 percent tax rate when combining state and federal taxes: 120 x .40
= 48. The company saves $48 million annually from taxes. That equals
2.4 percent of the $2 billion purchase price. Taking the dollar value of
buyouts of U.S. companies done this decade and multiplying them by the
average time a PE firm owns a business gets you $60 billion (for example,
$29 billion of deals done in 1990 times 4.5 years, times .024). I only mul-
tiplied the value of 2007 deals by 1.5 years since this is the likely average
considering that the most a PE firm could have held a company was two
years, and adjusted more recent years in a similar manner. I tacked on
another $10 billion because the deals done from 2005 to 2007 were at
much higher purchase multiples than was in Kliegman's example.

202 **finance leveraged buyouts:** A Professor Steven Davis-led study
showed PE firms eliminate 3.6 percent more jobs than competitors in
their first two years of ownership. They bought companies this decade
employing ten million people. Considering that the biggest job cuts
happen in the third year, I believe five hundred thousand jobs lost is a
reasonable number.

Appendix: The 1990s LBO Track Record

208 **Securities Data Corporation:** Top 10 1990s buyout chart found in
"U.S. Leveraged Buyout Market From 1980-2002" report compiled by
U.S. Bancorp Piper Jaffray M&A Insights, May 2003.

211 **$7.4 billion in fall 2000:** Looking at Citizens Communications Annual
Report, 10-K, for the year ending December 31, 2000, I found that
Citizens stock in the 3Q 2000, when the Valor buyout closed, ranged

from $13 to $19 a share. So I took $16 and multiplied it by the shares of common stock reported in the filing (266,372,768 shares) and added the $3.1 billion in long-term net debt. This gives Citizens roughly a $7.4 billion enterprise value in fall 2000.

211 **in mid-2006:** Looking at Citizens Communications Annual Report, 10-K, for the year ending December 31, 2006, I found that Citizens stock in the 3Q 2000, when the Valor sale closed, ranged from $12.38 to $14.31 a share. So I took $13.40 and multiplied it by the shares of common stock reported in the filing (322,538,000) and added the $3.46 billion in long-term debt ($4.32 billion in long-term debt minus $1.04 billion in cash). This gives Citizens roughly a $7.78 billion enterprise value in fall 2006.

211 **remained stagnant:** Windstream prospectus 424B3 filed April 6, 2007 says that "this increase [in phone lines] was driven by the acquisition of Valor and its approximately 500,000 access lines." When the PE firms acquired the GTE properties they had 520,000 lines.

211 **more than $200 million:** interview with an investor in one of the buyout funds that acquired Valor Telecom.

212 **20 percent of Vertis's sales:** Big Flower reported that for the six months ended June 30, 1999, digital services represented $164 million of its $852 million in sales, 19 percent.

213 **multiple for Saks:** Josh Kosman, "Despite Investcorp Efforts, Saks Proves a Costly Buy," *Buyouts Newsletter*, August 17, 1998.

213 **in the same markets:** interview with a person who was a Saks executive in the early 90s.

213 **annual rate of return:** interview with a source who has knowledge of the situation.

214 **failed miserably:** Kosman, "Despite Investcorp Efforts, Saks Proves a Costly Buy," in which I reported that it dropped less-expensive clothing lines and performance in Off Fifth Avenue stores was flagging.

214 **1990 leveraged buyout:** $1.5 billion price tag based on Capital IQ Saks report that said, "Deal Resolution: Proffitt's, Inc. (NYSE: PFT) completed the acquisition of Saks Holding on 09/17/1998. The equity was valued at $1503.06 million based on the closing price of $28.63 on 09/16/1998."

214　**roughly $2.3 billion:** based on Saks's 136,110,000 shares at $12.38 per share (average between high and low in third quarter 2005) and adding its $611 million in net long-term debt.

214　**smaller than Saks:** Saks had $1.27 billion in 1991 net revenue (based on *Buyouts Newsletter* article referenced above) and Nieman $1.21 billion in revenue and $61 million in operating earnings, according to its public filings.

214　**held a 40 percent stake:** Glenn Collins, "Kohlberg, Kravis Plans to Divest Remaining Stake in RJR Nabisco," *New York Times*, March 16, 1995.

215　**Corelle and OXO:** Thyra Porter, "World Kitchen's Growing Saga: Acquiring Brands—and Debt," *HFN*, June 10, 2002.

216　**by 50 percent:** Borden public filings showed chemical division's sales were $995 million in 1994, and Apollo said in its press release when buying the division that 2003 sales were $1.4 billion.

216　**in five years:** James Peltz, "In the Spotlight," *Los Angeles Times*, March 15, 1998.

217　**where it already competed:** LIN 1998 annual report says that seven of the company's eleven stations were in the top fifty of the November 1998 designated market area ("DMA") rankings of the Nielsen Station Index.

217　**toward smaller markets:** LIN as of year ended December 31, 2008 had fourteen of its twenty-seven stations in top fifty markets, a much smaller percentage than in 1998.

217　**LIN TV had focused on:** interview with Marvin Shapiro, managing director at investment bank Veronis Suhler Stevenson.

217　**from scratch:** Michael Malone, "Birth of a Station," *Broadcasting & Cable*, July 27, 2008.

218　**buying the business:** interview with Leon Humble, who headed ON's power division at the time of the sale.

218　**that are integrated circuits:** ibid.

218　**6.5 percent:** interview with a former ON executive who supervised financial affairs.

219　**or power-chip R & D:** interview with Humble, who headed ON's power division, and a top ON component chip executive at that time, and former ON executive who supervised financial affairs.

219 **side of the business:** interview with a former ON executive who supervised financial affairs.

219 **sold at higher prices:** interview with Leon Humble, who headed ON's power division at the time of the sale.

222 **Centennial into bankruptcy:** interview with Centennial CEO Michael Small.

222 **nearly tripled:** Cellular usage nationally grew from 86 million in 1999 to 252 million in 2007, according to the *Computer Industry Almanac.*

222 **Caribbean development:** interview with Centennial CEO Michael Small.

222 **financing talks:** "Centennial Communications Announces Pricing on $500M Senior Unsecured Notes Offering," Dow Jones News Service, June 17, 2003.

223 **incurring expensive penalties:** interview with a Centennial analyst.

223 **were ready to sell Centennial:** interview with Centennial CEO Michael Small.

223 **analog customers at once:** interview with a Centennial executive in its U.S. operations.

224 **split the market between them:** "Manville to Sell Riverwood Unit to Investor Group for $2.7 billion," Bloomberg Business News, October 27, 1995.

225 **against MeadWestvaco:** interview with an investment banker at large global bank who follows company.

Index